Lecture Notes in Computer Science

Edited by G. Goos and J. Hartmanis

236

TEX for Scientific Documentation

Second European Conference
Strasbourg, France, June 19–21, 1986
Proceedings

Edited by Jacques Désarménien

Springer-Verlag
Berlin Heidelberg New York London Paris Tokyo

Editor

Jacques Désarménien
Laboratoire de typographie informatique, Université Louis-Pasteur
7, rue René-Descartes, 67084 Strasbourg Cedex, France

Conference supported by

CNRS (Centre National de la Recherche Scientifique)
SMF (Société Mathématique de France)
Université Louis-Pasteur de Strasbourg

Program Committee

J. André	IRISA Rennes (France)
B. Beeton	Amer. Math. Soc. (USA)
H. Brown	Univ. Kent (Great Britain)
G. Degli Antoni	Univ. Milano (Italy)
D. Feingold	EDF Clamart (France)
D. Knuth	Stanford Univ. (USA)
D. Lucarella	Univ. Milano (Italy)
P. MacKay	Univ. Washington (USA)
J.-J. Quisquater	Philips Bruxelles (Belgium)
B. Schulze	Univ. Bonn (FRG)

Organizing Committee

J. Désarménien	Univ. Strasbourg (France)
R. Goucher	Amer. Math. Soc. (USA)
D. Lucarella	Univ. Milano (Italy)

Conference Chairman

J. Désarménien	Univ. Strasbourg (France)

CR Subject Classifications (1985): A.0, H.4.1, I.7.0

ISBN 3-540-16807-9 Springer-Verlag Berlin Heidelberg New York
ISBN 0-387-16807-9 Springer-Verlag New York Berlin Heidelberg

Printing and binding: Beltz Offsetdruck, Hemsbach/Bergstr.
2145/3140-543210

PREFACE

In this volume, the reader will find the texts of the contributions presented by the participants at the second European conference on *TEX for scientific documentation*, held in June 1986 at the *Centre culturel Saint-Thomas* in Strasbourg. TEX, a registered trademark of the American Mathematical Society, is the system for typesetting scientific texts by computer, created at Stanford by D. Knuth.

One will notice by reading the list of participants, that the European audience of TEX is so important that this system is being recognized as the reference in its field. Furthermore, it is significant to mention that researchers in other disciplines have used TEX for composing their works. Actually, one of the conclusive advantages of TEX seems to me to be its printing quality, comparable to that of texts composed by traditional means, but at much lower cost. This point is of course particularly important for scientific texts, as well as for texts with limited circulation. The presentation of R. Wonneberger proves this point. He suggested that all philologists interested in TEX should establish contact with him.

TEX is a bare product. That is its strength but also its weakness. First of all the strong point: It allows a great portability to all materials and for all operating systems; the final product depends only on the initial source and, of course, on the quality of the printer. The weakness then: The utilization of TEX alone is no doubt difficult; this is why most of its users have integrated it into a general environment of document preparation. Most of the contributions presented at the conference were related to this issue. This is the final evidence of the growing interest on TEX.

Moreover, the publisher Addison-Wesley displayed at the conference, and for the first time, the five volumes of the series *Computers and Typesetting* by D. Knuth. These assemble all original texts on TEX and on its companion METAFONT. This latter software was the heart of the report given by R. Southall. It is probable that before the next conference METAFONT will have been experimented by several people, possibly in conjunction with the problem of storing the character fonts needed by the laser printers.

In conclusion, I should like to thank those who helped me with the success of this conference: The *Centre national de la recherche scientifique* and the *Société mathématique de France* for their financial support, the *Université Louis-Pasteur*, the members of the Program Committee and of the Organizing Committee, and especially Ray Goucher who advertised this conference in the *TUGboat*—the TEX Users Group journal. I was also able to profit from Dario Lucarella who organized the preceding conference in Como. Finally, I think that all of the participants appreciated the efficiency and kindness of the secretary of the conference, Karen Trantham.

Strasbourg, June 1986 J. DÉSARMÉNIEN

TABLE OF CONTENTS

RUNNING TEX IN AN INTERACTIVE TEXT PROCESSING ENVIRONMENT

Wolfgang Appelt
Gesellschaft für Mathematik
und Datenverarbeitung mbH
5205 Sankt Augustin
Federal Republic of Germany

Abstract
We describe an implementation of TEX on a workstation with a high–resolution raster display. An editor, TEX and a screen preview driver are linked via an UNIX[†] *pipe, which allows a convenient interactive creation of complicated pieces of text.*

1. Batch and Interactive Text Processing

Text processing systems can be divided into two classes. The first class contains the so–called WYSIWYG–systems ("what you see is what you get"), the second one the formatting systems.

When using a WYSIWYG–system the appearance of a document on the display during the editing process is always identical to its printed form, except maybe some slight differences due to different resolutions of the screen and the printer. The *content* of a document and its *graphical representation* or *layout* are created simultaneously and interactively. The layout of the document is defined *apart* from its content and the text itself contains no instructions concerning its graphical representation, at least from the user's point of view.

When using a formatting system the appearance of a document will be more or less different from its printed form during the editing process. The author has to insert *processing instructions* into his text to inform the formatter about the desired graphical representation of the document. Formatting the document is usually not done interactively but via a batch process.

There is no general answer what kind of text processing system is better since both have their *pros* and *cons*. Since a lot of papers can be found on this topic we will not discuss it here into greater detail (see e. g. [MEY82]).

Our own experiences with TEX([KNU84]), which is a formatting system, and discussions with our users gave us the following impression: When an author

---

[†] UNIX is a Trademark of Bell Laboratories.

enters his text into the machine he usually concentrates on the *contents* of his paper and does not worry about its *appearance* or *layout*. TEX's way of operating, namely being basically a batch system that expects text with some "formatting instructions", is widely accepted by the users, especially if they are using a high level macro package as e. g. LATEX ([LAM86]). (Many users even prefer such a system to a WYSIWYG–system which distracts their attention from content to appearance.)

There are, however, two important exceptions to that general statement:

— If the author has to create a typographically complicated "piece of text", e. g. a mathematical formula or a table, or maybe if he wants to develop a tricky TEX macro, "immediate visual feedback" is essential. He is quite annoyed if he has to wait for printed output to see the result of his input even if such an "iteration loop" takes only a few minutes.

— If the author has finished the *contents* of his paper and the "only" thing left is a "little bit fine tuning" on the layout (e. g. eliminating the famous "`Overfull \hbox`"es, club or widow lines or ugly page breaks) he usually wants to perform this task in an "interactive" environment. Otherwise this task might be very time consuming, since a small modification one some page has often unpredictable and undesired effects on subsequent pages.

In other words: Even (or especially) for such a highly sophisticated formatting system as TEX there are sometimes situations where an operating mode "close" to a WYSIWYG–system is desirable.

2. Requirements for an Interactive TEXt Processing System

Creating an interactive text processing environment around TEX requires some special hardware and software facilities:

— To allow a screen preview of the formatted text a high resolution raster display is necessary. The size of the screen should be at least large enough to show a complete formatted page. For scientific publications a size of about 30 cm height and 20 cm width, which is approximately A4–size, is usually the minimum.

— Since the editor, TEX and the screen driver are to run and display their results simultaneously on the screen a multiprocess operating system including some kind of a window manager is needed.

— To achieve fast enough and guaranteed response times the system should run on a stand–alone workstation basis. The integration into a time–sharing environment would probably lead to some severe time problems.

A system fulfilling these requirements more or less satisfactory is the PERQ from International Computers Limited (ICL, UK). The PERQ is a graphical workstation with a raster screen (1024 × 768 pixels, height × width) of approximately A4 size, two megabyte RAM and about 34 megabyte secondary storage on a winchester disk. Graphical input is possible via a tablet and a three button puck.

ICL also sells a 1024×1280 screen for the PERQ which is nearly A3 size. This screen is very appropriate for a TEX implementation as described in this paper since it allows to display a complete formatted A4 page on one half of the screen leaving the other half for an editor and TEX window; see below.

The operating system is called PNX which is essentially UNIX Version 7 plus some System 3 facilities plus some extensions for using the special hardware facilities of the PERQ (e. g. graphical input/output). PNX has a rather convenient window manager: Several processes can run simultaneously in different windows on the screen; communication between processes in different windows is easily possible.

The PERQ has a 16–bit bit–sliced processor which especially supports fast raster operations on the screen. Processing speed is roughly about 0.5 MIPS. Since the PERQ system was designed in the early 80s it does not represent the latest state of the art in workstation technology.

3. The TEX Implementation on the PERQ

For a complete understanding of this chapter the reader should know the basic principles of the UNIX operating system (see e. g. [RIT78]).

The implementation of our system on the PERQ can be divided into two rather separate parts, the first one being the linkage of TEX and the screen driver, the second one the linkage of the editor and TEX.

The first step towards a previewing system was some recoding of TEX's input/output–system: we linked

term_in to *stdin*,
term_out to *stderr* and
dvi_file to *stdout*.

In other words, instead of writing the formatted text into a *dvi_file* TEX writes it to *stdout* which allows a linkage between TEX and the screen driver via a normal UNIX *pipe*:

```
tex | driver
```

Of course a *dvi_file* can be created by output redirection:

```
tex > dvifile
```

if printed output on paper is wanted. (Several hardcopy devices can be reached from the PERQ via ethernet.)

TEX and screen driver run within two different windows on the screen. The usual processing is on a pagewise basis, i. e. as soon as TEX has a compiled a complete page it *pipes* its output to the screen driver for showing the formatted text on the screen. Some recoding of TEX's buffering mechanism for *dvi_file* output was necessary to really achieve that pagewise processing.

If the driver has displayed a complete page it will usually wait until the user presses a button on the puck before it clears the driver window again and starts showing the next page.

Processing time for TEX and driver for a full A4 page is currently about 20 seconds; some reduction might still be possible. This may look a bit slow at first glance but the following should be considered: During the time the user reads the formatted text displayed in the driver window, TEX continues processing its input file and starts compiling the next page(s). When the user presses the button after he has read a page the next page will therefore usually appear "immediately". In other words, since proofreading a page usually takes considerably longer than 20 seconds, TEX and driver process the text faster than the user can read it, i. e. usually the system has to wait (when the *pipe* is full) and not the user.

Figure 1 shows a dump of the PERQ screen during a TEX run with screen previewing. Screen dumps are obtained by writing the screen bit map onto a file and printing this file on a Canon LBP 10 laser printer with 240 dots/inch. Each screen pixel is blown up to 2×2 pixels on the paper, i. e. the characters look a little bit "smoother" on the screen.

The TEX fonts for the screen, by the way, were produced by a rather quick and dirty method: We took the fonts for 200 dots/inch devices, which are on the standard distribution tape, and made 100 dots/inch fonts (which is rather close to the resolution of the PERQ screen) out of them by making one pixel out of each four. This brute and force method did not create nice fonts, of course, but it is better than nothing. When the new METAFONT and the Computer Modern Fonts are available we shall create new screen fonts.

We have, by the way, a preliminary version of the new METAFONT already running on the PERQ (the PNX adaptation was made by Seán Leitch who sent us his *change_files* by courtesy [LEI85]), but since we are still lacking font definitions, except of one "toy font", it is currently (March 86) not of much practical value for us.

This gave us a nice previewing system but for the situations mentioned above, where an interactive text processing is desirable, the integration of a text editor is necessary. We therefore included an editor into the *pipe*:

`editor | tex | driver`

The actual implementation, by the way, does *not* use the usual UNIX *pipe*, though the user will see no difference. What we did is, that the editor writes its output (the definition of *output* will be given in a moment) into an intermediate file and any time this file is modified, TEX will read it and process its contents.

The linkage between the editor and TEX could be realized by a few lines of C–code (see below) and some TEX macros which can be tailored to individual applications.

The editor we use is a rather simple full screen editor which was written by a colleague of mine at GMD [KRE84], not especially for our TEX implementation, by the way. We took this editor just for convenience since we had access to the source code. It should not be a great problem to substitute any other editor for it, maybe with some small modifications.

The definition of *output*, i. e. what the editor *pipes* to TEX, is rather trivial:

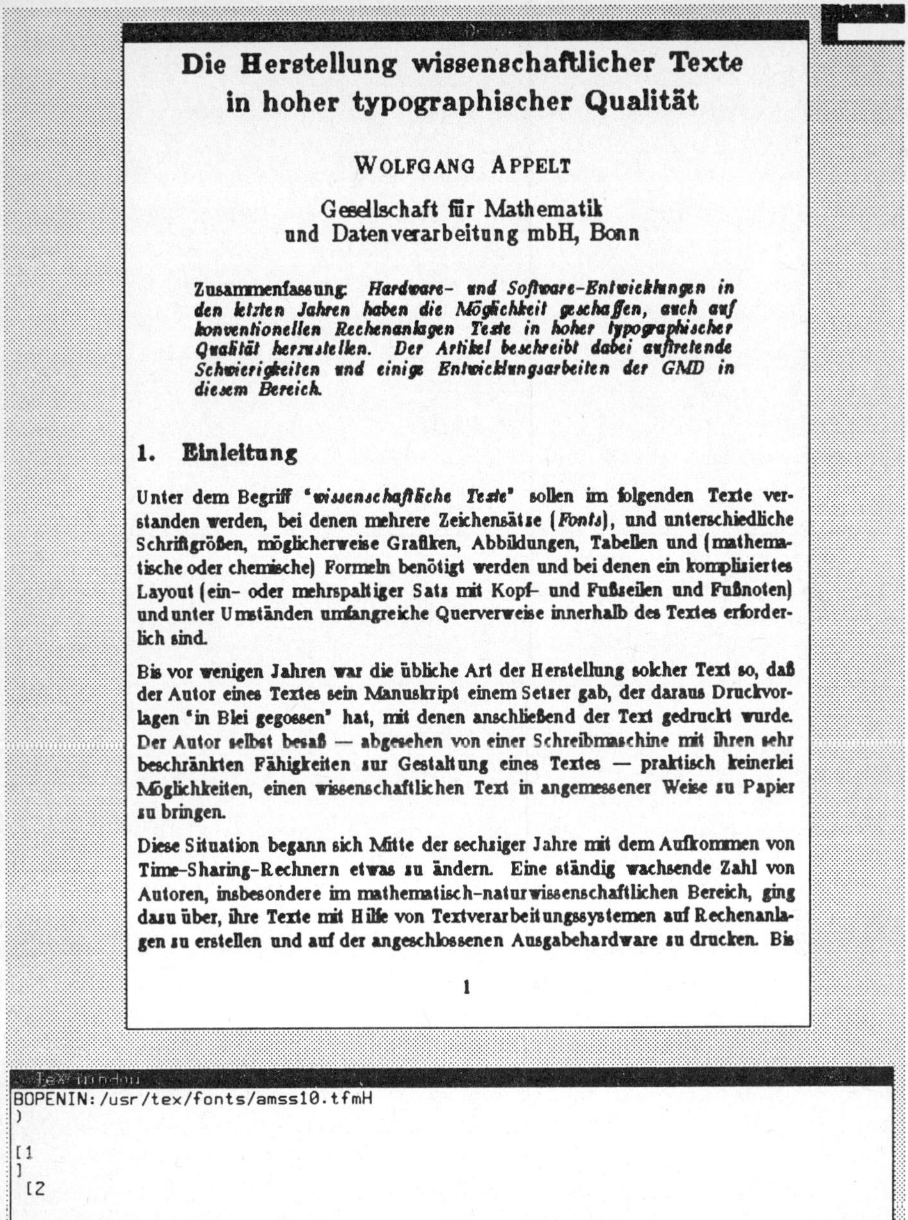

Die Herstellung wissenschaftlicher Texte in hoher typographischer Qualität

Wolfgang Appelt

Gesellschaft für Mathematik und Datenverarbeitung mbH, Bonn

Zusammenfassung: *Hardware- und Software-Entwicklungen in den letzten Jahren haben die Möglichkeit geschaffen, auch auf konventionellen Rechenanlagen Texte in hoher typographischer Qualität herzustellen. Der Artikel beschreibt dabei auftretende Schwierigkeiten und einige Entwicklungsarbeiten der GMD in diesem Bereich.*

1. Einleitung

Unter dem Begriff "*wissenschaftliche Texte*" sollen im folgenden Texte verstanden werden, bei denen mehrere Zeichensätze (*Fonts*), und unterschiedliche Schriftgrößen, möglicherweise Grafiken, Abbildungen, Tabellen und (mathematische oder chemische) Formeln benötigt werden und bei denen ein kompliziertes Layout (ein- oder mehrspaltiger Satz mit Kopf- und Fußzeilen und Fußnoten) und unter Umständen umfangreiche Querverweise innerhalb des Textes erforderlich sind.

Bis vor wenigen Jahren war die übliche Art der Herstellung solcher Text so, daß der Autor eines Textes sein Manuskript einem Setzer gab, der daraus Druckvorlagen "in Blei gegossen" hat, mit denen anschließend der Text gedruckt wurde. Der Autor selbst besaß — abgesehen von einer Schreibmaschine mit ihren sehr beschränkten Fähigkeiten zur Gestaltung eines Textes — praktisch keinerlei Möglichkeiten, einen wissenschaftlichen Text in angemessener Weise zu Papier zu bringen.

Diese Situation begann sich Mitte der sechziger Jahre mit dem Aufkommen von Time-Sharing-Rechnern etwas zu ändern. Eine ständig wachsende Zahl von Autoren, insbesondere im mathematisch-naturwissenschaftlichen Bereich, ging dazu über, ihre Texte mit Hilfe von Textverarbeitungssystemen auf Rechenanlagen zu erstellen und auf der angeschlossenen Ausgabehardware zu drucken. Bis

1

```
BOPENIN:/usr/tex/fonts/amss10.tfmH
)

[1
]
 [2
```

Figure 1: TEX and driver on the PERQ screen

Since it usually makes not much sense to take the complete file that is currently edited, only those pieces of text that the user explicitly selects within the editor will be forwarded to the TEX program. (Of course, it is not forbidden to select the whole file.)

Example: Suppose an author wants to compose a complicated formula "interactively". He then executes an UNIX shell script that opens three windows on the screen: one running the editor, another running TEX and the third one running the screen driver. Afterwards he will start entering his formula (or editing an already existing one) within the editor. If he wants to see what his input will produce he selects the corresponding lines of his input file, looks at the result in the driver window, edits again, selects again, edits again etc.

The user never leaves the editor window during this process. He only concentrates on editing his input and does not have to jump around between the three windows. The time required to see the formatted result within the driver window depends on the amount of selected text, of course. If the user selects only, say, a two lines formula, the formatted result appears "immediately" (meaning about one to three seconds).

Figure 2 shows such an editing process for a mathematical formula. The selected lines within the editor window are marked with an "@"-sign in the first column.

The procedure for the final "fine tuning" of the layout, as described above, could be done in a rather similar way. In this case the user might process the text from the start to the end. If e. g. he wants to insert an explicit page break somewhere he will do so and afterwards start processing of the remaining text from there on again until he has processed the complete paper. Of course, the processing time will be a bit longer in this case.

4. Future Developments

Except of the editor which is written in C all software is written in `WEB`, i. e. for installing the TEX system appropriate *change_files* were written. The screen driver is also realized as a *change_file* to the `DviType` processor. At some few places C–routines were used, especially the PASCAL–input/output was substituted by corresponding C–functions, since the PASCAL routines are considerably slower in PNX, and, of course, the graphical interface of the driver to the screen uses some PNX system functions.

Nevertheless, we regard the implementation easily portable to other systems, at least to UNIX systems with raster displays and window managers. There are, in fact, currently some efforts for porting our TEX implementation on the PERQ to other systems.

We are also working on the integration of graphics into TEX. To our opinion the creation of graphics within a document should be kept separate from the creation of the text and should be done by a dedicated graphics system, which in our environment will run in another window on the screen.

The merging of textual and graphical information will be done by the driver. Within the TEX input file the reference to the graphics will be realized by a TEX macro which will reserve the necessary empty space on the page and furthermore insert some "`\special`"–code into TEX's output. The driver will "execute" the "`\special`"–code by fetching the desired graphical information from the graphics

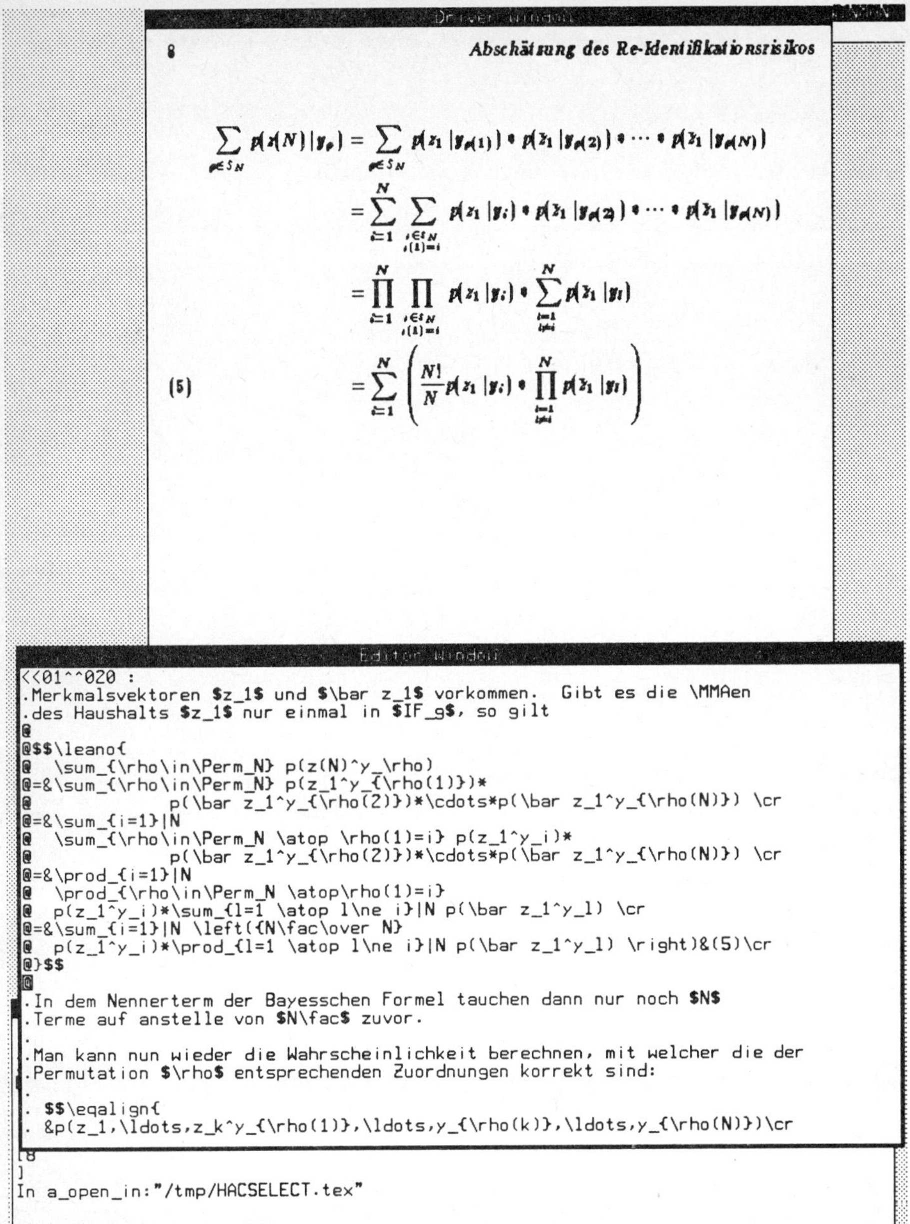

Figure 2: Creating a mathematical formula interactively

system (see [HOR86] for further details).

The user of the system might then easily edit textual and graphical information within the window of the editor resp. the graphics system until he has reached the desired result within the driver window.

References

KNU84 KNUTH, D. E.: *The TEXbook*; Addison–Wesley, Reading, Mass., 1984.

HOR86 HORN, K.: *Integration von Graphik in TEX*; In: Graphik in Dokumenten, Informatik Fachbericht 119, Springer–Verlag, Heidelberg, 1986.

KRE84 KREIFELTS, TH.: *hac – Ein bildschirmorientierter Texteditor für UNIX*; Benutzeranleitung; Interner Bericht der GMD, Sankt Augustin, 1984.

LAM86 LAMPORT, L.: *LATEX: A Document Preparation System*; Addison–Wesley, Reading, Mass., 1986.

LEI85 LEITCH, S.: *Implementing METAFONT on an ICL PERQ*; In: TEX for Scientific Publication, Addison–Wesley, Reading, Mass., 1985.

MEY82 MEYROWITZ, N., VAN DAM, A.: *Interactive Editing Systems*; ACM Computing Surveys, Vol. 14, No. 3, 1982.

RIT78 RITCHIE, D. M., THOMPSON, K.: *The UNIX Time-Sharing system*, Bell. Sys. Tech. J. 57 (6), 1978.

How to Please Authors and Publishers: A Versatile Document Preparation System at Karlsruhe*

Anne Brüggemann-Klein,
Peter Dolland, Alois Heinz

Institut für Angewandte Informatik
und Formale Beschreibungsverfahren
Postfach 6980
D-7500 Karlsruhe

Abstract

We introduce a document preparation environment which supports the authors in the production and publication of documents of high typographic quality. Our document model is compatible with the SGML-model standardized by ISO, and formatting can be done with TEX.

Keywords

Document models, document production, document publishing, SGML, ODA/ODIF, formatter, TEX, device driver, previewing, CRT composer

1. Introduction

Computer typesetting has become of great importance over the last years. Since the publishing houses began to demand "camera ready copies" from the authors, a lot of people have become interested in this new technology. It enables them to produce nicer documents than a typewriter can. This led to the development of efficient textprocessing systems like TROFF, SCRIBE and TEX.

In this article we introduce a system that tries to bring both parties under the same heading: The authors are enabled to use its facilities for their own purposes like getting a satisfying draft of what they have written, or the production of technical reports. But they do not have to learn and to insert into their text all the involved and device dependent markups the publishing houses might insist on! Nevertheless, when it comes to the production of documents in the finest typographic quality, our system ties up with the experience and the environment of the publishing houses. To their advantage, the authors' documents can be converted automatically into whatever layout they might wish to produce.

* This project has been partially supported by the Deutsche Forschungsgemeinschaft (Sto 167/1-1) and the IBM Corporation (L2/029 of the cooperation with the University of Karlsruhe)

Our system is based on a formatter independent document model which is compatible with the SGML-model standardized by ISO, see [SGML]. This enables us to edit our documents with the help of a syntax-driven editor. Its controlling syntax is a document itself and can be defined freely. Thus, it will be produced using the *same* editor. Afterwards, the documents can be marked with arbitrary MarkupMaterial, for example SGML- or TEX-commands.

As far as formatting and printing is concerned, our system is based on TEX. We shall briefly describe the TEX installations at our Institute. Especially, we introduce a previewing facility for TEX on the IBM PC screen and a general method for the development of drivers for CRT composers which are essential for printing documents in high typographic quality.

2. Publication of scientific documents today

For a long period of time traditional methods of hot-lead typesetting have provided a very high typographic standard in book printing. But some 15 years ago, these composition techniques became too expensive, especially for scientific documents which require skilled personnel for the composition of mathematical expressions, tables, diagramms ... .

Introducing computer typesetting the financial condition of the publishing houses became easier, but the typographical standard declined. In [K2] a careful investigation of this trend is given, where the *Transactions of the American Mathematical Society* are taken as an example, but cf. [MK] also.

Except for the typographic quality of the products, for the authors everything remained as it had been. The typesetting houses fed the authors' text, interspersed with formatting commands of a special formatting system, into the composition machine, and the authors only had to give clear instructions about their typewriter written texts as before.

A second alarming decline of the typographic standard that was combined with additional effort for the authors occured, when the typesetting houses decided to save the inhouse typing of the texts and instructed the authors to produce "camera ready copies" with their own local equipment. The idea was to use these documents for photographic duplication.

As a consequence of this publishing method, you can find dreadful contributions (from a typographical point of view) in conference volumes, where typewritten mathematical text is interspersed with handwritten special symbols which do not exist in the typewriter's font supply, see Figure 1 in [BHR]. Therefore, it is no surprise that some authors take refuge to some oldfashioned techniques of document production, see Figure 2 in [S].

In spite of all these defects in the typographic quality, the production of camera ready copies by the authors turns out to have some advantages. First of all, the authors are encouraged to use word processing systems of their own which provide them with better facilities in document preparation, e.g. easing corrections and renaming, generating indices automatically, managing bibliographies ... . On the other hand, word and text processing systems give them the aesthetic satisfaction to improve the typographic quality of all documents that are totally produced inhouse, like technical reports, instructional material, slides for lessons ..., compared with typewriter quality.

About "$\Longrightarrow$": As M we can choose the smallest set $A \in \mathfrak{M}$ with

$$\forall x\ (x \triangleleft A \longrightarrow x \in A) \quad \text{and} \quad \{\langle\langle r,s\rangle, \{\emptyset\}\rangle \mid Lsr\} \subseteq A\ .$$

With Lemma 2 we get of course

Lemma 3: For every formula α of the theory of types one can find a formula β_I of $\forall\exists\ldots\exists\ (0,1)$ with
α is satisfiable in a finite model
$\Longleftrightarrow$ β_I is satisfiable on a finite non empty subset U of N with interpretation of E by $\in^{\circ}_2$.

For getting a similar reduction for the satisfiability of α we need a representation of the coenumerable predicates on $\mathfrak{M}_2$, that means, of the complements of the recursive enumerable predicates on $\mathfrak{M}_2$.
Starting with equivalence (1) we have in the weak second order logic

$$\begin{aligned} Px_1\ldots x_\varrho \Longleftrightarrow \underset{M\neq\emptyset}{\exists M}\ \underset{Mq}{\forall q}\ (q=\langle \wp_1(q),\wp_2(q)\rangle \wedge R\,\wp_1(q)\wp_2(q)x_1\ldots x_\varrho \\ \wedge M\langle \wp_1(q),\wp_1(q)\rangle \wedge (\wp_2(q)=\emptyset \\ \vee \wp_2(q)=\langle \wp_1\circ\wp_2(q),\wp_2\circ\wp_2(q)\rangle \\ \wedge M\langle \wp_1(q),\wp_1\circ\wp_2(q)\rangle)).\end{aligned}$$

Instead of using the weak second order logic on $\mathfrak{M}_2$ we can use the first order logic on $\mathfrak{M}$:

$$\begin{aligned} Px_1\ldots x_\varrho \Longleftrightarrow \underset{m\neq\emptyset}{\exists m}\ \underset{q\in m}{\forall q}\ (q\in\mathfrak{M}_2 \wedge q=\langle \wp_1(q),\wp_2(q)\rangle \\ \wedge R\,\wp_1(q)\wp_2(q)x_1\ldots x_\varrho \wedge \langle \wp_1(q),\wp_1(q)\rangle \in m \\ \wedge(\wp_2(q)=\emptyset \vee \wp_2(q)=\langle \wp_1\cdot\wp_2(q),\wp_2\circ\wp_2(q)\rangle \\ \wedge \langle \wp_1(q),\wp_1\circ\wp_2(q)\rangle \in m)).\end{aligned}$$

For every coenumerable predicate $Qx_1\ldots x_\varrho$ on $\mathfrak{M}_2$ we have the representation

$$\begin{aligned} Qx_1\ldots x_\varrho \Longleftrightarrow \underset{m\neq\emptyset}{\forall m}\ \underset{q\in m}{\exists q}\ (q\notin\mathfrak{M}_2 \vee q\notin\Pi \vee \neg R\,\wp_1(q)\wp_2(q)x_1\ldots x_\varrho \qquad (2) \\ \vee \langle \wp_1(q),\wp_2(q)\rangle \notin m \vee \wp_2(q)\neq\emptyset \\ \wedge(\langle \wp_1(q),\wp_1\circ\wp_2(q)\rangle\notin m \vee \wp_2(q)\notin\Pi)).\end{aligned}$$

Here $\neg R\,\wp_1(q)\wp_2(q)x_1\ldots x_\varrho$ is formed by $\wedge$ and $\vee$ out of the atomic predicates $x=\emptyset$, $x\in\Pi$ and negated equations. The functions on both sides of the negated equations are formed out of $\lambda\emptyset$, n_0, $\wp$, $\wp_1$, $\wp_2$ and identity functions by substitution. With the same equivalences which we used in the proof of Lemma 1 we get now

Lemma 4: For every ϱ-ary ($\varrho \geq 1$) coenumerable predicate Q on $\mathfrak{M}_2$ one can find a $\delta \in N$ and a ($\varrho+\delta+1$)-ary quantifierfree expression R_2

Figure 1

1.3. Junctivity of weaving

In this section we define the operations intersection and union on trace structures and we investigate how weaving distributes through them. First, we give the definitions. For all trace structures T and U we define

$$T \cap U \;=\; \langle\, \underline{t}T \cap \underline{t}U,\; \underline{a}T \cap \underline{a}U \,\rangle \qquad \text{and}$$
$$T \cup U \;=\; \langle\, \underline{t}T \cup \underline{t}U,\; \underline{a}T \cup \underline{a}U \,\rangle \qquad .$$

Property 1.20

For all T and U, such that $\underline{a}T = \underline{a}U$, we have $T\,\underline{w}\,U = T \cap U$.

Proof

$$\begin{array}{ll}
 & T\,\underline{w}\,U \\
= & \{\text{ property } 1.12 \} \\
 & \langle \{x : x \in \underline{t}U \wedge x \restriction \underline{a}T \in \underline{t}T : x\},\; \underline{a}U \rangle \\
= & \{\, \underline{a}T = \underline{a}U\,,\; \text{property } 1.3 \} \\
 & \langle \{x : x \in \underline{t}U \wedge x \in \underline{t}T : x\},\; \underline{a}T \cap \underline{a}U \rangle \\
= & \{\text{ calculus } \} \\
 & \langle\, \underline{t}T \cap \underline{t}U,\; \underline{a}T \cap \underline{a}U \rangle \\
= & \{\text{ def. of } \cap \} \\
 & T \cap U
\end{array}$$

(End of property and proof)

Property 1.21

Weaving distributes through union and intersection of trace structures with equal alphabets.

Proof

For all T, T', and U, such that $\underline{a}T = \underline{a}T'$, we have

$$\begin{array}{ll}
 & U\,\underline{w}\,(T \cup T') \\
= & \{\text{ def. of } \cup,\; \underline{a}T = \underline{a}T' \} \\
 & U\,\underline{w}\,\langle\, \underline{t}T \cup \underline{t}T',\; \underline{a}T \,\rangle \\
= & \{\text{ def. of } \underline{w} \} \\
 & \langle \{x : x \in (\underline{a}T \cup \underline{a}U)^* \wedge x \restriction \underline{a}U \in \underline{t}U \wedge x \restriction \underline{a}T \in \underline{t}T \cup \underline{t}T' : x\},\; \underline{a}T \cup \underline{a}U \rangle \\
= & \{\text{ calculus } \}
\end{array}$$

Figure 2

From this point of view, the crisis of the typesetting houses has speeded up the development of software tools like TROFF, SCRIBE or TEX, which enable the authors to produce documents by themselves in a typographic quality which they hardly would have imagined to be so high some years ago.

But even these systems cannot ensure real top quality in typesetting. In order to realize the finest quality for documents, one still needs experts in typography who, for example, *design* the format of a book or a journal. Therefore, it makes indeed much sense to claim the competence of the publishing houses for layout design. Thus, the next aim of the publishing houses is to get the documents from the authors in a machine readable form, possibly interspersed with special markup material specified by the typesetting houses for further computer processing, see [EP].

But two dangers are hidden behind this evolution: First, the typesetting houses might impose particular markup rules on the authors that contradict their own view of the documents or are incongruous with the markup used in earlier versions. This, of course, adds some more difficulties to the author's job.

Second, the authors are again going to be completely subordinate to the publishing houses if they want to see a formatted version of their documents.

The first danger can be prevented by the invention of suitable document models which are designed for the special needs of both parties. We will describe these document models in the next chapter. On the other hand, the independence of the authors can be preserved by the development of a document workstation which is based on such a document model and enables the authors to get a satisfying formatted draft of their documents at any time they want. But in cooperation with a publishing house it shall be possible to print the document in the highest typographic quality. We are presenting here a concept of a document workstation that fulfils these requirements and is perfectly able to resolve the crisis between authors and publishers.

3. New document models

Before the publishers left the whole job of composing the documents to the authors, there was a very reasonable division of labour between authors and compositors. It was the authors' responsibility to put their ideas into well structured sentences and to make the logical structure of their documents clear to the reader by partitioning it into chapters, sections, paragraphs, tables .... It was the compositors' job to translate this logical structure into an adequate physical layout, in order to ensure the best possible readability.

In this way two views of a document arise. The first one is the authors' logical view. To them a document is a hierarchically organized structure consisting of logical objects. A book, for example, consists of a table of contents, a sequence of chapters, a bibliography and an index. A chapter in turn consists of a heading and a sequence of paragraphs, tables or figures, and a paragraph may consist of letters, special symbols and mathematical formulae.

The second view is that of the compositors. They design the optical layout of the logical units: For example, they begin a new chapter on a new page, choose bold 12 point letters for the headings, make an indentation of 3 pica for the first line of a paragraph and set the index in a double column format using an 8 point font.

The authors communicated the logical structure of their documents to the compositors implicitly by a preliminary optical layout, namely the way they wrote it down, and additional marginal notes which were interpreted by the compositors. In a computerized composing environment, however, such markups have to be interpreted automatically, i.e. the computer typesetter must get special formatting commands to produce the desired format.

Many text processing systems require a similar proceeding. The users have to intersperse their text with certain formatting commands which refer directly to the layout, like "center the following text in a new line." This way of proceeding makes it difficult or even impossible to change the layout style of the text afterwards.

For example, once the decision has been made to write section headings and subsection headings centered on a line of their own and once the corresponding formatting commands have been entered, only by a special *human* effort these different kinds of headings can be distinguished again in order to set, for example, the section headings as before but the subsection headings flush left.

Because almost all WYSIWYG systems use this method of determining the layout of the text at the moment the letters are entered, the original meaning of WYSIWYG, "what you see is what you get," has been converted to "what you see is all what you've got," see [L].

In the early 80's, the idea came up to markup the *logical* structure of the text instead of intermerging plain formatting commands, see [G]. Such a document with a ContentsRelatedStructuring can be read by a parser that replaces the *logical* delimiters by *special* MarkupMaterial like formatting commands. The parser knows from certain processing instructions called MarkupDirectives by which formatting commands the logical markup shall be replaced.

Thus, in a document with logical markup, a section heading is not marked by a "centerline"-command but by a designation of the type <begin section heading> "text of the section heading" <end section heading>, and the marks <begin section heading> and <end section heading> can later be replaced by formatting commands according to the MarkupDirectives which, for example, perform the centering of the included text.

As a matter of fact, it would be a tedious job to define new MarkupDirectives for each single document. Therefore, all documents of the same type or the same logical structure are grouped to a single document type (DocType). To the DocType "book," for example, could belong all documents which consist of a table of contents, a sequence of chapters, a bibliography and an index, where all chapters comprise a chapter heading and a sequence of paragraphs, tables and figures .... According to its hierarchical structure, such a DocType can be described by a context-free grammar.

So the MarkupDirectives are no longer associated with *single* documents; instead, they can be defined on a higher level for the Doc*Type*.

Therefore, at the very beginning of the document model comes the definition of DocTypes. To each DocType one can produce several ContentRelatedStructuredDocuments and define several MarkupDirectives. Each combination of a ContentRelatedStructuredDocument and a MarkupDirective can be used to yield a concrete document in layout form, see Figure 3.

From the viewpoint of typesetting houses this means that they expect from their au-

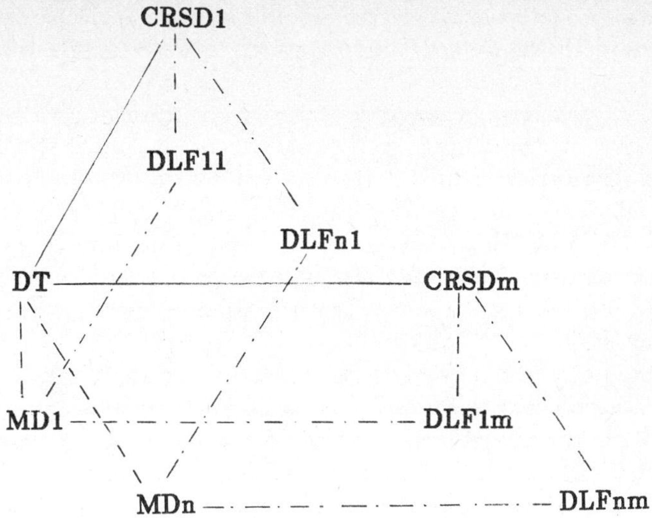

DT:	DocType
CRSD:	ContentsRelatedStructuredDocument
MD:	MarkupDirective
DLF:	Document in Layout Form

Figure 3

thors machine readable documents with logical markup and that they have to translate this logical markup afterwards in layout-related formatting commands.

No matter whether this is done automatically or by hand (as a provisional solution), the question arises whether the resulting perfectly high typographic quality is worth the additional trouble. Therefore, by standardization efforts it is tried to minimize the extra work.

The international standardization institutions ECMA and ISO are presently working out two document models which incorporate the ideas described above, namely ODA/ODIF (*Office Document Architecture/Office Document Interchange Format*) for the office area and SGML (*Standard Generalized Markup Language*) for the publishing area, including description languages and transmission rules, see [ISO] and [ECMA].

4. The concept of a document workstation environment

In the following we describe a project conducted at the Institut für Angewandte Informatik und Formale Beschreibungsverfahren at the University of Karlsruhe. Its aim is to provide authors with support in the production and publication of scientific documents.

The project deals with four components, namely the document workstation, the file server, the printing and formatting service, and a telecommunication interface.

From the users' point of view, the document workstation is the central constituent.

Here the (experienced) users can define new DocTypes and appropriate MarkupDirectives. But the main purpose is that users without any special knowledge in formatting languages and typography can choose a predefined document type and, by the help of an editor that is driven by this type, can edit documents of this type. Then they can use predefined MarkupDirectives to translate their ContentRelatedStructuredDocuments to a text data stream interspersed with formatting commands for the printing process.

The printing and formatting service provides formatters which are able to lay out scientific documents. It gets the text and the formatting commands from the workstation and enables the document to be printed on different output devices (paper, screen, foto film).

The communication between the workstation and the printing and formatting service is consciously designed as a batch system, in order to preserve the reasonable division of labour between the editing and the formatting processes. Therefore: no WYSIWYG! The authors should not continously be misled to worry about the layout while formulating the sentences. Instead, they should totally concentrate upon the contents. The printing and formatting service, however, has to make available a formatted draft copy of the authors' texts shortly after the editing session.

The file server stores DocTypes, MarkupDirectives, and documents, the latter in their different states as ContentRelatedStructuredDocuments, documents containing MarkupMaterial or formatted documents. Furthermore, the file server controls access rights and the communication between different authors working on the same document, saves different versions of documents and supplies a document retrieval interface.

In addition, a telecommunication interface must be available.

Summarizing, we provide the authors with a homogeneous and convenient environment which enables them to produce their own documents in a satisfying quality. As to the communication with the publishing houses, note that new MarkupDirectives can mark these documents with any markup the publishers could insist on, using the same ContentRelatedStructuredDocument, in order to achieve finest typographic quality. Thus authors may fulfil whatever requirements the publishing houses may impose on them in the future.

In the following sections we describe the single components of our project in more detail.

5. The printing and formatting service, or: TEX at Karlsruhe

The printing and formatting service of our project is based on TEX. TEX has been chosen for several reasons: First, there is no doubt that TEX gives the finest typographic quality of all formatters currently available. For example, the line breaking algorithm implemented in TEX is so efficient that only two hyphenations were necessary in the three pages of introduction to D. Knuth's TEXbook, see [K3].

Second, TEX generates a device independent output, which therefore can be typeset on a great variety of output devices. For the importance of device independent output see [B], for example.

As a very important matter of fact, the input language of TEX is powerful enough to allow a user-friendly interface to be built on it. And, last not least, TEX is widely spread at universities and institutions, thanks to the farseeing decision of D. Knuth to make TEX available as public domain software.

TEX has a long tradition at our institute. In September 82, TEX was running on a Burroghs B7700 which has been put out of service in the meantime. This was the first TEX installation in Germany. Today TEX is implemented on the following computers:

- TEX Version 1.1 on a Siemens S7881 under BS3000
- TEX Version 0.9999 on a Siemens S7561 under BS2000 (currently not in use)
- TEX Version 1.1 on a NCR Tower under UNIX
- TEX Version 1.1 on an IBM PC XT/AT under MSDOS (PCTEXby Personal TEX Inc.)

All these computers are interconnected by the LINK-net (*Lokales Informatiknetz Karlsruhe*), and text and binary files can be transfered between all of them. All scientists (and a great part of the technical staff) at the Institute have a terminal to the LINK-net in their offices.

Via the S7881, DVI-files can be transfered to an electrostatic plotter Benson 9424 which has a resolution of 254 dots/inch. It is also possible to output on an IBM matrix printer or an Epson LQ1500 via an IBM PC. Shortly, an IBM PC will be interconnected with a Corona Laser Printer which has a resolution of 300 dots/inch. The drivers for the IBM PC are by Personal TEX Inc. .

In order to have a previewing possibility, a driver for the screen of the IBM PC — equipped with a Hercules graphics card — has been developed. For that purpose, we first of all had to scale the PXL-files of TEX for the new resolution. We had got PXL-files for a resolution of 240 pixels per inch only, but the resolution of the screen was about 90 pixels per inch (in the horizontal). We therefore developed a special program (PXLSCALE) for converting given PXL-files for an arbitrary resolution into a new resolution. This program reads a PXL-file and converts it into an internal format, then calculates the new widths and heights of the characters, composes the new (in our case more coarse) raster and writes it back converting it into the external format again. The algorithm used for the evaluation of the new raster is rather primitive. A pixel in the output-raster is set black if it is covered by a certain amount of black pixels in the input-raster, otherwise it is set white. Furthermore, the algorithm obeys the rule of not to dissect parts of a character which should be connected. It does not pay attention to certain properties such as symmetry, perceptibility ... .

In order to improve the appearance of the scaled fonts we used another program which allows to edit PXL-files by hand. This editing was done for the most frequently used fonts only because it is not an easy work.

The driver program itself was developed by changing the program DVItype, which is a part of the TEX-system delivered on the distribution tape. The driver program interprets the DVI-files produced by TEX and displays them on the screen of the IBM PC in the same way they would be printed on paper but with resolution and quality reduced. All the programs described in this context are written in IBM-Pascal and were developed on IBM PC's which were placed at our disposal by the IBM Corporation, in a cooperation between IBM and the University of Karlsruhe.

For draft copies, technical reports, contributions to journals and proceedings, these output possibilities have shown to be sufficient in quality. But for the production of books it is most desirable to get the output on a CRT composer. Therefore, a TEX driver for a CRT composer DIGISET 400T20 is being developed in cooperation with a typesetting house at Karlsruhe.

In a CRT composer the light emitted by a cathode ray tube falls on a photographic film. Different from many laser printers, CRTs do not process bitmaps, but they control the processing of fonts by an instruction language which is similar to that of the DVI-files.

As to DIGISET composers, its instruction language enables the user to apply either Digiset fonts whose pixel patterns are on disk or user defined fonts whose pixel patterns are fed in together with the control commands.

Basically, a DIGISET driver for TEX can make use of both ways of processing the DIGISET offers. But if the DIGISET fonts shall be used, the proper TFM-files have to be produced for TEX. On the other hand, if TEX-fonts shall be used, the PXL-files must be converted into DIGISET format. Due to the high quality of the DIGISET fonts, it would be desirable to make the DIGISET fonts available. But for copyright-reasons, it is very difficult to get all the informations on DIGISET fonts which are necessary to derive the TFM-fonts for TEX without too much effort. Therefore, we decided to use the TEX fonts.

Thus, the job of writing a DIGISET driver consists of two major parts. First, the DVI-commands have to be translated into equivalent DIGISET command sequences. Second, the PXL-fonts must be converted to DIGISET format.

The first task has been settled by the program DVItoDIGI, see [J]. In order to test this program without having the PXL-fonts converted yet, we proceeded as follows. To each TEX-font we chose a DIGISET-font which was as similar as possible. These DIGISET-fonts were used by the driver instead of the original TEX-fonts.

After struggling with the faulty and incomplete documentation of the DIGISET composer, the program turned out to work well. But the differences between the printed fonts and those which had been used by TEX had dramatic consequences which made the output unacceptable, see figure 4.

Therefore, we started to solve the second problem, namely to convert the PXL-files into DIGISET format.

Two problems arose. Due to different systems of typographic measurements, the resolution of the TEX-fonts did not exactly fit any of the resolutions available on the DIGISET. To get the most out of the high resolution of the DIGISET, we decided to start with the best TEX-fonts we had which have a resolution of 600 dots/inch.

The closest approximation to this is the vertical resolution of 100/11.25 dots/Punkt on the DIGISET. Therefore, a TEX-character will appear by a factor of 0.99896 smaller than intended by TEX when printed on the DIGISET. In order to maintain the original proportions, all horizontal and vertical measures must be multiplied by this (small) factor.

The second problem is, that the vertical resolution of the DIGISET composer is 1.2 times greater than the horizontal one, whereas our PXL-fonts all come with identical horizontal and vertical resolution. Therefore the PXL-files have to be scaled vertically by a factor of 1.2.

The translation of PXL-fonts into DIGISET format is done by the program PXL-toDIGI, see [Sch]. This program first decodes a PXL-file and extracts to each character the matrix of the black and white pixels. Then the patterns are scaled vertically by 1.2.

3. SKELETON STRUCTURES FOR SETS OF ISO„ORIENTED OBJECTS

There are two well known skeleton structures which have proved to be useful for solving various problems volving rectangles: The segment tree of ÄBWÜ and the tile tree of ÄMcCÜ which was independently discovered in ÄEÜ but was called interval tree there. We show that both structures can be used in an algorithm to solve the rectangular visibility problem of the previous section.

The le] and right boundaries of all rectangles in the given set of n rectangles impose a *discrete raster* on the horizontal x„axis. We can assume that this raster is normed in such a way that it becomes a raster over a subset of integers. The horizontal projection of each of the n rectangles is a closed interval consisting of a contiguous sequence of elementary fragments. First we describe how these intervals are stored in a segment tree:

The *(empty) segment tree (skeleton)* is a binary tree of minimal height such that the i„th leaf both represents the i„th raster point and the closed open interval Ä$i, i + 1$), i.e. the i—th fragment. Each internal node represents the union of all fragments which belong to the leaves in the subtree deöned by it. Each closed interval Äi, jÜ, i.e. each consecutive sequence of fragments inclusive the two raster points i and j of the boundary of the interval can now be represented by the nodes which cover a subinterval of the given interval and are as close to the root as possible; the right boundary of a closed interval is represented by a leaf. It is well known that $O(\log n)$ nodes always sußce to represent an arbitrary interval. Each interval and the corresponding rectangle is associated with all those nodes whose union form the interval; i.e. each node has its associated *node list* of intervals. While the skeleton of the segment tree remains öxed these node lists change dynamically according to what intervals are currently active.

The following Figure 1 shows an example of a set of rectangles, the segment tree skeleton deöned by the set and the node lists of all nodes which are used to represent the intervals currently cut by the scan line.

We may furthermore assume that the internal nodes of the segment tree skeleton contain appropriate routing information to guide a search for a raster point. (One possibility is to assign to each internal node the minimal value represented by the leaves of its right subtree.)

The structure is semidynamic in the following sense: Initially, i.e. before the scan line meets the top boundary of the topmost rectangle, all node lists are empty. Whenever the scan line meets the top boundary of some rectangle r which has e as its le] and e as its right boundary the interval Äe, e'Ü is inserted into the structure. This consists of appending r's name to the node lists which represent interval Äe, e'Ü. Similarly, whenever the bottom boundary of some rectangle is met the name of the rectangle is deleted from all node lists which are used to represent the corresponding interval. Finally, *inverse range queries* can be posed: Given an edge e which is the le] or right boundary of some rectangle, we can determine the names of all (projections of) rectangles which contain e. Simply use the skeleton of the tree as a search tree for the Öraster point! e and report all names of rectangles (or:intervals) appearing in node lists on the search path.

When implemented appropriately the above structure has the following characteristics (cf.ÄBWÜ,e.g.):

Space required to store n intervals $S(n) = O(n \log n)$

Insertion time $O(\log n)$.

Deletion time $O(logn)$.

Query time $(\log n + k)$, where k is the size of the answer, i.e. the number of elements reported when answering an inverse range query.

We could directly use this structure as the structure L in the above given algorithm to solve the rectangular visibility problem:What remains to be shown is that we can perform visibility tests. They can be carried out as follows. In order to check whether or not a vertical edge e is visible at some scan point we determine all currently active intervals (ractangle projections) which contain the edge e. (This is an inverse range query with a raster point as query point). These intervals represent exactly those rectangles which may hide e. Thus, it sußces to evaluate the plane„equations of these rectangles at the scan point and determine the rectangle with minimal distance to the observer. If and only if this rectangle has e as its le] or right boundary the edge e is visible (at e'sintersection with the scan line).

Performing visibility tests as just described can, of course, be quite time consuming. For, the node lists may have length up to $O(n)$ which implies that a single visibility test may take time $O(n)$ as well. We can improve this if we maintain the lists of names of intervals representing rectangles in sorted order according to the relative distance to the observer: Each node list contains the intervals representing the currently active rectangles ordered as follows: Let (x, y) be a point where x lies in the interval of the node and y is the

Figure 4

Finally, the scaled bitmaps are coded to DIGISET format.

Because the DIGISET composer is located at a typesetting house in Karlsruhe, a situation that prevents us from accessing it freely, we had to test the program PXLtoDIGI without this composer. In order to test the scaling procedure, we printed the scaled characters on a lineprinter and inspected the product visually.

For the test of the coding procedure, a decoding program has been used which was originally developed for another purpose. The application of the coding program first and the decoding program afterwards did not affect the character patterns. Therefore, the coding procedure can be considered to be correct.

The program DVItoDIGI and PXLtoDIGI, as described above, are completely tested. Their extent is about 2600 resp. 2000 lines of source text. Both programs are linked together and must be tested again. We are planning to install the fonts generated by the program PXLtoDIGI on a disk in the typesetting house permanently. So we can save the transfer of the font data together with the DIGISET commands for each typesetting job. Furthermore, we are planning to install the program **METAFONT** by D. Knuth to get the PXL-fonts in that resolution that fits the DIGISET composer best.

6. The general concept of the document workstation

From a logical point of view, documents are — basically — hierachically organized structures. (Note that references do not disturb this hierarchical structure, because only their content(!) depends on the structure of the concrete document.) This philosophy has been incorporated into the general structure-editors NLS/Augment, later SRI International, of Englbart and the XS-1-family of Burkhart and Nievergelt, [M], the formatting system SCRIBE of B. Reid, [F] which forms the basis of the document editor of J.H. Walker, [M], and the TEX macro package LATEX of L. Lamport, [L]. In [Ki], an abstract document model is proposed which generalizes all these models. Also the standardized document models ODA/ODIF, [ECMA], and SGML, [ISO], follow this philosophy.

The theory of formal languages supplies an important tool for the description of hierarchical classes, namely the context-free grammars. Context-free grammars are commonly used in the syntax specification of programming languages. Here, a program simply is a string of symbols produced by the context-free grammar. In our philosophy, however, a context-free grammar, i.e. a document type, produces a derivation tree with the text of the document at its leafs. This derivation tree is precisely what we call a ContentRelatedStructuredDocument.

A syntax-driven editor has been designed, whose controlling syntax (i.e. the DocType) can be defined freely. But how can we describe the special grammars which correspond to DocTypes and are able to drive a document editor?

The crucial idea is that a context-free grammar again can be regarded as a document of a special type which is called DocTypeSpec, because it specifies DocTypes. Assume that the grammar/document DocTypeSpec has the *type* DocTypeSpec again. Then the situation becomes really nice, because one can use the *same* editor to define Doc*Types* (by driving it by the DocType DocTypeSpec) or to edit documents of a special type (by driving it by this type which must have been defined earlier).

7. The specification of the DocType "DocTypeSpec"

Our next job is the specification of the DocType "DocTypeSpec" which will be done in a (possibly) new version of an extended BNF-form. We start with a verbal description of the extensions.

We use a constructor for alternatives $[A_1, |A_2| \ldots |A_n]$, which means that precisely one of the expressions $A_1, \ldots, A_n$ has to be chosen. This gives us the possibility to summarize different rules with the same lefthand side as a single "object definition" (ObjDef).

As occurence indicators we use '*' (star), '+' (plus) and '?' (optional), which have to be prefixed to the operand. '*A' ('+A') means, that the expression 'A' has to be evaluated arbitrarily often (but at least once). '?A' means, that the evaluation of 'A' is optional.

By the way, introducing occurence indicators does not only make the grammars more readable, but also avoids unnatural asymetries in the derivation trees which stem from the use of recursion. We prefer prefix notation to postfix notation in order to support the interpretation of expressions from left to right.

Furthermore, we distinguish between two different kinds of terminals. In our notation, "internal terminals" are specific characters which are defined directly by the DocTypeSpecification. Such characters are delimited by simple quote marks ('...').

In order to avoid specifying a DocType down to the character level, it is convenient to introduce terminals which represent *content classes* of legal input by their identifiers. These "external terminals" are not specified further in the DocTypeSpecification. The evaluation of these external terminals initiates the DocTypeInterpreter — the kernel of our system — to call another program which takes over the control of the user's input. This may involve very different processes, for example the interpretation of regular expressions to fill up forms or also special editors as word-processors or graphic editors. Especially, external terminals could call the DocTypeInterpreter itself with a new DocTypeSpecification as controlling syntax, in order to include other documents. Naturally, such programms need suitable interfaces to the DocTypeInterpreter. External terminals start with a '#', followed by an identifier.

In figure 5 the Doctype "DocTypeSpec" is specified, which itself specifies all DocTypes.

Three external terminals are used. Their meaning is as follows:

- #ALPHA: any sequence of letters and digits
- #CHARS: any sequence of printable characters
- #EXTERN: any identifier of an external terminal

Note that the DocType "DocTypeSpec" itself belongs to the class of DocTypes it defines. Therefore, the specification of any DocType can be done by syntax directed editing itself.

As in the field of programming languages, there are additional syntactic constraints, which cannot be formulated in a context-free way. We should, e.g., postulate for the DocType "DocTypeSpec" that every ObjectName must be defined uniquely, i.e. occurs only once at the lefthand side of an ObjectDefinition.

Later on we will extend our DocType concept such that additional constraints can be integrated in the DocTypeSpecification.

```
DocTypeSpec   ::=  +ObjDef.

ObjDef        ::=  ObjName '::=' Sequence '.'.

ObjName       ::=  #ALPHA.

Sequence      ::=  Term *( '␣' Term ).

Term          ::=  ?[ '*' | '+' | '?' ]  [ ObjName | '#' #EXTERN
                   | '‘' #CHARS '’' | Alternative | '(' Sequence ')' ].

Alternative   ::=  '[' Sequence *( '|' Sequence ) ']'.
```

Figure 5

8. The interpretation of DocTypeSpecifications

One gets a specific ContentsRelatedStructure from a DocTypeSpecification by specifying for each iteration operator which is to be evaluated, how many iterations take place, and for each construct of alternatives which alternative has to be chosen.

Then a ContentsRelatedStructuredDocument consists of a ContentsRelatedStructure and the contents, which is fixed by evaluation of the external terminals.

Figure 6 shows, how the recursive structure of a DocTypeSpecification is mirrorred in the recursive structure of modules calling each other while interpreting DocTypeSpecifications. Interpretation here means that the system sets up a ContentsRelatedStructure according to a DocTypeSpecification in interaction with the user.

An object is interpreted by interpreting its defining sequence. Thereby references in the internal representation are established to enable the manipulation of an object as an entity. A sequence is interpreted according to the order of its Terms.

In the case a Term contains an occurence indicator, the user decides about the specific structure. The occurences of the Term's body have to be counted and the according number has to be stored at the beginning of the internal representaiton of the Term.

For the interpretation of the Term's body different possibilities exist according to the second alternative construct in the definition of the object "Term" in figure 5.

- An ObjectName causes the interpretation of the identified object. In this case the position of the corresponding definition has to be seeked.
- Internal terminals need not be taken over into the internal representation of a document, because they are elements of the DocTypeSpecification.
- External terminals initiate the call of a program under whose control the user can enter text or other data in a system buffer. The internal representation only gets a reference to these data.
- Subsequences cause their interpretations as a sequence. In contrast to the objects identified by names, their manipulation as an entity is not supported.
- Alternatives produce a menue which asks the user for selection. Depending on its choice, a number is stored in the internal representation of the ContentsRelated-

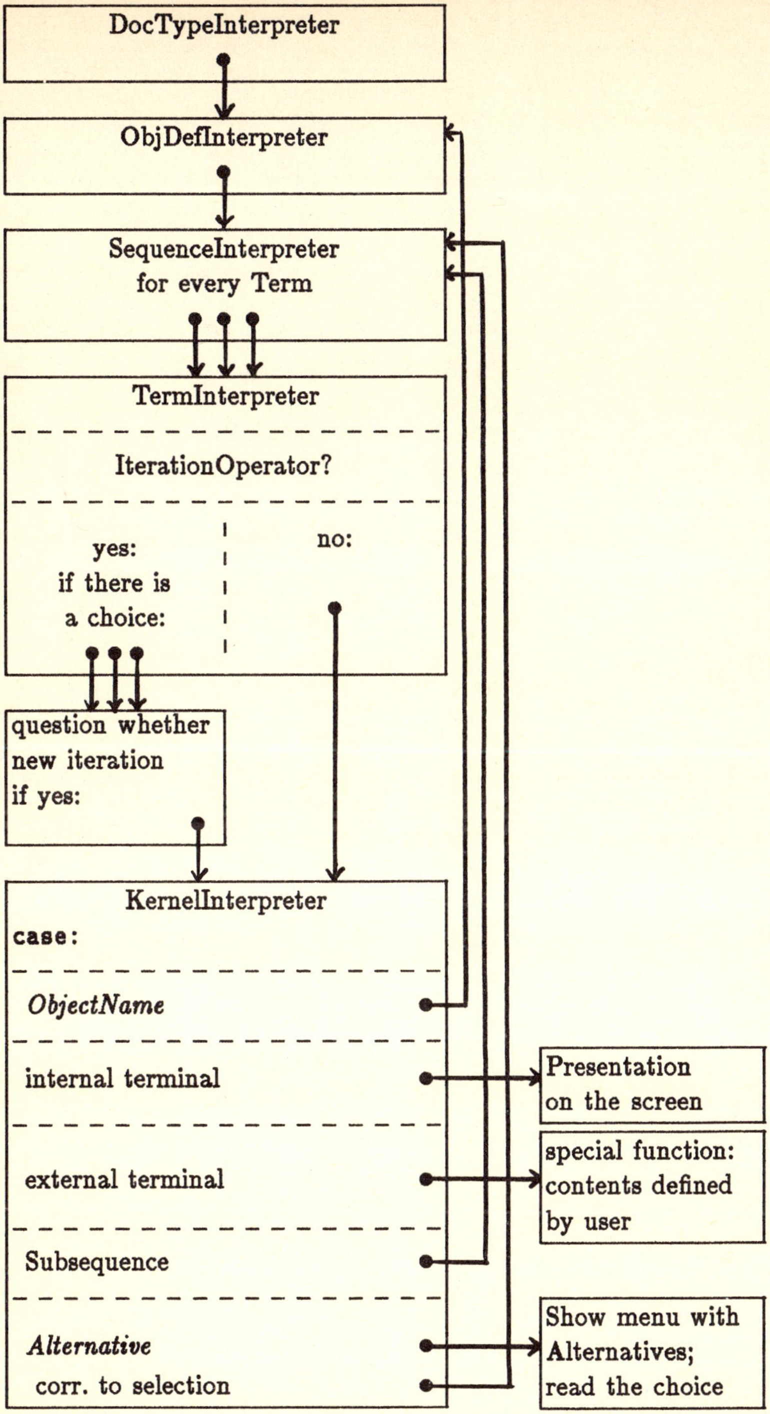
DocTypeInterpreter
ObjDefInterpreter
SequenceInterpreter
for every Term
TermInterpreter
IterationOperator?
yes:
if there is
a choice:
no:
question whether
new iteration
if yes:
KernelInterpreter
case:
ObjectName
internal terminal
external terminal
Subsequence
Alternative
corr. to selection
Presentation
on the screen
special function:
contents defined
by user
Show menu with
Alternatives;
read the choice

Figure 6

Structure. Afterwards, the selected subsequence is interpreted.

The DocTypeInterpreter does not fix the concrete layout of questions, warnings and error messages. This will be done by EditorDirectives depending on the DocType. Thanks to its separation from the contents, the ContentsRelatedStructure can be hold in the main memory. Therefore it is rather easy to manipulate this structure.

9. Integrating a reference concept

The function of ObjectNames is to point to an ObjectDefinition. If ObjNames appear in a DocTypeSpecification as strings without any additional structure, this reference character cannot be realized in the most efficient way. Therefore, to the terminal classes "internal terminals" and "external terminals" are added two further classes, namely "RefTypes" and "RefItemTypes."

- RefTypes cause the DocTypeInterpreter to read in a string similiar to the external terminals, called the Reference, but this Reference is separated from the regular contents and put into a special list structure if not yet existent. A pointer to the actual position in the ContentsRelatedStructure is implemented here, too. If the list already contains a RefItem for this Reference, the ContentsRelatedStructure gets an additional pointer to the position of the RefItem. RefTypes are notated by a '%', followed by a RefTypeIdentifier.
- RefItemTypes also cause the DocTypeInterpreter to read in a string which is added to the special list. If this Reference is already registered in the list, it must be refused with an error message. Otherwise, bidirected pointers are implemented between the corresponding positions in the list and in the ContentsRelatedStructure. In addition, all References which already exist get pointers in the ContentsRelatedStructure to the position of the RefItem. RefItemTypes are noted by a '!', followed by a RefItemTypeIdentifier.

Figure 7 shows different phases of the lists of the single RefTypes which can occur in a DocTypeSpecification. The RefType $A2$ did not get any Item so far. The RefType An has got a Reference called a, but there is no corresponding RefItem. RefType $A1$ has got several References and RefItems. The Reference x occurs twice, but no RefItem is there. On the other hand, there is a RefItem b, but no Reference to b. Finally, the RefItem a is a complete reference list: There exists a bidirectional pointer between the RefItem in the list and its position in the ContentsRelatedStructure and from there a pointer to the position of the RefItem.

Now we change the definition of DocTypeSpec using these new types of terminals, see figure 8. Note that the real difference to the previous specification is hidden behind the scenes, because here ObjNames are no longer simple character strings but references or RefItems, see the definition of ObjDef and Term.

This method solves the problem of multiple definitions of ObjNames, because RefItems with the same type and identifier are forbidden! Furthermore, the completeness of a DocTypeSpecification can be checked easily.

The new types of terminals make cross references an integral part of DocTypeSpecifications, see figure 9. Note that the automatic generation of chapter numbers, for example, does not fall into the domain of the DocTypeSpecifications, but of the editor directives.

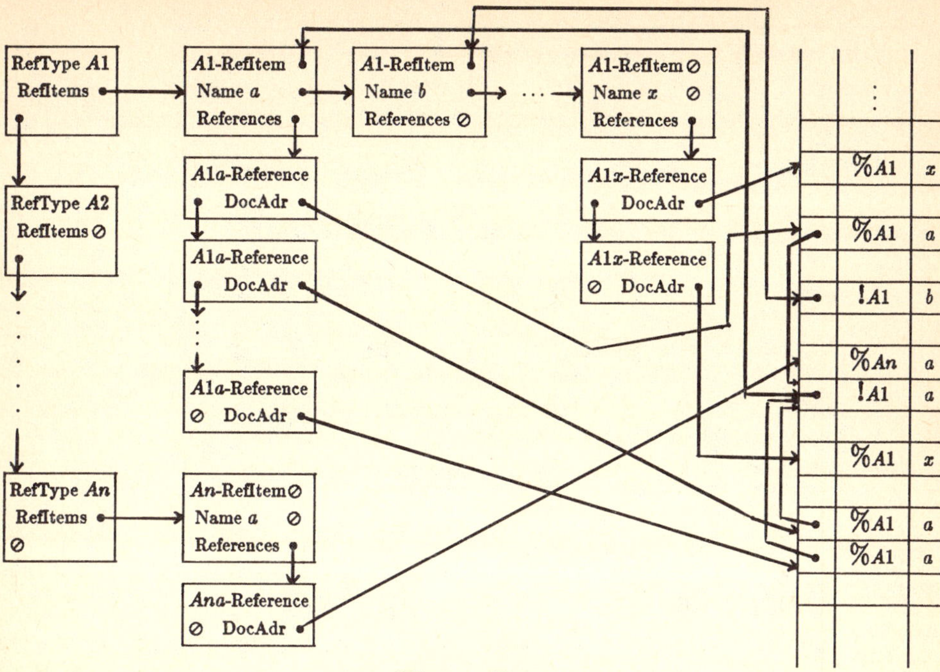

Figure 7

```
DocTypeSpec   ::= +ObjDef.

ObjDef        ::= !ObjRef '::=' Sequence '.'.

Sequence      ::= Term *( '␣' Term ).

Term          ::= ?[ '*' | '+' | '?' ]  [ %ObjRef | '!' #ALPHA
                  | '%' #ALPHA | '#' #EXTERN | '"' #CHARS '"'
                  | Alternative | '(' Sequence ')' ].

Alternative   ::= '[' Sequence *( '|' Sequence ) ']'.
```

Figure 8

Because References are only stored by positions, not by contents, a change of a RefItem immediately propagates to the corresponding References. Therefore, a Reference to chapter 4 becomes a Reference to chapter 5 automatically, when the insertion of a new chapter changes chapter 4 to chapter 5.

10. The configuration of the document workstation

So far we have demonstrated how DocTypeSpecifications and ContentsRelatedStructuredDocuments can be edited in a uniform way by interpreting DocTypeSpecifications. Therefore, the kernel of the document workstation is the DocTypeInterpreter.

```
Report        ::= Header +Chapter Bibliography Appendix.

Header        ::=   < not yet specified >.

Chapter       ::= !ChapNo #Heading GenText *Section.

Section       ::= !SectNo #Heading GenText *Section.

GenText       ::= *[ #Text | %ChapNo | %SectNo | %LitRef ].

Bibliography  ::= #Heading *( !LitRef BibText ).

BibText       ::=   < not yet specified >.

Appendix      ::=   < not yet specified >.
```

Figure 9

The DocTypeInterpreter passes control to special functions if he meets an external terminal. In general these special functions have two output streams, namely the screen and a system buffer for document contents, and one input stream, namely the keyboard. But there may be special functions for the batch processing of input streams as well, for example in order to translate a SGML-document into a ContentsRelatedStructured one. Also other kinds of interaction with the user, like menue choices at the alternative constructs are done by special functions; in the latter case the user's input has to be transfered back to the DocTypeInterpreter.

The next problem is how to display the contents of the document beeing edited on the screen in an adequate manner. For this purpose, the DocTypeInterpreter has a DocType "EditorDirectives" at its disposal which corresponds to the DocType of the document. These EditorDirectives provide for an adequate representation of such differently structured documents like a short novel or an application form.

To get a formatted output of a document, the ContentsRelatedStructuredDocument must be translated into a sequential data stream consisting of the text and interspersed formatting commands. This job is done by the MarkupGenerator which reads the DocTypeSpecification, the ContentsRelatedStructuredDocument and a MarkupDirective which is, like the EditorDirectives, a ContentsRelatedStructuredDocument of a special type again. These MarkupDirectives correspond to the type of the document that has to be formatted and contains the information about the correspondence between logical parts of the document and MarkupMaterial.

The complete configuration is shown in figure 10. More detailed information about EditorDirectives and MarkupDirectives can be found in [D].

11. The file server

What will be the task of the file server within the document system?

First it has to manage all the different types of objects, namely DocTypeSpecifications, MarkupDirectives, ContentsRelatedStructuredDocuments, text streams with formatting commands (TeX input files), and formatted documents (DVI-files) with all

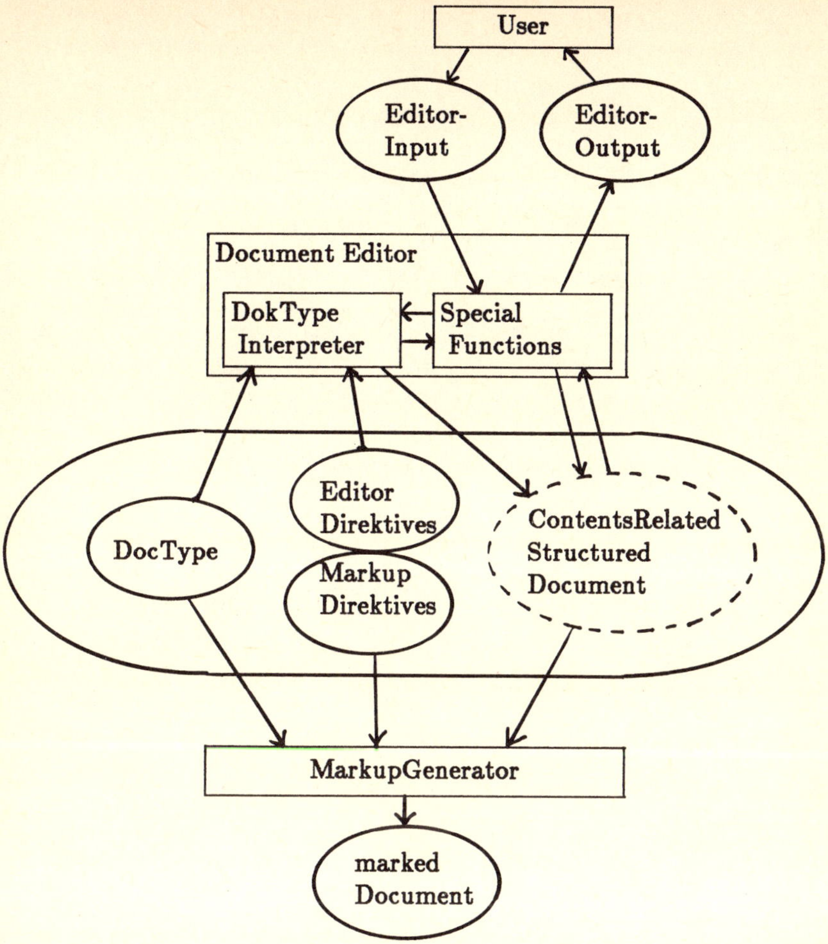

Figure 10

the relations between them. Furthermore, all the informations regarding one special document have to be kept in a database. These informations are

- (short) name of the document
- document type
- author(s)
- title
- abstract
- dates of creation and updates
- date of release (for publishing)
- number of recalls
- notes
- a.s.o.

The system should support several users at the same time but separate their document data areas. Users should be able to give authorization to other users for reading and/or writing their files. One should be able to pass queries to the database — even from the outside via mail — like the following

- which are the titles of all the available documents by author XYZ?
- which are the titles of all the documents published after DATE?
- which ist the abstract of document DOC?

The answers to these questions should be given by the system and sent back to the questioner. Also formatted documents should be sent to interested readers.

An an important conceptual question had to be answered: Should the file server (or the database system) know anything about the structure of DocTypes and documents? We say "No." So the cooperation between file server and editor can be very loose. The functions of the file server in this case will be essentially the following

- read document type
- write document type
- read structured document
- write structured document.

The file server can manage all types of objects but it cannot interpret them. In fact, it doesn't need to worry about DocTypes because the design of our editor a priori makes sure that all the documents are consistent with their types!

Therefore, the following realization can be considered. The objects are stored in a hierarchical file system as it is possible with the UNIX operating system, and the bibliographic data are stored in a relational database system. There will be a number of globally defined DokTypeSpecifications, MarkupDirectives ... which cannot be seen by a user exept through the workstation.

Users can define and store their own DokTypeSpecifications, MarkupDirectives and ContentRelatedStructuredDocuments with the help of the editor in some subdirectories of their home directories. There the formatted documents and the DVI files will be stored, too. The relation between DocTypeSpecifications, MarkupDirectives, ContentsRelatedStructuredDocuments, text files with formatting commands and formatted documents will be established by means of *name conventions*.

The user's home directory will contain a subdirectory *.documents*, were the database files and the files for DocTypeSpecifications reside. For each type there will be a subdirectory named with that type containing one *.structures* subdirectory, several MarkupDirectives for that type and for each MarkupDirective a further subdirectory containing formatted documents and corresponding DVI files which are composed according to DocTypeSpecifications in the *.structures* subdirectory. The organization of the file system is shown in figure 11.

Updates to the file system and to the database will be made by the editor only. Queries can be posed using the editor or special programs. There will be one special user to whom queries can be posted via mail. These queries will then be collected, the answers computed and mailed back automatically.

Acknowledgement

The authors wish to thank Rolf Klein for his engagement. He read a first draft of this paper and gave many useful hints which made it more understandable.

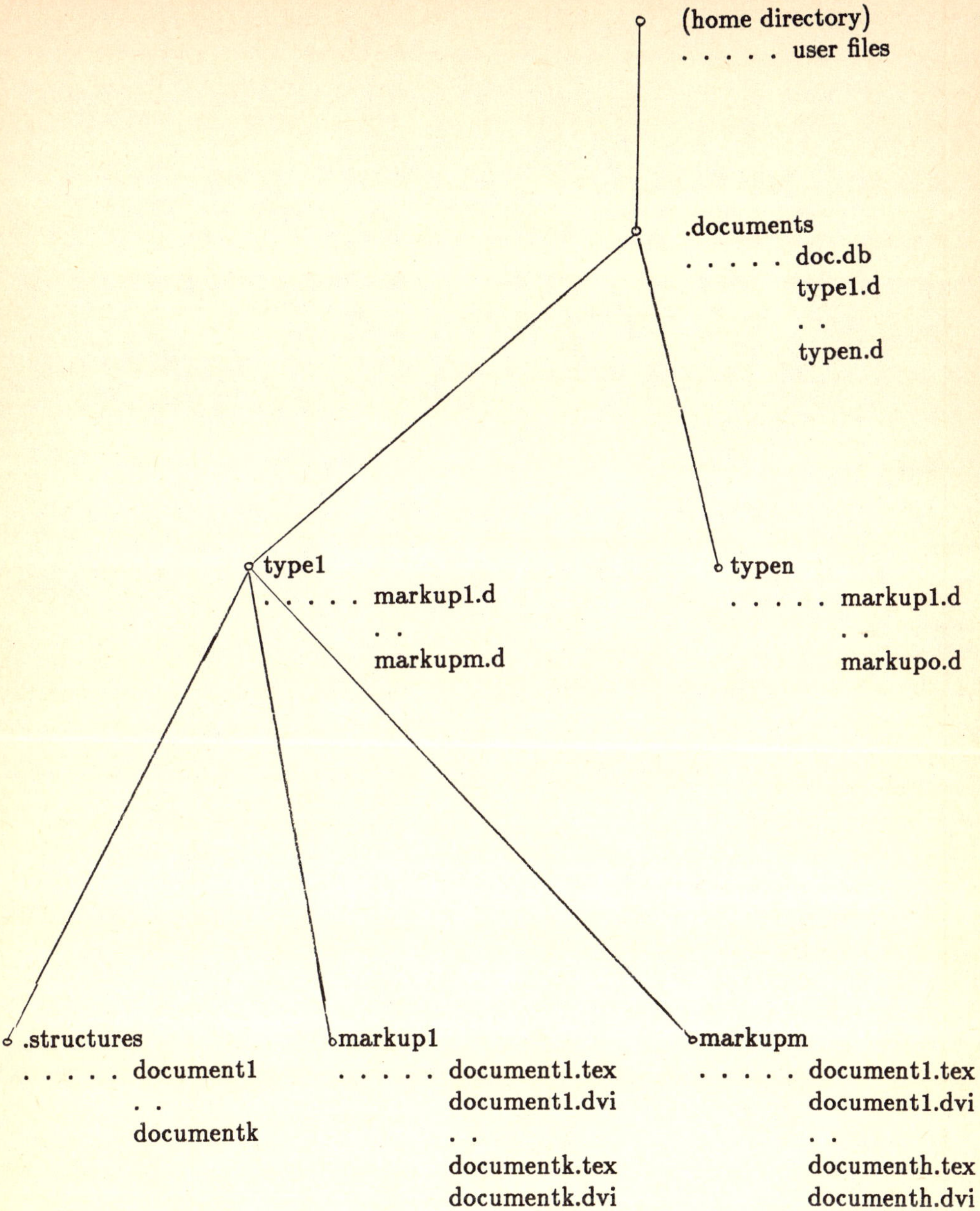
(home directory)
. . . . . user files
.documents
. . . . . doc.db
type1.d
. .
typen.d
type1
. . . . . markup1.d
. .
markupm.d
typen
. . . . . markup1.d
. .
markupo.d
.structures
. . . . . document1
. .
documentk
markup1
. . . . . document1.tex
document1.dvi
. .
documentk.tex
documentk.dvi
markupm
. . . . . document1.tex
document1.dvi
. .
documenth.tex
documenth.dvi

Figure 11

12. Literature

[B] H. Brown: From Text Formatter to Printer, in J.J.H. Miller (ed.): Protext 1, Boole Press, 1984

[BK] A. Brüggemann-Klein: TEX-Treiber für Lichtsatzanlagen, Institut für Angewandte Informatik und Formale Beschreibungsverfahren, Universität Karlsruhe, interner Bericht, 1986

[BHR] E. Börger, G. Hasenjäger, D. Rödding (eds.) Logic and Machines: Decision Problems and Complexity, LNCS 171, Springer, 1984

[D] P. Dolland: Konzeption eines Dokumentenarbeitsplatzsystems, Institut für Angewandte Informatik und Formale Beschreibungsverfahren, Universität Karlsruhe, interner Bericht, 1986

[ECMA] Standard ECMA-101: Office Document Architecture, 1985

[EP] Elektronisches Publizieren technisch-wissenschaftlicher Texte, interner Bericht über ein Forschungs- und Entwicklungsvorhaben, gefördert durch die Kommission der europäischen Gemeinschaften und das Bundesministerium für Forschung und Technologie, 1985

[F] R. Furuta, J. Scofield, A. Shaw: Document Formatting Systems: Surveys, Concepts, Issues, Comp. Surv., Vol 14, No. 3, 1982

[G] C.F. Goldfarb: A Generalized Approach to Document Markup, SIGPLAN Notices of the ACM, 1981

[ISO] ISO/DIS 8879

[J] C. Jäger: Dokumentation zum Programm DVItoDIGI, Diplomarbeit, Institut für Angewandte Informatik und Formale Beschreibungsverfahren, Universität Karlsruhe, 1984

[Ki] G.D. Kimura, A.C. Shaw, The Structure of Abstract Document Objects, Comp. Sc. Dep. FR-35, University of Washington, Seattle, WA98195, Technical Report No. 83-09-02, 1983

[K1] D.E. Knuth: Semantics of Context-Free Languages, Math.Syst. Theory 2.2 and 5.1, 1968 and 1971

[K2] D.E. Knuth: TEX and **METAFONT**, New Directions in Typesetting, Digital Press, 1979

[K3] D.E. Knuth: The TEXbook, Addison-Wesley, 1984

[L] L. Lamport: LATEX, User's Guide & Reference Manual, Addison-Wesley, 1986

[M] N. Meyrowitz, A. van Dam: Interactive Editing Systems, Comp. Surv., Vol 14, No. 3, 1982

[MK] P.A. MacKay: TEX's Coming of Age, in in J.J.H. Miller (ed.): Protext 1, Boole Press, 1984

[PK] M.F. Plass, D.E. Knuth: Choosing Better Line Breaks, in J. Nievergelt, G. Coray, J.-D. Nicoud, A.C. Shaw (eds.): Document Preparation Systems, North Holland, 1982

[S] J.L.A. Snepscheut: Trace Theory and VLSI Design, LNCS 200, Springer, 1985

[Sch] S. Schuierer, Dokumentation zum Programm PXLtoDIGI, Institut für Angewandte Informatik und Formale Beschreibungsverfahren, Universität Karlsruhe, 1985

AN IMPROVED USER ENVIRONMENT FOR TEX*

Peehong Chen   Michael A. Harrison
Jeffrey W. McCarrell   John Coker   Steve Procter

Computer Science Division
University of California
Berkeley, CA 94720, USA

Abstract

This paper describes the enhancements we have made at Berkeley to the TEX environment. The goal of the enhancements is to shorten the edit-compile-debug cycle in preparing TEX documents. An important step in cutting down debugging time is the development of a DVI previewer on a workstation with a high resolution bit-mapped display. Yet another approach we took is the integration of TEX with a powerful display-oriented editor whereby the editing, compiling, and certain pre- or postprocessing of a document may be automated. We present some of the important results of our work in this paper with a general critique on TEX that underscores our motivations.

1. Introduction

This paper is a report on the improvements we have made at Berkeley to the TEX document preparation environment. During the past few years, TEX [8] has evolved at Berkeley as an alternative to the standard UNIX text processing system `troff` [10] and its preprocessors. We enjoy doing our writings in TEX because it has a number of advantages over other systems, some of which we see are its extensibility (macros), mathematics, and the high quality output. Unfortunately, at the same time we have also discovered some disadvantages of and inconveniences in using TEX. The fact that TEX is batch-oriented often makes it very expensive to reprocess a document with only few changes. Another criticism we consider valid is its lack of graphics support, although a "hook" is available (`\special`) and many proposals have been made over the years in the public forum such as the `tex-hax` mailing list.

* This work has been sponsored by the U.S. National Science Foundation under Grant MCS-8311787 and by the U.S. Defense Advanced Research Projects Agency (DoD), ARPA Order No. 4871, monitored by Naval Electronic Systems Command, under Contract No. N00039-84-C-0089. Additional support was provided by the State of California MICRO program under grant number 532422-19900.

In 1984, a team was formed at Berkeley to conduct research in document preparation systems, with the improvement of TeX as our primary goal. The work we have done in the project comprises two phases. In phase one we took the obvious approach to make enhancements by integrating TeX and its accessory programs with an interactive editor. Furthermore, on our workstations we developed a DVI previewer and other TeX-related tools to shorten the edit-compile-debug cycle. In the second phase, which is still under development, we are taking a more ambitious approach that attempts to design and build a brand new system based on TeX. The idea is to stick with TeX's source language including its macro facility and formatting algorithms but, in addition, making it incremental and more user friendly. Moreover, editing tables, graphics, and raster images will be an integral part of the system. We call this new environment Visually-ORiented TeX, or VORTeX.

The two approaches are actually interrelated. The first phase started earlier with porting TeX to the SUN workstation and developing a DVI previewer under its window system, followed by integrating all TeX-related software in a display-oriented editor. By now it has produced a number of programs which are useful in and of themselves. They have also become important prototypes and special subsystems for the ultimate VORTeX environment.

This paper is concerned with the results produced by phase one of our project, as the objectives and design of the VORTeX system itself is discussed elsewhere [4]. We first give a general critique on TeX from the user's point of view in the next section, pointing out its strengths and weaknesses as compared with other systems. This also serves as a background for later sections which discuss some of the important enhancements we have done.

Section 3 describes the functionalities and technical aspects of `dvitool`, the DVI previewer we have been developing on the SUN workstation. Working with a window-based system, one can have a text editor operating on a source file, also have available a console or shell window in which to run additional jobs, and have a third window displaying the formatted output all at the same time. Our program for previewing DVI files is called `dvitool` which supports keystroke commands, pop-up menus, scroll bars, and other standard user interface in a window paradigm.

Section 4 discusses the TeX integration with GNU Emacs [13]. For the time being, most of us use Emacs as our editor-of-choice in preparing source files. Emacs allows one to customize it by writing programs in a Lisp dialect. This turns out to be an extremely powerful language, and we have constructed very large programs which aid in the use of TeX. In addition to doing obvious things such as matching braces automatically, the user can receive a great deal of assistance in working with bibliographies. It is possible to avoid the use of multiple passes with LaTeX/BibTeX [9,11] and a great many other important facilities can be made available through the use of our system. Discussions in this section are concentrated on high-level abstractions of the design and its basic functionalities.

Finally some concluding remarks are given in Section 5 on our experience with building this improved TEX environment. Notes on what we expect to do in the future, especially with VORTEX, will also be mentioned.

2. A Critique

We have chosen to base the VORTEX system on TEX for a number of reasons which center around TEX's unique advantages. One of these is the concept of a device independent file which gives the same results on different output devices, and the only limitation is the resolution of the device. We also are committed to getting the highest possible quality from our systems. TEX has outstanding algorithms for dealing with the basic problems of computerized typesetting. In particular, the line breaking algorithm is excellent and the hyphenation algorithm gives impressive results for relatively small table sizes.

TEX's greatest strength is its handling of mathematics. It is in processing mathematics that the advantages of a source-based system such as TEX become very noticeable. In a seminar given at Berkeley, students were asked to typeset a page of complicated mathematics from a textbook. This was not terribly difficult to do using TEX. On the other hand, with Xerox Dandelions available some students attempted to set the same page using the processing facilities available as part of the STAR system [1]. It took much longer, and the results were very disappointing in terms of appearance. This has lead us to believe that typesetting mathematics without a source language is in general a painful task. Even with the notion of *plagiarizing*, (i.e. by copying template formulas from what's available in system's database), which is supported by some WYSIWYG (what-you-see-is-what-you-get) systems like LARA [6], the potential tampering by the user will still put its final quality in question. The output produced by TEX on mathematics exceeds the levels of all but the best hand compositors, and it can be truly said to be an "expert system" in the production of mathematics.

Unfortunately, TEX has weaknesses as well. There is no graphic facility whatsoever. The system is oriented to batch operating systems. TEX has facilities for setting tables, but these are primitive, and the construction of tables in TEX is an enormously difficult and time-consuming chore. The situation is somewhat ameliorated with LATEX [9] which makes producing tables almost as easy as using `tbl` and `troff`.

TEX achieves its flexibility by being a macro-based system. That is, the user writes macros to accomplish what one wishes to do. Such examples of course are the `plain` package and the LATEX macro package. There is a very poor human interface in the macro system, and it requires a high degree of wizardry to use it.

While the source based systems have been impressive in the quality of their output for difficult typesetting jobs like mathematics, the situation is reversed with the WYSIWYG editors. Here excellent human interfaces have been developed. Users find it easy to learn the systems for simple word processing or even for the construction of graphics and the preparation of tables. The software for the Macintosh [7] is especially noteworthy in this regard. On the other hand, these systems cannot do mathematics well and they do not generally produce high quality results comparable to those obtainable from TEX.

3. TEX without Paper: Dvitool

Dvitool, a TEX output previewer running on the SUN workstation, is an integral part of the Berkeley TEX environment. Our primary goal for dvitool was to provide a means to view the DVI representation of a TEX file without printing it. In our large community, printing takes a long time and is particularly frustrating when debugging a macro. The section describes dvitool's basic functionalities, its user interface, and the future directions.

3.1 Functionalities

One of the first things dvitool does when executed is look for a user specific customization file. The customization file describes initialization parameters which are mostly window system specific, for example, the placement and size of the window dvitool runs in. After dvitool has started up, the image it presents of the DVI page is 1.45 times the size of an 8.5 by 11 inch sheet of paper. This scale factor means that when dvitool is made as big as the screen allows, the full width of the page and about 60% of its height will be visible. The scale factor is largely historical, but it is also practical. It turns out that at our screen resolution (80 dots per inch) that 1.45 times normal size is close to the lower bound of usability. Any smaller and the fonts would be illegible. Even at 1.45 times normal, dvitool's fonts cannot be called satisfactory.

Once the page is painted, the user can scroll an arbitrary amount either vertically or horizontally. The default action is to scroll 1/3 of the window size. There are also commands to position on any edge of the page, so one keystroke positions the bottom of the page at the bottom of the window. The complete DVI page is read in at one time, so that new views of the same page are instantaneous.

The user can move back and forth across pages as well. Since a new DVI page must be read and painted, there is a short delay, typically 4 seconds in our environment. Pages are cached, however, so that once a page has been viewed, viewing it again is nearly instantaneous. The memory penalty for page caching is about 6K bytes per page, which is not too prohibitive on our workstations with 4 megabytes of memory. The user can limit the number of cached pages and dvitool internally sets the limit whenever it cannot obtain enough memory to cache another page.

"Wildcard" searches have been implemented on any of TEX's ten \count variables. These are not full regular expressions; they just match any field so the user can go to the first page in chapter 4, for example. Commands also exist to view the first and last pages of the file. The movement commands are reminiscent of a text editor.

We've also implemented a global magnification scheme in `dvitool`. TeX's `\magnification` macro magnifies the size of individual letters on the page, but keeps `\hsize` and `\vsize` in true dimensions so the pages always come out 8.5 by 11 inches. `Dvitool`'s magnification, on the other hand, is global. It simply magnifies the entire page. There are 6 steps available, corresponding to TeX's 6 magsteps. This feature is particularly nice for aging eyes. We implemented discrete steps of magnification rather than a continuous spectrum because new magnifications require new fonts.

`Dvitool` can also report information about the DVI image, though this ability isn't quite as useful as it sounds. DVI files were designed to be a compact representation of a typeset page. There isn't a lot of extraneous information in them, so there isn't much that `dvitool` can report. About the most useful feature is that the user can select a character with the mouse and ask what font that character is set in. Even this is of limited usefulness, however, because the user has to correlate the font name in the TeX document which may have gone through arbitrary macro expansion to the system's name of the font that dvitool knows about. For example, TeX users in our environment have to know that TeX uses `amitt` for italic fonts. LaTeX users have to correlate `amitt` with emphasized text as well.

A companion program for `dvitool` we've developed is called `texdvi`. As the name implies, in one step TeX is executed and then the output is previewed using `dvitool`. `Texdvi` is smart enough to start up a new `dvitool` or to signal a running `dvitool` to preview the newly formatted output. However, `dvitool` will not be invoked if the DVI file was not changed. In addition, if there were errors during the TeX job, `texdvi` asks the user if he still wants to preview the potentially flawed DVI file. The new DVI image displays the text at exactly the point that was displayed earlier. This is very useful for debugging because of automatic repositioning. There are similar mechanisms for working with LaTeX and SliTeX (i.e. `latexdvi` and `slitexdvi`). In fact the program is set up in a way that with the formatter replaced by any TeX dialect, say FooTeX, the program `footexdvi` only has to be a symbolic link to `texdvi`.

3.2 User Interface

The user interface to `dvitool` has undergone many changes. Our window environment offers many ways to invoke commands. We finally decided on two: keystrokes and menus. The reason is that inexperienced users of `dvitool` expect to use the mouse to perform commands in a window environment, while advanced users find the menus cumbersome. We provide both so that `dvitool` is both easy to learn for the novice and responsive to the expert. We provide clues to help the user graduate from novice to expert level. For example, all of the menu commands also contain the matching keystroke commands as a hint to the user. We also provide an on-line help facility which is itself a DVI file.

We rejected having "buttons" as our user interface. Buttons can be thought of as menus which are statically displayed. They are fixed areas inside the window that the user points to and clicks on with the mouse to invoke a command. The standard placement for buttons is a row of them either across the top or down one side of the window. The idea was rejected for two reasons: we wanted to devote as much screen real estate as possible to displaying the DVI page, and we didn't want to force the user to be continually switching from the keyboard to the mouse.

As part of `dvitool`'s customization facility, keystroke commands can be redefined by the user to look like the key bindings of his/her favorite text editor. This feature is particularly important because users frequently switch from the editor to `dvitool` and back.

3.3 Future Directions

`Dvitool` was developed on the SUN workstation and runs under their proprietary window system [2]. Some care has been taken to isolate the system dependent parts of the code, but any program which must deal intimately with a non-standardized graphics interface is inherently not very portable. `Dvitool` is typical in this respect. We expect to begin work on a port to the X window system [5] soon.

Over time, the the user interface to `dvitool` has become more editor-like. Since it is possible, and indeed desirable, to have both your text editor and `dvitool` on the screen at the same time, we've tried to make them as homogeneous as possible. Planned additions to `dvitool` include negative magnification (shrinking) and a word search facility. Ligatures present problems for the word search routines. At the DVI level, ligatures such as the two characters "ff" are printed as a single character. Certainly we could create a translation table at compile time to do that mapping, but that solution is necessarily dependent on external and potentially changeable information.

Another problem is how to search for math text. How would the user tell `dvitool` to look for x_3, for example? The obvious solution of having `dvitool` recognize the TeX syntax for that expression implies that `dvitool` would have to be able to parse the TeX language which is a task far beyond its scope.

4. Integrating TeX with Emacs

One way to enhance the TeX environment is to customize a display-oriented text editor whereby the editing, compiling, and certain preprocessing or postprocessing of a document may be automated. Since in general a modern display editor is interactive, this approach turns out to be a remedy for TeX's lack of interaction with the user. Our editor of choice is GNU Emacs [13] which is the latest implementation in the Emacs family of editors [12]. GNU Emacs supports Emacs Lisp (or ELisp) in both interpreted and compiled forms. ELisp is very close to a full Lisp implementation: general list and attribute processing are available as part of some 900 system primitives and functions for various editing purposes.

The enhancements we've made to TEX in Emacs are basically two macro packages: *TEX-mode* and *BIBTEX-mode* [3]. The combined system is about 6,000 lines of ELisp code which is split into eight different files according to functionalities. Only the most essential parts are loaded initially; other files are loaded on demand. The first package, *TEX-mode*, is an aid to editing, spelling checking, compiling, previewing, and printing TEX and LATEX/SLITEX [9] documents. *BIBTEX-mode*, on the other hand, is an interface to editing BIBTEX [9,11] databases. Perhaps more importantly, the two modes are integrated to yield a very nice bibliography system for both types of documents.

A major focus of our design is a clean and uniform abstraction for both document structure and desired functionalities. The document structure refers to the types of objects and their interrelationships in a document that must be made explicit to the user. Functionalities are the possible operations which may be performed on certain objects. The two are bridged together by a set of commands which is uniform across the board in terms of naming and key bindings. Because there are so many commands in the system, the hope is to make them not only useful but easy to remember as well.

4.1 Document Structure

At the source level, *TEX-mode* makes the distinction between a *document* and a *file* by acknowledging that a TEX or LATEX document may involve multiple files connected by `\input` or `\include` commands. *TEX-mode* views a document as a tree of files with edges being the connecting commands. The root of a document tree is called the *master file*. Operations involving the entire document must be started from the master file. The processing sequence is the preorder traversal of the tree. In *TEX-mode*, each individual file has a link to the master to assure any global commands initiated in its buffer will always start from the master. The link to master also makes it possible to separately compile any component file or a part of it. The technique used in *TEX-mode* to do separate compilation is discussed in Section 4.2.4.

The next level of abstraction is a *file*, or when loaded in Emacs, a *buffer*. Objects of even smaller granularities include *regions* and *words*. A *region* is a piece of text, including any white space, bounded by a marker and the current cursor position (i.e. *point* in GNU Emacs). A *word* in *TEX-mode* is a piece of text with no white space in it.

At the output DVI level, the distinction is less complex. The only abstractions are the DVI file as a whole and subranges of one extracted out as another file. Normally DVI files themselves are not visited in Emacs. Therefore in a buffer bound to the TEX source `foo.tex`, the implicit operand for operations such as *preview* and *print* is `foo.dvi` instead of `foo.tex`. With the abstractions, it is possible to preview or print a DVI file partially as well as in its entirety.

Furthermore, *TEX-mode* maintains the notion of *document type* which may be either TEX, LATEX, or SLITEX in our current version. The type information is needed when the user tries to execute operations involving programs which are type-specific, such as the formatter (i.e. `tex`, `latex`, or `slitex`) and the document filter (i.e. `detex` or `delatex`). However, such information is implicit to the user except for the first time — once specified it will be saved as a comment line in the document to be read by later invocations. In other words, from the user's point of view, operations in *TEX-mode* are generic. For instance, an operation is known as *format* at all times instead of as `tex`, `latex`, or `slitex` under different situations. *TEX-mode* does operator overloading implicitly by consulting the type information.

4.2 Functionalities

Operations in our enhanced TEX environment fall into one the following categories: (1) delimiter matching, (2) bibliography processing, (3) spelling checking, and (4) compiling-debugging-previewing-printing. All four are defined in *TEX-mode* with the exception that the second also relies on *BIBTEX-mode.*

4.2.1 Delimiter Matching

A rather complete delimiter matching mechanism is implemented in *TEX-mode.* First, automatic delimiter matching applies to a pair of parentheses, brackets, or braces (i.e. `(...)`, `[...]`, or `{...}`). That is, whenever a self-inserting closing delimiter (i.e. `)`, `]`, or `}`) is typed, the cursor moves momentarily to the location of the matching opening delimiter (i.e. `(`, `[`, or `{`). *TEX-mode* gets this for free simply by modifying Emacs' syntax table entries.

The matching of other delimiters is less straightforward. Matching delimiters such as quotes (i.e. `` `...' ``, ``` ``...'' ```, and `"..."`) and TEX dollar signs (`$...$`) cannot be done automatically by syntax entry modifications. For example, the symbol `'` is the right quote as well as the apostrophe. Modifying syntax entries in the normal way is inappropriate because we don't want the cursor to bounce in the case of apostrophes. Matching double quotes (`"..."`) and TEX dollar signs (`$...$`) is even harder because the opening and closing delimiters are identical in those situations.

Semi-automatic Delimiters

TEX-mode introduces the notion of *semi-automatic matching.* To get semi-automatic delimiters inserted, one types some special commands and the text between a bound and the current cursor position will be enclosed by a pair of delimiters. The bound may be explicit or implicit. For the first case, which is called *zone matching* in *TEX-mode*, the user consciously sets a zone marker and closes it at the other end by typing the command that corresponds to the delimiters wanted. For the second case, an implicit bound refers to the white space before or after a word. *TEX-mode* calls this scheme *word matching* . Symbols like `` `...' ``, ``` ``...'' ```, `$...$`, and `$$...$$` as well as groupings for fonts and boxes such as `{\it ...\/}`, `{\tt ...}`, `\hbox{...}`, and `\vbox{...}` are all built-in semi-automatic delimiters in *TEX-mode*. For instance, typing the command **C-c i** (`tex-word-it`) will automatically enclose the previous word in `{\it ...\/}`, with ... being the word.

Automatic Delimiters

Matching identical opening and closing delimiters is a difficult task. The situation is further complicated by the TEX dollar sign because a pair of single dollar signs (`$...$`) denotes *math mode* in TEX whereas a pair of double dollar signs (`$$...$$`) means *display math mode*. A correct mechanism not only has to know which self-inserting `$` or `$$` is an opening delimiter and which is a closing one but also must be clever enough so that the second `$` in `$$` does not match the one preceding it. Furthermore, a dollar sign may be escaped (i.e. `\$`) in TEX which must be treated as an ordinary symbol rather than a math mode delimiter. *TEX-mode*'s dollar sign matching mechanism is designed to handle all cases correctly. A similar but less complex mechanism applies to the matching of double quotes (`"..."`).

LaTEX Delimiters

One of the most commonly used commands in LaTEX is a pair of `\begin` and `\end` which is normally used to embrace a large piece of text under a certain *environment*. Environments can be nested in the obvious way, just as in any block-structured language. With several levels of environments in place, proper indentations become essential to readability.

TEX-mode has a facility that opens and closes LaTEX environments automatically with proper indentations inserted. For example, with one command, you can get

```
\begin{enumerate}
  █
\end{enumerate}
```

where █ denotes the current cursor position. Most LaTEX environments are predefined and there is an operator which prompts you for an environment and its associated arguments interactively.

Customization

All delimiter matching schemes mentioned above can be customized. A new pair of delimiters may be defined statically by putting the information in Emacs' profile (`.emacs`) to have it available for every *TEX-mode* session. Alternatively, the user can enter the information interactively to *TEX-mode* so that a new delimiter pair is bound for only one particular Emacs session.

4.2.2 Bibliography Processing

BIBTEX is a bibliography preprocessor for LaTEX documents. Under the LaTEX paradigm, one makes citations in the source by referring to entries defined in bibliography databases. A BIBTEX database is a file with the name suffix '`.bib`' which contains one or more bibliography entries. To get the final output, the user first runs `latex` on the source to produce some reference information which is passed to `bibtex` to generate the actual bibliography. A second run of `latex` looks up the bibliography and produces cross reference information based upon which the last `latex` does the actual substitutions.

TEX-mode makes it possible for BIBTEX to work on plain TEX documents as well. It bypasses the first `latex` and invokes `bibtex` directly. It works with multiple files involved in a document by recursively examining `\input` commands in plain TEX files and `\includeonly`, `\include`, and `\input` commands in LATEX files. Furthermore, it prompts you for corrections at the places where citation errors are found. In addition, a database lookup facility is available for making citations. The implications are:

1. The same mechanism not only works for LATEX documents which BIBTEX was originally designed for but for plain TEX documents as well.
2. To get the final LATEX output, the user only has to invoke one or two `latex`'s manually — depending on non-citation symbolic references being present. To get the final TEX output, only a single run of `tex` will suffice. This is due to the automatic invocation of `bibtex`, the error correcting facility, and the automatic substitution mechanism.
3. Due to the lookup facility, the user does not have to memorize or type in the exact entry names in order to make citations. The system prompts you one by one the matching entries found in the specified bibliography database. The selected entry will be interpolated into the source automatically.

In our environment there is a powerful IBM 3081 mainframe which we often use for large jobs. Currently it supports TEX and LATEX but not BIBTEX. However, using our bibliography system in Emacs, we are able to get all bibliographical references resolved in our local machine (VAX/UNIX), send the document as a single file to the 3081 computer over the network, execute `tex` or `latex` there, and get the resulting DVI file back. In fact, a fair amount of work needs to be done before a `.tex` file is sent to the remote machine. For instance, the conversions between special characters used in the two systems and between stream-based files (UNIX) and record-based files (IBM 3081 takes 80 columns per line) must all be realized beforehand. It would be impossible to take advantage of the remote machine's fast speed if our preprocessing facility were not available.

Finally, bibliography database files can be manipulated using *BIBTEX-mode*. It has all fourteen BIBTEX bibliography entry types predefined so that to insert a new entry the user only has to specify its type. A skeleton instance of the specified type will be generated automatically with the various fields left empty for the user to fill in. A set of supporting functions such as *scroll*, *field copy*, *entry duplicate*, ..., etc. is provided to facilitate this content-filling process. Other major features of the mode include a facility to make a draft bibliography for debugging and previewing purposes and an extended abbreviation mechanism that allows one to abbreviate chunks of text and to browse abbreviations defined in any `.bib` files.

4.2.3 Spelling Checking

The *TeX-mode* spelling interface allows one to check the spelling for a word, a region, a buffer, or the entire document. It is specially tailored to TeX and LaTeX documents: keywords and commands of TeX will first be filtered out by a program called `detex` and those of LaTeX by `delatex`, before being sent to the system's spelling program. The user will be able to scroll the list of misspelled words and make corrections, including using a dictionary lookup facility. To avoid screen redisplay overhead, searching under low speed connections ($\leq$ 2400 baud) is implemented for scrolling and replacing any misspelled words in the buffer. That is, if an instance is not visible in the current window, only the line containing it is shown in a tiny window at the bottom of the screen.

4.2.4 Compile-Debug-Preview-Print

A number of TeX related programs can be invoked from *TeX-mode*. These external programs are executed uniformly in Emacs' inferior shell process. The generic operators are *format*, *display*, *view*, and *print*. The first two are overloaded based on the document type. The *display* operator is a pipeline of formatting followed by previewing (i.e. `texdvi`, `latexdvi`, or `slitexdvi`). The *view* operator is bound to a previewer such as `dvitool` described in the Section 3. The other two operators are self-explanatory.

The notion of master file plays an important role here. Both *format* and *display* operate on either the entire document, a buffer, or a region in buffer. A document preamble and similarly a postamble can be associated with the master to contain the document's global context. To separately compile a component file or its subregion, a mechanism is available in *TeX-mode* that includes in a temporary file the document's preamble and postamble with the selected text inserted in between. The system will then run *format* or *display* on this temporary file. This technique is primarily for debugging purposes as there is no provision for linking separately generated DVI files into one big DVI file. However, for users wanting only a quick look at a relatively small portion of a document in the debugging phase, this automatic facility turns out to be very valuable.

A DVI file can be previewed or printed in its entirety. *TeX-mode* can also invoke the program `dviselect` so that arbitrary pages within a DVI file may be extracted and only these selected pages will be previewed or printed. This is another useful tool for avoiding unnecessary work in a batch oriented environment like TeX.

Another support for debugging is a mechanism which automatically positions the cursor to the line and column where the error occurs. Also available are little tricks like commenting out a region by a single command and recovering it by another command.

4.3 Commands

The bridge between objects and their corresponding operations is the set of commands available to the user. The central issue here is the uniformity in both naming and key bindings.

By and large, the two modes obey the naming convention that a function name consists of three parts: prefix (`tex-` or `bibtex-`), generic operator, and abstract object. The corresponding key binding will be the **C-c** prefix, followed by **C-** and the first letter of the middle part, then the first letter of the last part. One example is the *TEX-mode* function `tex-format-document` with its corresponding key binding being **C-c C-f d**. *BIBTEX-mode* deals with a simpler set of objects such as bibliography entries and their component fields. The function to duplicate the previous entry, for instance, is called `bibtex-dup-previous-entry` which is bound to **C-c C-d p**. There are variations to this convention due to the constraint of limited keys, but all converge to the central idea of uniformity.

5. Conclusions

The environment described in this paper has proved to be useful to users of TEX and TEX-like programs. With `dvitool` and the various editing functions in *TEX-mode*, for example, the edit-compile-debug cycle has been cut down drastically, besides saving on paper expenditure. The abstract document structure which *TEX-mode* supports and the special techniques it uses have made possible a simple form of separate compilation, which also contributes to avoiding unnecessary processing overhead. Furthermore, the bibliography subsystem based on the two Emacs modes has become a valuable tool in writing TEX and LATEX documents.

Other subsystems that have been built but not mentioned in this paper include a bitmap editor for the TEX PXL and GF font formats. This program is very useful for tuning special fonts such as digitized raster images. We have also written a DVI driver for the Xerox Raven laser printer and a font converter from PXL to the Xerox Interpress format. One of the things we have not added yet to the system, but will do so soon, is the automatic construction of indices, etc.

Even though this enhanced Berkeley TEX environment is far from being ideal — graphics is still absent and table writing is still inconvenient — among many other missing but desirable features, we expect to have all of this functionality available in the final VORTEX system. Our experience with the subsystems built so far has been of significant value to the design of VORTEX. We distribute this software from Berkeley, and it is currently running in approximately 30 universities and industrial sites.

6. References

[1] *8010 STAR Information System Reference Library, Release 4.2.* Xerox Office Systems, El Segundo, California, 1984.

[2] *SunView Programmer's Guide, Release A of 17.* Sun Microsystems, Mountain View, California, February 1986.

[3] Peehong Chen. *GNU Emacs TEX-mode and BIBTEX-mode.* Technical Report, Computer Science Division, University of California at Berkeley. To appear.

[4] Peehong Chen, John Coker, Michael A. Harrison, Jeffrey W. McCarrell, and Steve Procter. The VORTEX document preparation environment. Submitted for publication.

[5] Jim Gettys and Ron Newman. *Xlib - C Language X Interface: Version 9.* MIT Project Athena, Cambridge, Massachusetts, 1985.

[6] J. Gutknecht. Concepts of the text editor Lara. *CACM*, 28(9):942–960, September 1985.

[7] L. Johnson. *Macintosh MacWrite Manual.* Apple Computer, Inc., Cupertino, California, 1983.

[8] Donald E. Knuth. *The TEX Book.* Addison-Wesley Publishing Co., 1984.

[9] Leslie Lamport. *LATEX: A Document Preparation System. User's Guide and Reference Manual.* Addison-Wesley Publishing Co., 1986.

[10] Joseph F. Ossanna. *Nroff/Troff User's Manual.* Computer Science Technical Report 54, AT&T Bell Laboratories, Murray Hill, New Jersey, October 1976.

[11] Oren Patashnik. *BIBTEXing.* Computer Science Department, Stanford University, Stanford, California, March 1985.

[12] Richard M. Stallman. EMACS: the extensible, customizable self-documenting display editor. In *Proceedings of ACM SIGPLAN/SIGOA Symposium on Text Manipulation*, pages 147–156, Portland, Oregan, June 8–10 1981.

[13] Richard M. Stallman. *GNU Emacs Manual.* Free Software Foudation, Cambridge, Massachusetts, second edition, March 1986.

THE VORTEX DOCUMENT PREPARATION ENVIRONMENT*

Peehong Chen   John Coker   Michael A. Harrison
Jeffrey W. McCarrell   Steve Procter

Computer Science Division
University of California
Berkeley, CA 94720, USA

Abstract

VORTEX (Visually-ORiented TEX) is a TEX-based document preparation environment being developed at Berkeley. The system will have three major features: (1) Both source and target representations of a document will be maintained and displayed. Changes made to one representation will propagate to the other automatically. (2) It will reformat and redisplay a document incrementally. (3) A high degree of interactivity and a good user interface will be provided. Our approach is to derive an internal representation based on which transformations between source and target can be realized efficiently. This paper describes the objectives and motivations of the project. An outline of the internal representation as well as VORTEX's basic functionalities and user interface is presented.

1. Introduction

During the last ten years, there has been a significant amount of work done in text processing and document preparation systems. Detailed classifications of these systems can be found in [7]. For our purposes, it is sufficient to consider two different series of developments. In one, which we call the *source-based model*, documents are prepared with interspersed editing commands. The system is then run, usually in batch mode, and the results observed. Typical processors of this type include `nroff/troff` [15] and the associated UNIX subsystems and preprocessors. This group also includes Scribe [17], which has one of the nicest user interfaces of this type of system. The high point of this group in terms of output quality has been the TEX [13] family of processors.

* This work has been sponsored by the U.S. National Science Foundation under Grant MCS-8311787 and by the U.S. Defense Advanced Research Projects Agency (DoD), ARPA Order No. 4871, monitored by Naval Electronic Systems Command, under Contract No. N00039-84-C-0089. Additional support was provided by the State of California MICRO program under grant number 532422-19900.

A second major development has been the *direct manipulation model*, which includes processors of the so-called "what-you-see-is-what-you-get" (WYSIWYG) type. This started with the Bravo editor [14], and subsequent systems such as Etude [11], Tioga [19], and Lara [10] have been developed at various research institutions. Also, with personal workstations becoming common place, a number of commercial WYSIWYG systems like STAR [1], MacWrite [12], and Interleaf [2] have already penetrated many homes and offices. One thing common to the all these systems is the absence of a source language for describing documents. Everything is specified on-line by invoking menus and buttons so that a large number of details are hidden.

Each of these trains of development has important advantages and disadvantages. By and large, the output quality produced by source-based systems is higher than that by WYSIWYG editors. This is because most source compilers are batch-oriented, which means the formatting can be better optimized. Direct manipulation systems are limited, in this regard, by certain constraints in terms of response time. However, being batch-oriented often makes source-based systems poor in their user interface and expensive in the processing time. It is in the area of user interfaces that WYSIWYG systems seem preferable.

VORTEX is an attempt to combine the best features of both paradigms. We believe the ability to deal with multiple representations of the same document is extremely important. There are simply some aspects of document preparation which are much better dealt with at the source level, while others are better dealt with by direct manipulations. More precisely, the major focuses of VORTEX are the following:

- *Multiple Representations.* Both source and target representations of a document will be maintained and presented. The source representation refers to a TEX document in its original unformatted form whereas the target representation means its formatted result. The user can edit both representations using a *text editor* and what we call a *proof editor*, respectively. Changes made to one representation will propagate to the other automatically.
- *Incremental Processing.* The system will reformat a document and redisplay it on the screen incrementally. That is, only the part of the document or the subregion of the screen that's affected by recent changes will be reprocessed.
- *User Interface.* The system will be running on, but not restricted to, a workstation with a high resolution bit-mapped display. It will have a high degree of interaction with the user. Unnecessary details will be hidden especially in the proof editor whose major usage is to modify document appearance. The user interface is so designed that in the case where only conventional terminals are available, the system can still be used as an incremental TEX compiler.
- *TEX Compatibility.* Given a TEX file, VORTEX can produce a DVI file which generates the same printed image as if a standard version of TEX had been run. This DVI file is "equivalent to a standard DVI file modulo `\special` commands".

- *Composite Objects.* The system will support not only text, math, and tables, but also non-textual objects such as graphics and raster images. There will be a high-level tool for each special object and all special tools will integrate with the base system coherently.

The rest of this paper is a sketch of some considerations we have made to realize these objectives.

2. Architecture

The VORTEX system will be an integration of a number of modules sharing a common internal representation (IR) for the document. Some of the important modules include a text editor, a formatter, a proof editor, and a DVI generator. Each of these modules performs as least one transformation from one representation of the document to another. The IR comprises three parts, call them IR_S, IR_T, and IR_I, which correspond to the internal representations of the source, target, and some intermediate information, respectively.

The display of VORTEX in a window-based system will have at least three windows: text window displaying the source, proof window displaying the target, and message window for receiving input or displaying messages. Different files of a document can be bound to separate buffers displayed in different subwindows as a tiled partition of the text window. In a conventional terminal display, there will only be a text window and a message window; the proof window will be missing and its editor will be disabled.

The text editor is responsible for maintaining a window which displays the document in its unformatted source form. It performs the mapping from the images displayed on the text window to IR_S, its internal representation, and vice versa. In addition to performing standard text editing operations such as insert and delete, it also invokes the formatter upon the user's request. The formatter is a mapping from a source file to IR (initial round), or from IR to IR', a reorganization of IR (later rounds).

After this transformation, the proof editor will be invoked which maps IR_T to the physical screen positions of the images. The primary purpose of this editor is maintaining a window which displays the document in its target (formatted) form. Hence it also performs the mapping from screen positions to IR_S, but not IR_T. This is because modifications to the document's output appearance must be translated to the corresponding TEX code in the source representation, as represented by IR_S. The correct structure for IR_T will only be generated by the formatter. Finally the DVI generator is a mapping from IR_T to TEX's standard output format, the DVI representation.

There will be some special editors for non-textual objects such as tables, graphics, and raster images. Specific argument syntax will be defined for TEX's "hook", the `\special` command, so that particular objects will always be manipulated by their corresponding editors. These will be direct manipulation editors which are invoked whenever their respective objects are selected in the base editors.

VORTEX's basic flow of control starts from the formatter, it constructs or reorganizes IR until the selected output page is encountered. Then IR_T is mapped to the screen as formatted images and the two base editors are activated. As editing goes along in both windows, changes will always be reflected in the text window and IR_S simultaneously. If any of the special objects is selected, its corresponding editor will be invoked. At any given time, the two windows may or may be synchronized in terms of the images displayed. Explicit commands must be given in either window to make the two representations and their respective screen images synchronized, which may involve some scrolling, or even reformatting. If reformatting is required, the formatter is invoked and the whole process starts over again.

3. Internal Representation

There are two major problems which VORTEX's IR needs to face. One is the *multiple representation problem* [16]; our representation must provide the necessary correlation between the TEX source which makes up the user input (IR_S) and the target page representation (IR_T). The data structure must, as well, provide a means of restricting changes to the document so that the formatter can recreate the minimum portion of the document possible, making the TEX formatter incremental.

TEX stores information that is used in calculating line and page breaks, etc. in boxes, which don't correspond in any obvious way with the source. The only real correlation is that if one types a letter (and it's not part of a control sequence or some other command structure), it should be able to be found on some page of the output. We need to relate source tokens to output boxes through the IR in a much stronger way. Output boxes are nested; a character is contained within a line which is contained within a paragraph which is contained within a page. We would also like to maintain this hierarchal organization with the source, since characters and paragraphs have an obvious hierarchal structure in the source.

To allow the formatter to operate incrementally, we need a way of restricting the changes to a document to minimize the amount of box rebuilding necessary. This is aided by a hierarchal organization, since with one we can easily move upward to higher levels in the document. For example, if a word is added to a paragraph, that paragraph needs to have line breaks recomputed, but the pages before the current one are safe. Later paragraphs may have to be moved around, but unless they themselves change, their already computed line breaks are safe.

3.1 The *IR* Hierarchy

The preceding considerations imply a hierarchical model and thus we chose the tree as the basic data structure. Of course, we need to modify the standard tree paradigm to make it more useful for our purposes. From the highest level, the IR for a document can be viewed as a tree of *file* nodes, each of which is the root of a subtree whose leaves form the actual content of a source file as a chain of text (IR_S). Embedded in this gigantic forest is a box structure (IR_T) which corresponds to the currently formatted pages. The file nodes as well as several other types of nodes which are not part of IR_S or IR_T are collectively called the IR_I.

Most nodes in the IR are doubly linked with their neighbors either horizontally, vertically, or both. The primary reason for this strong connection is to make the propagation of changes, syntax-directed editing, and incremental reformatting efficient. A substantial amount of work done previously by the formatter will be saved in the IR, since it organizes the original text and the resulting boxes into a structure where changes can easily be restricted. For instance, if the user changes a letter of a word in a paragraph, it is easy to determine that only the line breaks of that paragraph will need to be recalculated and, if the change is simple and the paragraph remains the same length, nothing else will need to be recomputed. The premise for this optimization is based upon the context saved in the embedded IR_T which is linked to the nodes in question.

3.2 What Lives In The *IR*?

The information that needs to be represented in the IR is the same as that which TEX uses in its horizontal, vertical and math lists, with a few additions. IR_S contains the simplest possible information: the actual text. In addition, the target representation also needs to be related to it. At the target level, TEX only knows about rules and characters, we generalize this to boxes so that we can maintain more output state information (these boxes make up the IR_T). In addition to the linking pointers, a box in IR_T contains the image and its position relative to the origin of a page. A box also contains a number of attributes such as its dimension, the type and size of current font, etc. which can be queried or modified by the proof editor. Another important piece of information is the TEX code which corresponds to certain operators for modifying certain box attributes.

The formatter generates IR_I nodes on top of the IR_S. For instance, the text `{group}` in IR_S will be linked to a common parent in the IR_I of type *group* by the formatter. These IR_I nodes, together with all IR_S entries, will be related to the IR_T structure. However, some IR_S and IR_I nodes may not have associated boxes in IR_T and similarly some boxes may not have corresponding nodes in IR_S or IR_I. For example, a *group* node would have no output representation and therefore no box in the IR_T; and a page box would have no single representation in the IR_I.

So far we have seen two types of IR_I nodes: *file* (`\input`) and *group* (`{...}`). Some other types include *par* (`\par` or a blank line), *math* (`$` and `$$`), *cs* (control sequence), *special* (`\special`), etc., which should all be self-explanatory. These nodes are the minimum necessary given the structure of TEX documents. We may add others later to make optimizations for the formatter, but these are the ones we think will be necessary to describe a TEX document, and to relate the IR_S and the IR_T. This IR_I along with the IR_S and the IR_T form the concerted whole, the IR, that will allow us to overcome the multiple representation problem.

4. Functionalities

Generic operations for the two base editors include (1) *sync*, (2) *insert/modify*, (3) *move/scroll/search*, (4) *select*, (5) *cut/paste*, (6) *attribute*, and (7) *file*. These operations can be classified as *destructive* or *non-destructive*. Destructive operations modify the IR and mark the corresponding nodes *dirty* while non-destructive ones only traverse through IR, inspecting the node content. Among the generic operations, (1), (2), and (5) are destructive, (6) and (7) may or may not be destructive, and the rest are non-destructive.

Sync is the command which invokes the formatter to bring the target representation up to date. As mentioned earlier in Section 2, changes made to the proof window will propagate to the text window immediately, but not to the proof window itself. In other words, any modifications done in either editor will only be reflected in the source window in real time. Some hints will be shown in the proof window to indicate any images known to be dead. One technique considered is to paint the dead regions in a different gray tone, but this can only be approximations because in many cases the scope of a dead region is very hard to determine without reformatting.

Insertions will be modeless; text can be inserted at the current cursor position without having to invoke any *insert* command. *Modifications* will be syntax-directed based on the IR_I hierarchy. For instance, an attempt to delete just one delimiter of a group (`{...}`) will be prohibited because otherwise the remaining text will be syntactically invalid.

The *move* type is a collection of cursor moving operations. VORTEX will support all of the standard ones such as moving forward and backward either horizontally or vertically. *Scrolling* is a special case of cursor motion. It can be either *monolithic*, affecting only one window, or *synchronized*, where both windows are forced to display approximately the same text. The latter case may imply a *sync* operation if the two representations are out of phase in terms of the content to be displayed. Yet another special case of cursor moving is *searching*. A variety of searching schemes will be supported including ordinary search, regular expression search, incremental search, and a very special kind called logical search. Logical searching allows one to go to arbitrary pages, sections, chapters, or other logical entities in a formatted document easily and will apply to the proof editor only.

A ring of selection buffers will be maintained. *Structural selections* correspond to traversing $IR_S \cup IR_I$. Starting at the IR_S, each additional *select* points to a higher order object in the hierarchy. For example, one selects a letter, two does it for a word, three for a group, etc. *Arbitrary selections*, on the other hand, are simply a consecutive chunk of text in IR_S. That is, one explicitly sets a marker at one place and moves the cursor to a second, and the text between the marker and current cursor position becomes a selection when the *select* command is called. Each new selection pushes the old ones into a ring buffer. This buffer may be used by some operators like *cut/paste* as implicit operands. Specific operators of the cut/paste type include *erase* (remove everything in the current selection), *copy* (duplicate the current selection to another place), and *move* (a *copy* followed by an *erase*).

Attribute operations are specific to the proof editor. There are primarily two types within this category: *query* and *modify*. For each object selected, queries can be made on its attributes such as *mode* (math, horizontal, etc.) *font* (type and size), *dimension* (height, width, depth), *operators* (cut, paste, etc.) and the corresponding *TEX code* (to be mapped back to the source), etc. Some of the attributes can be modified based on the operators registered and the result will propagate to the IR_S automatically. Operators registered for IR_T nodes are largely appearance fixing commands like change of margins, fonts, breaks, and glue.

Finally *file* operations like *read* and *write* are self-explanatory.

5. User Interface

The two base editors are homogeneous in the sense that they are manipulating essentially the same abstract object (document). But at the same time they are also heterogeneous because their underlying representations are in fact different. From the user's point of view, there should be only one system with a uniform user interface rather than having to work with two editors with two sets of protocols. Furthermore, it is a desirable feature that any functions be realized by both mouse/menus and keyboard input. The primary reason for this consideration is that it makes VORTEX still useful even with only conventional terminals available. Given the complication, a variety of interesting issues have emerged in the design of VORTEX user interface.

Standard cursor moving keystroke commands (e.g. **C-f** for forward, **C-b** for backward, **C-p** for up, **C-n** for down) will be supported. But an easier method is simply to drag the mouse and point at the desired position. However, this technique is restricted to the current visible window. To access text outside the current window, a scrolling facility must accompany the mouse dragging. Making selections is another good example. For structural selections, one mouse click, for instance, selects a character, two consecutive clicks does it for a word, three for a group, etc. The keystroke version for this may be some special command which takes an optional prefix argument as the indicator for the depth of traversing in the *IR* hierarchy. Thus the command itself selects the character after the cursor, with prefix argument 1 it selects a word, with 2 it does it for a group, etc. In another case, scroll bars will be available for mouse lovers, but conventional scrolling commands bound to keystrokes will also be provided.

What is important here is that the same paradigm will work in both types of windows, although the objects returned as a result of similar commands may be different. For example, four consecutive mouse clicks in the text editor may return the current file while in the proof editor the same command may select the current page being displayed in its window. This is a footnote to the fact that the two editors are dealing with two different representations: there is no such notion as a *page* in the source and similarly no such notion as a component *file* within a target. Nontheless, from the user's point of view, it suffices to have a uniform interface to the same generic operators. The returned results, though may not necessarily be the same, can always be approximated asynchronously using the *sync* option.

6. Formatting and Display

The key strategy in VORTEX's incremental formatting (compiling) is the idea of structure-oriented editing which works on the IR hierarchy rather than on individual characters. This is an approach taken by a number of programming environments such as [4,6,18]. Incremental compilers assume *a priori* the existence of an underlying internal representation which must be created initially by a non-incremental process. VORTEX's formatter plays the dual role of constructing the IR initially and maintaining it afterwards. Its non-incremental part will also be invoked whenever the incremental part finds itself unable to proceed, thereby providing a graceful escape from any unexpected situations.

In VORTEX, IR_S is a stream of text. Some of its entries will be marked *dirty* by the two editors after some editing. When *sync* is invoked, the formatter starts parsing from the leftmost dirty entry in the IR_S. As it goes along, IR_I nodes will be created and new boxes will be generated and merged to IR_T. It will mark an IR_T box as being one of the following types: *same*, *relocate*, *new*, or *dead*. The reason for this is to provide the necessary information for the proof editor's redisplay algorithm to work incrementally.

The formatter will skip consecutive clean IR_S entries as soon as the first entry with a corresponding IR_T box marked *same* is encountered. It resumes the computation upon reaching a dirty entry with the necessary context retrieved from the IR_T boxes linked to its neighbors. The formatting terminates at a point when no dirty entries are found in the remaining IR_S, or the selected page has been generated, or an error is detected. At this point, if there are no errors found, the proof editor will be invoked to redisplay its window. Otherwise the text editor will be positioned to the error spot and a diagnostic message will appear in the message window. The user can then make fixes and reiterate the process.

The proof editor redisplays its window based on the type of IR_T boxes visited. It starts from the box which corresponds to the top of the selected page. It ignores any boxes marked *same*. *Relocate* boxes will be copied to their destinations and *new* boxes will be rendered. Finally *dead* boxes will be erased. All these will be executed using *Bit-Blt* operators [5], an efficient set of primitives for bitmap graphics. A similar idea but much more complicated in magnitude has been implemented in Yale's PEN editor [3].

The text editor, on the other hand, is based on an ordinary textual window whose redisplay algorithms are relatively well known [8,9]. VORTEX's text editor will take a similar approach in this respect.

7. Conclusions

We believe TeX is an excellent system, but is based on a batch-oriented software technology. VoRTeX is a system that attempts to integrate the best features of TeX with interactive editors, incremental processing techniques, and a uniform and friendly user interface. We have sketched in this paper a possible design to realize the objectives of VoRTeX. Although some of the ideas will not be verified until the system is implemented, our initial study on the efficiency and storage requirements has indicated that the basic model we have derived is feasible.

We also expect to support graphics and other non-textual objects in our system. Among the work being done are the design of a VoRTeX-specific syntax for `\special`'s argument list, a direct manipulation table tool, and an object-oriented graphics editor.

8. References

[1] *8010 STAR Information System Reference Library, Release 4.2.* Xerox Office Systems, El Segundo, California, 1984.

[2] *Interleaf Publishing Systems Reference Manual, Release 2.0, Vol. 1: Editing and Vol. 2: Management.* Interleaf, Inc., Cambridge, Massachusetts, June 1985.

[3] Todd Allen, Robert Nix, and Alan Perlis. PEN: a hierarchical document editor. In *Proc. of ACM SIGPLAN/SIGOA Symposium on Text Manipulation*, pages 74–81, Portland, Oregan, June 8–10 1981.

[4] Malcolm Crowe, Clark Nicol, Michael Hughes, and David Mackay. On converting a compiler into an incremental compiler. *SIGPLAN Notices*, 20(10):14–22, October 1985.

[5] James D. Foley and Andries van Dam. *Fundamentals of Interactive Computer Graphics.* Addison-Wesley Publishing Company, Reading, Massachusetts, 1982.

[6] Christopher W. Fraser. Syntax-directed editing of general data structures. In *Proc. of ACM SIGPLAN/SIGOA Symposium on Text Manipulation*, pages 17–21, Portland, Oregan, June 8–10 1981.

[7] Richard Furuta, Jeffrey Scofield, and Alan Shaw. Document formatting systems: survey, concepts, and issues. *Computing Surveys*, 14(3):417–472, September 1982.

[8] James Gosling. A redisplay algorithm. In *Proc. of ACM SIGPLAN/SIGOA Symposium on Text Manipulation*, pages 123–129, Portland, Oregan, June 8–10 1981.

[9] B. S. Greenberg. *The Multics Emacs Redisplay Algorithm.* Technical Report, Honeywell Inc., 1979.

[10] J. Gutknecht. Concepts of the text editor Lara. *CACM*, 28(9):942–960, Sep. 1985.

[11] Michael Hammer, Richard Ilson, Tim Anderson, Edward J. Gilbert, Michael D. Good, Bahram Niamir, Larry Rosentein, and Sandor Schoichet. The implementation of Etude, an integrated and interactive document production system. In *Proc. of ACM ACM SIGPLAN/SIGOA Symposium on Text Manipulation*, pages 137–146, Portland, Oregon, June 8-10 1981.

[12] L. Johnson. *Macintosh MacWrite Manual.* Apple Computer, Inc., Cupertino, California, 1983.

[13] Donald E. Knuth. *The TEX Book.* Addison-Wesley Publishing Company, Reading, Massachusetts, 1984.

[14] Butler W. Lampson. *Bravo Manual.* Xerox Palo Alto Research Center, Palo Alto, California, 1978.

[15] Joseph F. Ossanna. *Nroff/Troff User's Manual.* Computer Science Technical Report 54, AT&T Bell Laboratories, Murray Hill, New Jersey, October 1976.

[16] Charles L. Perkins. *The Multiple Representation Problem.* Master's thesis, Computer Science Division, University of California at Berkeley, Dec. 1984.

[17] Brian K. Reid. *Scribe: A document specification language and its compiler.* PhD thesis, Computer Science Department, Carnegie-Mellon University, Pittsburgh, Pennsylvania, October 1980.

[18] Tim Teitelbaum and Thomas Reps. The Cornell program synthesizer: a syntax-directed programming environment. *CACM*, 24(9):563–573, Sep. 1981.

[19] Warren Teitelman. A tour through Cedar. *IEEE Software*, 1(2):44–73, April 1984.

EasyTEX: TOWARDS INTERACTIVE FORMULAE INPUT FOR SCIENTIFIC DOCUMENTS INPUT WITH TEX

Ester Crisanti (*)
Alberto Formigoni (*)(**)
Paco La Bruna (*)
(*) *Te.Co.Graf., Milano (Italy)*
(**) *Università degli Studi di Milano, Dipartimento di Scienze dell'Informazione (Italy)*

Abstract

TEX presents some difficulties in preparing scientific texts because of an input language with many commands to remember, a linear language used to describe non–linear objects (formulae), a non–interactive processing and the need to re-process the whole text also after small modifications.

EasyTEX's Formula Processor attempts to give a solution to these problems, allowing interactive, pop–menu driven formulae input and editing and producing a file suitable for TEX processing.

EasyTEX is thought to be an integrated environment for scientific document preparation able to work both as a stand–alone system and as a TEX front end. This project is being carried out in steps, or releases, the first of which, the Formula Editor, is now completed.

Formulae may be interactively input using EasyTEX and then inserted into source files for TEX processing by means of the \input *command.*

EasyTEX is now implemented on IBM and compatible PCs, using various types of graphic resolution (including IBM PC basic graphics) for its bit–mapped display.

1. Introduction

As it is well known, the TEX typesetting system allows the creation of high quality documents, performing automatic formatting and allowing a so–called *fine tuning* of particular typographical items on the base of commands (*Control Sequences*) the typesetter intersperses within the text.

TEX is particularly useful in typesetting scientific texts, containing formulae and tables, because of a reduced complexity in the description of such text elements and the possibility of using (also pre–defined) macros.

The language used to describe to TEX the document layout is of *procedural mark–up* type and processing is of batch type.

TeX, along with other similar systems, allows lower typesetting costs in the typographical world. But, moreover, TeX has introduced a new possibility in preparing high quality documents: the author can be himself the typesetter of his texts with a relatively low effort. This is also an important contribution to the circulation of scientific *grey literature*.

Though TeX reduces the complexity of typesetting and offers a powerful tool to high quality documents authors, some difficulties remain:

1) the typesetter must know an editing language to input the document text;
2) the typesetter must know TeX commands and language syntax to direct all processing;
3) it is quite difficult to foresee the final document layout while entering the text;
4) there is the inconvenience of seeing all TeX commands within the text;
5) the whole text must be reprocessed even after little modifications to the text, in particular while modifying TeX commands during the layout adjustment.

All these difficulties made us think about the opportunity of developing an *interactive system* offering an user–friendly interface based on commands easily chosen from pop–up menus. Such a system, called *EasyTeX*, should provide interactivity for all principal TeX commands and features. EasyTeX functional characteristics are presented in the proceedings of the conference "Protext II" on the Text Processing Systems [7].

EasyTeX's idea grew up and became that of an integrated environment for document preparation, particularly for scientific documents, which might also stand as an interactive TeX front end. This is the reason why EasyTeX's architecture is made up of three integrated environments: a Word Processor (*WP*), with all main facilities offered by TeX; a Formula Processor (*FP*), to simplify formulae input; a Box Processor (*BP*), to introduce a (although limited) text–image integration. Interactivity was planned to be it's main characteristic, along with user–friendliness, for all TeX principal functions, though allowing any other TeX command to be specified through so called *passive commands*.

Another important characteristic of EasyTeX had to be the possibility to run on largely diffused and low cost workstations; we decided to implement EasyTeX first on the *IBM PC* and compatibles with standard graphics under *MS–DOS*.

On the way, we realized that such a project should have been accomplished by two or three steps, or releases. We planned to first complete the *FP* only as a Formula Editor for TeX documents formulae interactive input; then to integrate the *FP* with the *WP*, offering a first version able to work also as a stand–alone system; and, finally, to introduce the *BP* and a *mouse* user interface.

The first step is now completed and this work intends to present EasyTeX as a *Formula Editor* for TeX documents formulae interactive input. A description of all functions now implemented will be done, along with some functional aspects related with the user–interface and mathematical structures handling and some peculiar architectural solutions.

2. Functional description

EasyTEX's *FP* allows single formulae input, manipulation, storing and translation to TEX source files. Such files may then be *\input* into TEX documents either in *math text style* or in *display style*.

These operations can be performed easily because interactivity allows the immediate display of the commands effect on the formula and pop–up menus drive the user in the commands selection.

The *FP* also guides the user during input, so that, for instance, a fraction input will be made easy by the cursor movements: the latter, when closing with the *return* key the numerator, moves to the place where the denominator will be placed, and so on.

TEX mathematical fonts are used on the screen, which is handled in a bit–map way; this makes the user see the exact layout the formula will have when processed by TEX within a document.

2.1 Entering a formula

Let us suppose to input the formula:

$$V(x) = \int_0^1 \frac{e^{-x}}{1+e^x} dx.$$

Let us see how to do and how EasyTEX works during this phase; to simplify the description, only the input sequence will be presented, omitting menu operations. After invoking EasyTEX, on the screen will appear:

1) on the top the menu line;
2) in the middle the cursor, as a box;
3) on the bottom the image of the default virtual keyboard, that is *italic* for letters and most used mathematical symbols for other keys.

The first step is to write $V(x) =$. This is simply done stroking the corresponding keys. We get so the following result:

$$V(x) = \Box\,.$$

We have now to input the integral. A simple selection of the *integral* menu element will give:

$$V(x) = \int^{\Box}\,.$$

Not only the integral symbol has been displayed, but also the cursor is conveniently positioned to input the upper limit and the size of the font in use has been reduced (from Text style to Script).

After writing the upper limit, this structure must be ended to begin entering the lower limit. This is simply done by stroking the *return* key. The result will be:

$$V(x) = \int_{\Box}^{1} .$$

Now, after entering the lower limit, on the screen there will be:

$$V(x) = \int_{0}^{1} \Box .$$

Similarly, the fraction argument and the exponents will be input with the cursor and menu guide.

2.2 Roots, Fractions and Blocks

These structures are characterized by dynamically dimensioned symbols. EasyTEX interactively processes these structures, automatically dimensioning and centering symbols and characters during input and always presenting on the screen a formatted formula. For example, entering the formula:

$$\sqrt[3]{\frac{e^x}{x}}$$

would be done as follows:

1) the *Root* menu element is selected, yielding:

$$\sqrt[\Box]{}$$

2) *3* and *return* will give:

$$\sqrt[3]{\Box}$$

3) the *Fraction* menu element is selected, giving:

$$\sqrt[3]{\frac{\Box}{}}$$

4) e^x is input, using the *Exponent* menu element, giving:

$$\sqrt[3]{\frac{e^x \Box}{}}$$

5) a *return* will give:

$$\sqrt[3]{\frac{e^x}{\square}}$$

6) x and then *return* (to close the denominator), will give:

$$\sqrt[3]{\frac{e^x}{x}\square}$$

7) and, finally, another *return* (to close the root), will give:

$$\sqrt[3]{\frac{e^x}{x}}\square .$$

The structure consisting of dynamically dimensioned delimiters with their argument is called *Block*. This automatic mechanism may be selected through the *Block* menu element, instead of stroking delimiters directly from the virtual keyboard. In fact, in the latter case, delimiters will not be dynamically dimensioned.

For instance, if we want, instead of

$$(\sum_{i=0}^{\infty} x_i)^2$$

to obtain

$$\left(\sum_{i=0}^{\infty} x_i\right)^2$$

we can do that simply using EasyTEX's *Block* structure.

2.3 Matrices and Tables

EasyTEX also allows matrices and tables input. These structures are handled interactively through menu and allow an easy input of such difficult text elements.

2.4 Accents

EasyTEX allows the use of several mathematical accents, such as $\hat{a}$, $\ddot{A}$, $\ddot{y}$, $\vec{\beta}$, etc.

Normally, a single character is accepted; in this case the accent is simply selected from the menu after the character to be accented.

2.5 Editing commands

EasyTEX's *FP* offers two levels of editing: the character or symbol level and the structure level. In the first case, the cursor moves from a character or symbol to another, respecting the philosophy used for input. So, going back to the formula

$$V(x) = \int_0^1 \frac{e^{-x}}{1+e^x} dx\square ,$$

pressing the $\leftarrow$ key would make the cursor move first on the x, then on the d, then following e^x, then after the x of the e's exponent, and so on.

In the second case, the cursor moves structure by structure, and pressing $\leftarrow$ key would make the cursor move first to contain dx, then to contain $\frac{e^{-x}}{1+e^x}$, then to contain $\int_0^1$ and, at last, to contain $V(x) =$.

In the same way operate commands like *insert, move, copy*, etc.

The *FP* is always in *insert mode*; the alternative state, *replace*, may be used to replace parts of a formula already introduced. Replacing parts of a formula causes EasyTEX to reformat the whole formula interactively.

The *FP*, before executing an editing command, checks the correctness of the context in which that command must act. Some operations, in fact, cause error messages to be displayed because they do not respect the syntactic structure of the formula. For instance, removing a numerator in a fraction is not allowed, while replacing the numerator is.

The *FP* may be, anyway, requested to omit structural checks on mathematical constructs.

3. Architectural aspects

The *FP* architecture was defined as independent functional modules, communicating by means of status data.

The modules constituting the *FP* are: *Command handler, Memory manager, Formatter and Filter*.

The Command handler: performs interfacing with EasyTEX's *Supervisor* and other Processors; receives, through the Supervisor, all inputs from the *User interface*; coordinates, by means of status data the execution of the Memory manager, the Formatter and the Filter.

The Memory manager is built up of a set of routines which allow the creation and handling of the tree data structure, also implementing a virtual memory mechanism.

The Formatter interactively handles the formula creation and manipulation with respect to all problems concerning with symbols and characters positioning and spacing.

The Filter updates the formatted formula image on the screen in correspondence with all modifications and optimizing redisplaying time.

Some peculiar aspect concerning the data structure, formatting and the table driven execution architecture will now be presented.

3.1 The tree structure

The internal representation form of a non–ordinary text, such as mathematical formulae, requested a careful study to satisfy different conditions: to allow fast handling and processing by the system, to make easy the data transfer from main memory to disk without making response times heavy and to have a structure which could properly organize mathematical formulae.

Analyzing mathematical formulae, configurations similar from a structural point of view were found; for instance, the integral and summation operators are both constituted by four objects: a symbol, a lower limit, an upper limit and an argument. Every formula then can be described as a finite combination of such objects, called *basic constructs* and *specific constructs* [13].

Associating to every base construct the root of a tree data structure and to every specific construct the related child nodes, we obtained a data structure describing in a simple and convenient way a formula.

For instance, the formula

$$\int_a^b f(x)dx$$

is mapped into the tree:

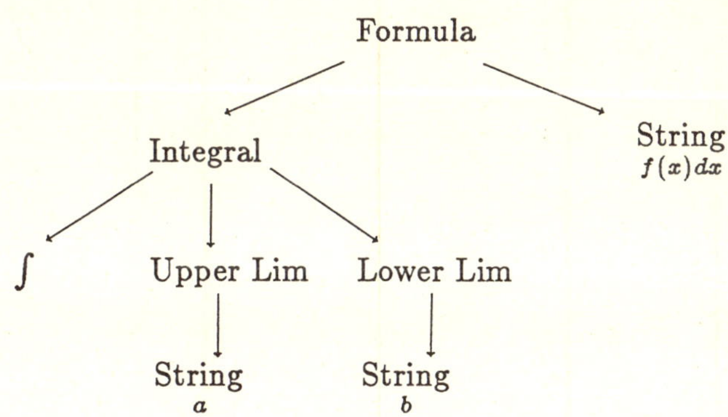

Such an association procedure may be iterated on all elements constituting a mathematical formula to obtain a tree structure completely describing it.

3.2 The Formatter

The technique used to format mathematical formulae is similar to the one used by TEX. In fact, every formula is regarded as a box, itself built up by smaller boxes down to *atomic* — i.e. no further splittable — boxes, corresponding to single characters and symbols.

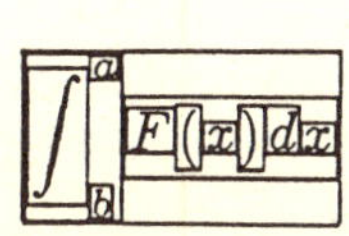

Every box has a rectangular shape and has three associated sizes, *height, depth* and *width*, used by the Formatter to build the formula image.

The tree data structure used by the *FP* allowed to implement the Formatter module in a compact and efficient way. In fact, every tree node is associated with a formula element and, at every moment, the formula (and tree) element box has updated sizes. Some other data, such as the (x, y) coordinates of the box reference point, are present in the node data in two forms: absolute and relative. Absolute data are used for fast formatting and redisplaying when no changes occurred, after a formula modification, to the box dimension and position; relative data are used for fast formatting and redisplaying when, due to changes occurred to some parent tree node, absolute box data have to be updated (*heredity* mechanism).

The most important difficulty in implementing the Formatter was in handling *conflict* situations between boxes. We define a conflict situation in formatting boxes when, modifying the dimension or position of a box, a partial overlapping between two adjacent boxes occurs. For instance, introducing a fractional order on a root, a conflict arises between the fraction box and the root symbol box (vertical conflict) when the denominator is input. Conflict detection and resolution were implemented and their algorithms inserted in the Constructs Table.

3.3 A table driven system

EasyTEX's *FP* and TEX Interface are characterized by a table driven structure. In order to set memory managing and formatting free from different types of mathematical structures, suitable and simple algorithms were defined and put in a *Constructs Table* (*CT*). The *CT* is organized in a bidimensional array in which every entry corresponds to a construct (basic or specific). The table contains both structural information (font type, child nodes number and type, etc.) and references to the algorithms used for formatting.

Due to the *CT* use, the Memory manager and the Formatter are *context free* and operate, on the different structures, in a parametric way.

This solution offers some advantages, such as a simple compilation of a new *CT* entry if a new construct has to be added; a lower number of duplicated data in the nodes, such as child nodes number, structural check information, etc.(they are gathered in the table element); a simpler implementation of a *heredity* mechanism for formatting and redisplaying purposes, and so on.

Such a mechanism has also been studied for the TEX Interface. the *TEX Interface* is the EasyTEX's module that performs the *translation* from the internal format (*EasyTEX Document File* format) to the linear format suitable for TEX processing.

A translation table has been implemented by means of which every tree node is translated, in a parametric way, to a TEX *Control Sequence* (for instance, the *integral* node into *int*) and every character is mapped either in a character or in a Control sequence (for instance, α into *alpha*).

The final result is that, if a new mathematical construct has to be added (say, trigonometric functions or set operators), only the *CT* and the TeX Interface table must be changed.

4. Future developments

As we already said, (at least) two other steps are planned in EasyTeX's development. The first of them, the implementation of the *WP* and its integration with the *FP*, should be completed on next October; the *BP* integration and a mouse user interface should be available on next February.

We received some other suggestions about EasyTeX's extensions, such as the integration of another environment devoted to *graphs design*, useful in industrial project design; we are now evaluating the opportunity of such extensions.

We were also requested to design a *Document Data Base*, based on a Local Area Network among PCs and a host system and using *CD-ROMS*, able to solve documentation (also technical) problems in industrial organizations. Such a system, based on TeX and EasyTeX, is following the experience we made with *SDDS* [3], together with Mondadori publishing company, CILEA and Università di Milano, Dipartimento di Scienze dell'Informazione as one of the DOCDEL experiments supported by the Commission of the European Communities.

Acknowledgements

The authors of the present work intend to give particular thanks to:

Prof. Gianni Degli Antoni, Director del Dipartimento di Scienze dell'Informazione dell'Università degli Studi di Milano, for the initial idea of EasyTeX and for his support and encouragements during the project study and development.

Gloria Gazzano for her precious advice based on her experience in editors project.

Mauro Beneduci, Marcello Casu and Giorgio Valtolina, respectively for their works in the study and implementation of the User Interface, Font Manager and TeX front-end.

Special thanks also to Giovanni Canzii for his support in TeX interfacing problems and in typographical characters handling, and to all those who somehow gave suggestions useful to the project development.

References

1) J. André, Y. Grundt, V. Quint "*Towards an interactive math mode in TEX*" Proceedings of the First European Conference on "TEX for Scientific Documentation" Como, Italy, Addison–Wesley ed., (may 1985).
2) G. Canzii, D. Lucarella, A. Pilenga "*A Scientific Document Delivery System*" Electronic Publishing Review (june 1984).
3) G. Canzii, G. Degli Antoni, S. Mussi, G. Rosci "*S.D.D.S.: Scientific Document Delivery System*" Proceedings of the First European Conference on "TEX for Scientific Documentation" Como, Italy, Addison–Wesley ed., (may 1985).
4) G. Canzii, G. Degli Antoni, D. Lucarella "*TEX come standard per i CD ROM*" atti del convegno "Text Processing", AICA, Milano, Italy (nov. 1985).
5) G. Canzii, A. Formigoni, E. Crisanti "*EasyTEX: un ambiente integrato per la preparazione di testi scientifici*" atti del convegno "Text Processing", AICA, Milano, Italy (nov. 1985).
6) G. Canzii, D. Lucarella, A. Pilenga "*TEX come sistema di document delivery*" in "Office Automation: metodi e tecnologie", AICA informatica, Masson, Milano, Italy (1986).
7) E. Crisanti, A. Formigoni, G. Gazzano, P. La Bruna "*EasyTEX: an integrated environment for scientific document preparation and interactive TEX front-end*" "Protext II", Proceedings of the Second International Conference on Text Processing Systems, Miller ed., Dublin, Ireland (oct. 1985).
8) A. Formigoni "EasyTEX: un ambiente integrato per la preparazione di testi scientifici", graduation thesis in Computer Science, University of Milan (aa. 1984–85)
9) L. Kernighan, L. Cherry "*A system for typesetting mathematics*" CACM, vol.18 (1975).
10) D. Knuth "*The TEX book*" AMS and Addison–Wesley (1984).
11) M. Levison "*Editing Mathematical Formulae*" Software Practice and Experience, vol.13 (1983).
12) V. Quint "*Editing mathematics on the buroviseur*" in "Office Information System", Naffah ed., St. Maxim, North Holland, (1982).
13) V. Quint "*An interactive system for mathematical text processing*" Technology and Science of Informatics, vol.2 n.3 (1983).
14) V. Quint "*Interactive editing of mathematics*" "Protext I", Proceedings of the First International Conference on Text Processing Systems, Dublin, Ireland (oct. 1984).

A Multilingual TÊX

Michael J. FERGUSON
INRS-Télécommunications
Montréal, Canada

Abstract

This paper discusses a modification to TeX that allows for multilingual hyphenation on a paragraph by paragraph basis using standard TeX fonts. Although this is a sufficient for most applications, it does not of itself solve spacing, linguistically unique characters, text input, nor multilingual message problems. A discussion of these problems, with special emphasis on solutions through TeX modifications, is included. These suggestions are followed with a plea for standardization.

1. Introduction

This paper discusses a very efficient modification of TeX, that we refer to as TÊX, that allows multilingual hyphenation, including words with accented letters, using **standard TeX fonts**. The features and difficulties with the present system are discussed in Section 2. Although in the TeX context, the solution to the hyphenation problem, especially for words involving accented letters is primary other concerns quickly become apparent. A number of these have already been discussed by Désarménien [1] for TeX in a French enviroment. This paper is primarily concerned with these issues in terms of obtaining consistent elegant modifications of TeX where necessary and a discussion of some of the difficulties encountered.

Désarménien has shown that the special conventions of French spacing are adequately handled at the TeX format level without modifications to TeX itself. He pointed out that some letters, such as " Ê " were not terribly pleasing in their accented form and argued for inclusion of better designed forms in the fonts. He modified the standard TeX fonts to include some of the accented letters used in French. A further discussion of the inclusion of additional letter forms and their accented alternatives is found in Section 3.

After acceptable output is obtained, the next issue that arises is with respect to the ease of input. This assumes, of course, that the present input procedures are sufficiently simple that a user will even attempt to obtain output. TeX has been traditionally input through a text editor and a character oriented terminal. In such an environment, the order and number of keystrokes for creating an accented character, such as "ô" along with its appearance on the screen, is important. This will be briefly discussed in Section 4.

A system is not truly multilingual until its messages, and even its commands are available in each language. Programming languages have been remarkably resistant to linguistic modification and one suspects that TeX will be the same. A brief discussion of some of the problems of so modifying TeX is given in Section 5.

Extensions to TeX, in keeping with the inviolable integrity of the TeX program [2] file must be introduced via WEB [3] change files. A short discussion of some of the problems and a partial solution is given in Section 6.

The paper ends with a plea for cooperation and standardization.

2. TeX extensions – TêX

TêX is obtained through a modification to TeX itself rather than by a program or format written in TeX and has been in continual use, for French/English, at INRS-Télécommunications and Bell-Northern Research (Montréal) since early 1985. The primary purpose was to allow for multilingual hyphenation without any modification of the standard fonts supplied with a TeX system. The modification has two parts – the introduction of multiple pattern and hyphenation exception sets and the allowing of hyphenation of words containing accented letters, *ie* letters that were obtained using TeX's `\accent` primitive. An example would be "éléphant" which was written "`\'el\'ephant`". Briefly the features of the extension are:

- A new **primitive** integer parameter `\language` has been introduced. The value of this parameter controls the set of language `\patterns` and hyphenation exceptions actually in force when hyphenation is attempted. This parameter defaults to zero and hence never need be mentioned in unilingual installations.

- Hyphenation exceptions are language dependent.

- Words with accents, such as "l'épicerie", will be hyphenated correctly. These modifications of TeX will work, with accented letters such as " é " built using TeX's accent primitive or resident in the font. In addition they will work whether the letter is accessed as a single character or as a ligature.

- `\lccode` 1 and 2 are now used to indicate which characters are accents. Note that `\lccode` 0 indicates a non letter.

- Any number of languages may be used. The `trie_op` table has been extended to 16 bits from its current size of 8 bits. The present bilingual (French/English) running at INRS-Télécommunications uses, 238 `trie_op` locations. French alone uses 108 and English alone 181.

- The changes are upward compatible — a standard `plain tex` can be built into a format file by a modified `initex`. However, the format file has been modified so that a non-extended `plain.fmt` will cause a "fatal format error" if used with TEX.

There is one major and a few minor restrictions. The **major restriction** is

⋆ all words in a paragraph are hyphenated according to the `\language` in force at the end of the paragraph.

TEX operates on entire paragraphs at once – the major reason why it does such an excellent of line breaking. Although each character contains information about its font, it does not contain any information about the `\language` in force. Thus the **single** value of `\language` when the the paragraph is being processed is the one that controls which patterns will be used. The most obvious solution is to extend a character node to include a byte for the `\language`. This would have the virtue of also extending TEX's main memory pointers to be 24 bits and hence allow for a rather dramatic increase in main memory. It would be up to the compiler to pack this efficiently.

Some of the minor restrictions, at least in terms of French/English but not necessarily for all languages are as follows. It is not clear which ones need be relaxed for which languages.

⋆ Discretionary hyphenation spellings, as required in German, are not automatically included. These probably could be added, in special format to the `\patterns`, and handled during hyphenation much as ligatures. This would mean an additional extension to TEX.

⋆ Accents must be in the same font as the characters in the word to be hyphenated. This can probably be relaxed by allowing TEX to ignore a character font if the character has an `\lccode` of 1 or 2.

⋆ Accents may not be placed on ligatures.

⋆ Characters built up through hboxes rather than the accent primitive are not allowed in hyphenatable words. It is not obvious how to relax this constraint.

⋆ A new value of `\language` determines both a set of hyphenation patterns and exceptions. There is no provision for using an additional set of hyphenation exceptions with an already existing set of patterns. For instance, if it were really important that "Random House" hyphenation be used rather than "Websters", a set of patterns for both would be required.

To change hyphenation rules it is only necessary to change the value of `\language`. However, since accents and certain characters may be legitimate in one language and not others, it may also be desirable to modify certain `\lccodes`. There are checks in TEX to prevent disasters if `\language` is somehow not within the range allowed.

2.1 Multilingual Patterns and Hyphenation Exceptions

The incorporation of multiple pattern lists and hyphenation exceptions is done by modifying the appropriate data structures as follows:

- Each hyphenation pattern is prefaced with the current `\language` value before inserting it into the pattern trie.
- Each hyphenation exception is prefaced with the current `\language` value before entering it into the exception hash table.
- When a word is to be hyphenated, each pattern is prefaced with the current `\language` value before attempting to find a match.

In order to put patterns in correctly and safely, a rather rigid, but simple, procedure involving the value of `\language` is used. In contrast to the present TEX, `\patterns` may (must!) be called several times, at least once for each language. This gives room for `\language` to be modified between calls. On the last set of patterns, the trie is compressed. All pattern inputs, except the last are indicated by adding 1000 to the value of `\language`. Thus `\language=1001` indicates that this is the second language and it is not the final set of patterns, while `\language=1` indicates that this is the second language and it is the final set of patterns. The complete set of rules are:

- `\language` must start at 0 mod 1000. and be increased by no more than 1 as each new language is added.
- If `\language>=` 1000, then the present pattern set that is being input is **not** the last. For example

  ```
  {\language=1000 % English (0)
  \patterns{ ... }
  }
  {\language=1001 % French (1)
  \patterns{ ... }
  }
  {\language=2 % Spanish (2)
  \patterns{ ... }
  }
  ```

  would input patterns for three languages, with the values given in the parentheses to be used to invoke hyphenation in that language. The grouping braces are optional ... but make \language local. The accented letters are put in the normal way that accents are invoked in TEX, namely with forms such as ´ or ˆ. These forms were locally redefined to drop the correct character into the patterns.

Note again that the value of \language mod 1000 may increase by at most 1 each time patterns is called. This is to prevent unused language values existing. If this is violated, an error will occur. Since initex is already inside \patterns, the only possible action is to abort and correct the problem in the input file.

The first set of patterns initializes the pattern memory while the final set produces the compressed trie memory. If \language never goes below 1000, the compressed trie will **not** be written. This will show up in the "stats" at the end of initex with a trie memory size of 0.

A new variable lan_max, which is saved in the format file, indicates the maximum number of languages that have been initialized using \patterns. lan_max is modified **only** when \patterns is called. If \language exceeds lan_max, a pleasant error message results, and \language is reset to 0. It will maintain that value within the group where the error message occurs.

2.2 Modifications for Hyphenating Words with Accented Characters

The modifications that allow for the hyphenation of accented words are as follows:

- Designate accents with \lccode of 1 or 2.
- Make accent kerns implicit so that they disappear before the word is sent to the hyphenation routine.
- Reconstitute the accents after the hyphens are returned from the hyphenation routine.

The net effect of this is that hyphenation patterns will be applied to words involving accents. This means, for instance, that the word "considérions" has the hyphens "con-sid-é-ri-ons" if the English patterns in Plain are used, but is hyphenated as "con-si-dé-rions" if the French patterns are used. Note that the English patterns insert two incorrect hyphens and miss another. In addition there will never be a hyphen inserted between an accent and its following character since that case has never been given an odd number.

Two \lccodes were used to allow for different placement of the same accent symbol – for instance above or below the accented character. Initially it was thought that the cedilla " ¸ " would require such special treatment but that turned out not to be the case. The second value could be used for language dependent accent placements. However this is of limited utility at the moment as there is no way, other than recompiling TEX to modify the accent placement routine.

3. Font Definition and Printing of Special Characters

A "special character" is arbitrarily defined as a letter or punctuation that does not appear in the TEX's standard Roman fonts. The "guillemets" for quotations in French, *ie* « guillemets », are examples of punctuation. The « » here have actually been made from the ⟨⟩ in the mathematic fonts. They do not really have the correct shape. Whether they are adequate is a matter of conjecture. There are several ways to introduce additional special characters into TEX.

- Build a composite form using TEX's `\accent` primitives. TÊX will hyphenate in this case.

- Build a composite form by shifting `\hbox` and `\vbox` forms. TÊX will not hyphenate in this case.

- Replace a character in the standard TEX font with the desired form. This approach does not appear to allow for all of the forms required for French [1] let alone allow extension to multiple languages.

- Add the special characters to the upper 128 locations in the font. This is probably the most desirable approach for the long run especially if it is possible to cover all of the Roman alphabet based languages with 256 characters. However doing this will require a number of extensions to TEX. Specifically

    - Several tables that are presently 128 must be extended to 256. These include tables for `\lccode`, `\uccode`, `\sfcode`. If the mathematics fonts are extended, then the `\delcode` table must also be increased. These changes are quite straightforward. If the special characters are to be allowed in TEX command sequences and/or processed syntactically by TEX, then several more tables must be changed. These are discussed in Section 4.

    - The TEX commands `\uppercase` and `\lowercase` rely on the the simple numeric relation between the upper and lower case versions of a letter in ASCII coding. A similar relationship for the upper and lower case letters in the upper 128 locations would allow a simple modification to these routines. If simple relations are not maintained, two additional tables relating upper and lower case will be required.

Non universal changes in character locations in fonts will be detrimental to the electronic interchange of documents. Clearly such extensions should be done in some international forum.

4. Text Input

The output of special characters in text is quite a bit simpler than the input of those characters. TeX, with perhaps the table extensions for characters in the upper 128 locations of a font table as indicated in the previous section, adequately handle these output problems. The input problems are complicated by

- ⋆ the number of keystrokes and order of input,
- ⋆ whether the special character is generated as a single character on the terminal screen,
- ⋆ and whether it is required that special characters be allowed in command sequences.

The first two complications are intimately bound to the particular terminal, keyboard, and text editor in use. Very few non-English keyboards have all of the special and accented letters required by a specific language. Special characters are obtained either directly with one stroke, or indirectly with three strokes using a `<backspace>` or `<accent>` key. The `<accent>` key stops the advance of the carriage and allows for superposition. An " é " is thus formed in any of the following ways – `<é>`, `<accent><'><e>`, `<accent><e><'>`, `<'><backspace><e>`, or `<e><backspace><'>`. In standard TeX input, one uses `<\><'><e>`. the number of keystrokes is 3 but the input order is constrained. There does not appear to be any universally agreed upon input procedure nor any particular set of displayable special characters.

A possible solution to the first two complications, and the one currently in use at INRS-Télécommunications is to have a TeX preprocessor that converts the special characters to their composite TeX form. For most operating systems, this step can be imbedded in a command procedure so that it is relatively transparent to the user. However, the actual TeX file cannot be processed directly by TeX. A slightly more sophisticated form of this procedure is to convert automatically between a TeX form and an editing form upon entry and exit from the text editor. This has the advantage of ensuring that the file that is kept is processable directly by TeX but gives rise to some minor complications with a system crash during editing.

The third complication is much more severe. It basically requires that the number of possible input characters be increased from the ASCII standard of 128 to 256. The changes to TeX to accomodate this are extensive. Simple changes involve the increase to 256 of the single and active character control sequence tables along with the `\catcode` table. A slightly more complex one involves modifications of TeX's hash tables. One change that appears to be quite difficult, and may in fact impose a restriction to 254 input characters rather than 256 involves the use of the character values 128 and 129 to indicate `\span_code` and `\cr_code` while processing alignments for tables. This internal coding appears to require that at least two input code values not be used. This effectively restricts the maximum number of inputs to 254. **The recommendation is that special characters be not allowed for command sequences and that the files be pre/post processed during input/output of the text editor.** The danger is that characters that are single keystrokes will sneak into TEX definitions and create errors.

5. Multilingual Messages and Primitive Commands

TÊX generates only English error messages and/or instructions. INRSTEX [4] generates bilingual messages with the appropriate message determined by the value of `\language`. Except for `\versionfrancaise` which invokes the French forms, spacing, messages, and hyphenation, the commands used are English. Thus `\beginlist` ... `\endlist` are used in both versions for lists. It would have been quite simple to invoke a large `\let` list to create equivalences but this was not done, primarily so that a knowledge of the other command set was not required when editing a document in the other language. **It is not recommended that multiple language commands be a part of TÊX either.**

Conceptually a change in the messages from English to another language merely requires the translation of the appropriate strings in the WEB program. Two types of strings exist – those that are printed directly, such as "`Please type the name of your input file`" and those that are retrieved from the `pool` file. Those strings printed directly are a part of the TEX program and those in the `pool` file are incorporated in the format file. The `pool` file accounts for almost of the message strings and WEB takes care that the PASCAL and `pool` files match. This means that it is virtually impossible to add a new language without recompiling TEX and INITEX. At this point it is also not clear the best procedure for incorporating `\language` dependent messages.

6. Change Files and TEX Modifications

TEX is written in WEB and has been placed in the public domain but at the same time declared to be unchangeable. In keeping with this spirit, TÊX is produced using WEB's change file mechanism. Unfortunately, to actually produce a running version of TÊX, a system change file, in this case one for a VAX/VMS system, was also required. Since WEB only allows **one** change file, this meant that the TÊX change file and the VAX/VMS change file had to be merged. It also means that additional modifications, for example involving multiple language messages, would require further merging. To facilitate this merging a set of EMACS [5] routines were written that do the following:

- Compare a change file with the original file and number the change sections according to the section numbers that would appear in an **unchanged** woven version of the file.

- Merge two change files and note when there are identical section numbers in each file. If there are identical section numbers, it is possible that the change files could conflict and/or the order of the changes in a particular section are not consistent with the original. These potential errors are corrected by hand editing. The TEX and VAX/VMS change files conflicted in only two sections. In both cases only the merge order had to be changed.

These routines do not solve the multiple change file problem but they do make it possible to incorporate TEX simply into system change files.

7. Suggestions for Cooperation

It is clear that TEX is a powerful typesetting and document preparation system which is capable of operating in multiple languages. One of TEX's most important attributes is its portability and openness. The intent has always been to allow for TEX files to be processed by any TEX system and obtain identical output. Although this is compromised somewhat by different format files, it can be totally destroyed by incompatible fonts and incompatible extensions. Our experience has convinced us that modifications such as those incorporated in TEX are necessary for the smooth working in a multilingual environment and even in a unilingual environment when using standard TEX fonts and accented characters. It is important that there be cooperation amongst the various groups so that interchange of documents in different languages be possible with the minimum of additional environmental information.

References

1. J.A. Désarménien, "How to run TEX in a French Environment: Hyphenation, Fonts, Typography", *Proc. First European Conf. on TEX for Scientific Documentation*, D. Lucarella, Editor, Varenna, Italy, May 16-17, 1985.

2. D.E. Knuth, **TEX: The Program**, Addison Wesley, 1985 – also available in WEB file form on the TEX distribution tape.

3. D.E. Knuth, "The WEB System of Structured Documentation", Computer Science Dept. Report, Stanford University, 1982 – also available on the TEX distribution tape.

4. M.J. Ferguson "The INRSTEX Reference Manual", INRS Technical Report No. 84-19, 1984

5. R.M. Stallman, "EMACS: The extensible, customizable self-documenting display editor", *Proc. ACM SIGPLAN/SIGOA Conf. on Text Manipulation*, pp 147-156, Portland Ore., June 8-10, 1981 – the EMACS actually used is the *James Gosling* version.

INRSTȆX: A Document Preparation System for Multiple Languages

Michael J. FERGUSON
INRS-Télécommunications
Montréal, Canada

Abstract

This paper discusses a system for the preparation of documents, primarily but not exclusively scientific, in several languages. It can be viewed as a very large extension of Plain *or as a simpler version of LaTeX. Care has been taken to maintain syntactic consistency and to separate the document formatting chores from the document preparation housekeeping chores. This paper is not a complete description of INRSTȆX but rather describes its capabilities and chooses lists and combined text/graphics for some detailed comments.*

1. Introduction

INRSTȆX is a system to aid in the preparation of documents in several languages using ordinary fonts. The first, rather primitive, version was developed using TeX78 in 1982. The present version is based on TeX82 and was completed in 1984. It has been in continual use since that time at INRS-Télécommunications and Bell-Northern Research (Montréal). The key enhancement since 1984 has been the inclusion in 1985 of a graphics capability that allowed for printing complete documents without **any** cutting or pasting. This latter capability has dramatically increased the commitment to the system. The particular version referred to in this paper uses a VAX/VMS computer and a QMS Laser Printer, but is easily modifiable for other configurations. The two languages actually used are French and English.

INRSTȆX has been designed to sit on top of `Plain`. All of the commands, except `\footnote`[†] are identical those described in the TeXbook. INRSTȆX believes that groups should be designated and syntactically consistent. Groups in INRSTȆX are defined by either braces {...}, `\begin...` `\end...` pairs, or the mathematic groups implied by \$...\$ or \$\$...\$\$. In some cases `\begin...` `\end...` synonyms of `Plain` commands that imply grouping have been defined. An example

[†] The footnote macro has been modified to be similar to that used in the TeXbook. The net effect is that the result is nicer and its use identical to `\footnote` in `Plain`.

is \beginmidinsert ... \endmidinsert for \midinsert ... \endinsert. Unlike LATEX [1], INRSTEX believes that entities such as sublists should be defined explicitly by a \beginsublist ... \endsublist or by the designated abbreviations \bsl ... \esl rather than being determined by depth of environmental nesting. Like LATEX, entities may be nested and work correctly. Thus it is possible to have lists consistently spaced inside narrowed text.

Like LATEX, INRSTEX is intended to make it easy to get off the ground in the use of TEX. Indeed, when working within a particular document format, the effort to produce a document is much simpler than working with Plain directly. Even the modification of a document format is relatively simple. "Elementary" TEX is probably best seen through a INRSTEX or equivalent filter than through Plain.

It is difficult in a short paper, or even a long one, to give the flavor and/or appreciate the power of a system. Short descriptions tend to all sound the same, giving the impression that any particular system is capable of everything – easily! Sometimes little features, that seldom show up except through use, create large architectural problems. For instance, the requirement that a message to the terminal, that included a command such as \LaTeX, not expand it into its horrible form of L\kern -.2em \raise .3ex \hbox {\sc a}\kern -.09em T\kern -.1667em \lower .5ex \hbox{E}\kern -.125em X necessitated a ring buffer of token lists – totally hidden from the user. As part of its user friendly attitude, INRSTEX does send out reassuring messages when processing such items as section heads or cautionary types such as when the user inserts a " " " rather than a " ‘ ‘ " or " ’ ’ ".

The basic capabilities of INRSTEX will be described in Section 2. The bilingual features are described in Section 3. Since there is not enough space to describe everything in detail, two aspects will be described to give a flavor. Section 4 describes INRSTEX's approach to lists while Section 5 describes INRSTEX's approach to combining text and graphics. INRSTEX's table making macros which are both unique and very simple are described in the July 1986 issue of TUGboat [2]. Details of all of the INRSTEX kernel features are described in [3]. Section 6 contains some observations.

2. INRSTEX Features

INRSTEX really consists of a number of complementary packages. The packages, all relatively independent, are as follows:

- the INRSTEX macro package kernel. This includes all the facilities needed for
  - section and chapter heads,
  - lists,
  - **easy** tables,
  - *floating* figure and table insertions,

  - footnotes,
  - automatic generation of table of contents, list of figures, and list of tables,
  - automatic numbering of equations, section heads, etc.,
  - symbolic referencing of equations, sections, etc.,
  - optional margin notes to aid in keeping track of symbolic references,
  - automatic generation of citation lists (IEEE style only) without any preprocessing,
  - a multicolumn format with a relatively simple method for column balancing,
  - a *subdocument* feature for building large documents in pieces.
  - an `\every...` for almost all features. This allows for some simple document style changes. For example `\everyfootnote` will define a token list that is invoked whenever a `\footnote` is produced.

- additional packages for special forms. The modular form of the kernel allows for modifications of what is inside and out. At the present these include

  - a verbatim style using `typewriter` fonts for such things as program listings,
  - a several document styles including a <<PAPER STYLE>>, <<BOOK STYLE>>, <<REPORT STYLE>>. Some of these are rather specialized.
  - TeXGraph, a graphics system for drawing figures and inserting external figures. This uses the graphics primitives of the QMS Laser printer and is to be enhanced quite soon to write `PostScript` [4]. It is *inside* rather than outside the TeX system.
  - memo macros **including** graphics for letterhead,
  - slide making **including** graphics for letterhead,

- templates for various styles. This makes their use as easy as filling in blanks and is very important for making the system accessible to unskilled users.

- **Multilingual TÊX** [5], an **extension** to TeX, that allows for language dependent hyphenation tables and hyphenation of accented words while using ordinary fonts.

- INRSprint, a printing program for the QMS Laser printer that does font management and interprets graphics `specials`.

INRSTÊX may be viewed from several perspectives.

- At the user level, it is a set of procedures that augment the `Plain` macros supplied with TeX. These aid the author in building a document by making shuffling of such things as sections, equations, figures, and tables sufficiently painless that they will be done. It helps the secretary/typist by making it easier to respond to changes. To work most effectively, the author, at the *pencil* input level, should be aware of the power of the system.

- At the document formatting level, parameters and features are available to modify various spacings, headers, footers, etc.

- At the document design level, the various internal formatting forms are available **independently** of the housekeeping functions which are used for the automatic generation of section, equation, and figure numbers, or such things as the table of contents.

3. English and French — Together

INRSTEX supports both English and French document preparation, and is easily extendable to other languages. It does this through the generation of messages and various forms from within the INRSTEX kernel and its various additional packages. Through the TEX [5] extension of TEX, language dependent hyphenation of words, with and without accents, is allowed. An example of a kernel form language variation is the change from "Chapter" to "Chapitre" when a `\chapterhead` is called in French rather than in English. `\englishversion` calls the English forms and `\versionfrancaise` the French forms.

4. Lists

To obtain a flavor of the philosophy and style of INRSTEX, this section will discuss in some detail the list capabilities of INRSTEX. `Plain` supplies two commands for lists, `\item`, and `\itemitem`, that create list items with indentations of one and two times the paragraph indentation in force when they are called. Thus a `\parindent=0pt` will totally destroy a list. INRSTEX supplies a complete set of commands for three levels of lists. It does not have any special forms for numbered or non-numbered lists but rather lets the user do this as necessary using standard commands and counters. It is easy to add these using TEX definitions as necessary (see Section 4.2 for an example of an automatically numbered list). Unlike LATEX, the depth of a list is explicitly stated. Thus it is possible to start with a `\beginsublist` rather than a `\beginlist` if `sublist` indentation is required or even to skip a level while inside a list. Lists and their associated items can appear in either vertical or internal vertical mode. They also work in multicolumn format and in conjunction with modifications of the page margins.

The commands `\beginlist`, `\beginsublist`, `\beginsubsublist` or the approved abbreviations `\bl`, `\bsl`, and `\bssl` start lists and matching `\endlist`, `\endsublist`, `\endsubsublist`, or the abbreviations `\el`, `\esl`, and `\essl` terminate them. Mismatches cause error messages. As each \begin... \end... pair form a *group*, it is possible to change the fonts or any other parameter and that change affects only the present group and all of its internal groups. This is an important benefit of designating lists instead of list items. All items in a list are introduced by \listitem <list_item_mark> followed by the actual body of the list. As usual there is an approved abbreviation \li.

The main text of a list is indented a fixed amount according to the value of the \listindent, \sublistindent, or \subsublistindent as the case may be. The list item herald, if it exists, is placed the value of the \listitemmarksize to the left of the indented list. All spacings between list items and between lists are controlled by parameters that are specified in the INRSTÊX default file. In fact this file has **all** the parameters, including those set in Plain, in one place.

INRSTÊX also supplies three token lists \everylist, \everysublist, and \everysubsublist whose contents are emptied inside the list group every time the corresponding \begin...list is called. These may be used for changing the list indentations, fonts, or individual item skips. Anything done in an outer list is of course valid in the sublists. Thus \everysublist={\eightpoint \it } will force all sublists to be set in \eightpoint with a default of italic. There are three additional token lists \e@verylist, \e@verysublist, and \e@verysubsublist for the document designer†.

One of the most useful list macros is a \samplemark{<example>} which sets the size of the present list indentation to that of <example> plus 1en. This makes it quite simple to create labeled lists or compensate for a number such as [1467] during a very long bibliography. The list commands can be, and are, used as the basis of specialized lists such as citation references.

An example of small but important INRSTÊX feature is the protection of list item baseline skips from external influences. INRSTÊX has a \spacing{<size>} macro where <size> is in number of lines and may be fractional. It turns out that lists look rather terrible if they are double spaced. An \everylist may override this protection if desired.

4.1 An Example List

Things to note about lists are

- There are three levels of lists, *lists*, *sublists*, and *subsublists*.
    - ∘ A list, sublist, subsublist starts a group. The group localizes the effect of changes.
    - ♣ List items are indicated in the same way at all levels.

† INRSTÊX protects its internal macros with an **@**. However the **@ always** appears as the second letter and never replaces any letter. This makes conversions between internal and external forms rather easy and readable.

◇ Display mathematics is acceptable within lists. This is an example.

$$\oint_{|z|<1} \frac{e^{-kz}}{(1-z)} dz$$

It can also have a second paragraph that is a part of this item. This paragraph could even have a narrowed portion

Wise men lay up knowledge but the babbling of a fool brings ruin near. **Proverbs Ch. 10, Vs. 14**

• It is possible to tighten the list here but it would not do much good as this is the last subitem.

Note: The **Note:** herald is so large that it sticks **into** the actual list item. This can be seen on this line.

⋆ This is a more normal size herald.

The previous list is produced by

```
\beginlist
\li $\bullet$ There are three levels of lists, {\it lists},
      {\it sublists}, and {\it subsublists}.
\beginsublist
\eightpoint
\li $\circ$ A list, sublist, subsublist starts a group.
        The group localizes the effect of changes.
\li $\clubsuit$ List items are indicated in the same way at
        all levels.
\li $\diamond$ Display mathematics is acceptable within lists.
        This is an example.
    $$
     \oint_{\vert z\vert < 1} {e^{-kz} \over (1-z)} dz
    $$
It can also have a second paragraph that is a part of this
item. This paragraph could even have a narrowed portion
\beginnarrowtext .5in
\tenpoint \it \noindent
Wise men lay up knowledge but the babbling
of a fool brings ruin near.
\bf Proverbs Ch.~10, Vs.~14
\endnarrowtext
\li $\bullet$ It is possible to tighten the list here
    but it would not do much good as this is the last
    subitem.
\endsublist
```

```
\li {\bf Note:} The {\bf Note:} herald is so large that it sticks
         {\bf into} the actual list item. This can be seen
         on this line.
\li $\star$ This is a more normal size herald.
\endlist
```

4.2 A Numbered List

This automatically numbered list

1. You shall have no other gods before me.
2. You shall not make for yourself any graven image.
3. You shall not take the name of the Lord your God in vain.
4. Remember the sabbath day, to keep it holy.
5. Honor your father and mother.

Exodus Chap. 20, Verses 3-13 (Abridged)

is actually produced by

```
\newcount\listnum
\def\lin{\advance\listnum by 1 \li \the\listnum. }
\everylist = {\listnum=0}
\beginlist
\tightenlist
\lin You shall have no other gods before me.
\lin You shall not make for yourself any graven image.
\lin You shall not take the name of the Lord your God in vain.
\lin Remember the sabbath day, to keep it holy.
\lin Honor your father and mother.

\hfill {\it Exodus Chap. 20, Verses 3-13 (Abridged)}
\endlist
```

The \tightenlist is used to reduce the inter list item spacing since nearly all of the items are one line. Note the blank line before the reference. List items may be several paragraphs long.

This list is so short that it is probably just as easy to hand number it using \li <number>. The listing could have been made alphabetic by replacing \the\listnum by \alphabetic{\the\listnum}. Whether the construction is necessary depends upon the frequency of the lists. Usually bibligraphic lists are automatically numbered.

5. Text and Graphics – TeXGraph

INRSTeX has been recently extended to include a graphics capability and the merging of external plot and figure files. Documents may now be produced without any cutting or pasting of any sort. The importance of this capability cannot be overestimated. There is seldom a final version of any document. Although TeX was initially accepted because it allowed for the typesetting of mathematical equations, it has now become essential because it produces **complete** documents.

The graphics merging is accomplished through TeX and the interpretation of \specials by the INRSprint printing driver rather than through a special external page building system. The \specials interpretation capabilities of INRSprint are quite modest. Unlike LaTeX, which creates its pictures using small graphics elements in special fonts, INRSTeX uses graphics primitives supplied by the laser printer. This results in more compact and versatile drawing and can grow as laser printer capabilities grow. The current version of TeXGraph assumes a QMS laser printer and writes specials in its QUIC [6] language. This limits the capabilities to vector graphics, circular arcs, and various pattern fills. A new version will write in PostScript [4] and is anticipated to have many more primitives available – ellipses, splines, and arbitrary rotations appear to be possible.

5.1 TeXGraph Capabilities and Requirements

TeXGraph allows for the inclusion of plot files and the overlay of text as necessary. This text overlay may be printed either horizontally, vertically, or both, thus allowing for the labelling of axes with TeX fonts. Angular text printing is not available in QUIC. From the user view all that is required to input a plot file, centered on the page with the appropriate space left is to use \centerplotfile{<filename>}. The <filename> file will have been previously converted to QUIC and will have been preceded by a comment that gives TeXGraph the plot size information required to leave the appropriate space. TeXGraph reads only the size information from the plot file and produces error messages if the file is not found or the size information is not present. Neither case stops the processing. A file may be inserted at an arbitrary place in the text by using

```
\beginTeXgraphics % starts TeX Graph -- abbreviated \btg
\includefile{<filename>}
\endTeXgraphics  % ends TeX Graph -- abbreviated \etg
```

In fact the \includefile{<filename>} will insert a file at the present location while creating graphics.

To insert a plot file, INRSprint must be able to interpret the file name and insert the contents of that file at its present location.

5.2 TeXGraph Primitives

TeXGraph has a number of capabilities that range from primitive to powerful.

- Drawing primitives consist of commands for circles, circular arcs, line vectors, vectors with arrowheads, and erasing vectors, and fill patterns.

- There are commands for changing whether the distances specified are to be interpreted absolutely, with respect to an origin or relatively with respect to the present position.

- There is a command to change the (pen)width of the drawn lines and to change the interpreted scale of the units of distance.

- There is a command to change the default units. However, since arbitrary scaling of units is allowed, this command is of limited use except for those that visualize distances in different dimensions. The dimensions available are those available in INRSTEX.

- There is a "graphical segment" which can be placed at any specific location. Distances inside a graphical segment are interpreted with respect to the segment origin. The distances inside a segment may be either relative or absolute with respect to the segment origin. There is a *segment scale* which allows for segments to be scaled relatively with respect to an overall graph.

- Text, with all the capabilities of INRSTEX may be written either horizontally or vertically (up) on the page. This allows for the such things as labelling graphs.

- TEXGraph attempts to keep track of the maximum extent of a graph. These are available after the graph is terminated in the variables `\hgraphsize` and `\vgraphsize`. `\hgraphskip` and `\vgraphskip` will cause a horizontal or vertical skip of the appropriate graphsize.

- All of TEX's definitional capabilities are available. These can be used to replace a complex structure by a single command or, although it is frowned upon, to change the surface syntax of TEXGraph.

- Explicit use of grouping through {}, or `\begingroup`, `\endgroup` pairs is not allowed. This will foul up the positional record keeping inside. Groups may be produced only through the use of segments, namely the `\beginsegment...` `\endsegment` pair.

5.3 Simple TEXGraphics

TEXGraph will allow for rather sophisticated graphics. You can use the definition capabilities of INRSTEX to create libraries of symbols and neat forms for future use. The units of the dimensions are implicit, but changable. The default is inches. Thus `h:<number>` is the distance in the horizontal (to right) and `v:<number>` is the distance in the vertical (down) direction. The locations are absolute distances with respect to an origin in the upper left hand corner. Thus directions in TEXGraph and TEX are identical.

The following diamond box is a simple example

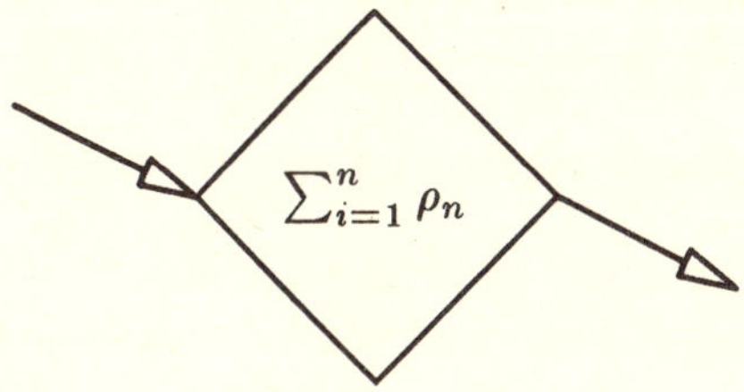

and was put in place with

```
$$
\centergraph{
   \btg
     \move h:0 v:.5   % moves penup to (0,.5)
     \lvec h:.5 v:0   % draws a line to (.5,0)
     \lvec h:1 v:.5
     \lvec h:.5 v:1
     \lvec h:0 v:.5
     \move h:-.5 v:.25 \avec h:0 v:.5 % left arrow vector
     \move h:1 v:.5 \avec h:1.5 v:.75 % right arrow vector
     \textref h:C v:C %sets the reference point dead center in text.
     \move h:.5 v:.5
     \htext {$\sum_{i=1}^n \rho_n$} % horizontal text box
    \etg}
$$
```

The command `\centergraph{<...>}` uses the information about plot size to center the graphics horizontally and to leave enough room vertically. Note that there are no angular restrictions on the arrow vectors. Arrowhead types supplied are .

5.4 Text in Graphs

Text may be written either horizontally (left to right) with `\htext{<text>}` or or vertically (upwards) with `\vtext{<text>}`. These commands `\htext` and `\vtext` create a TEX `\hbox`. The reference point for this box, specified by `\textref h:<L C R> v:<T C B>`, where one of the choices in the `<...>` specify one of the nine reference points shown below:

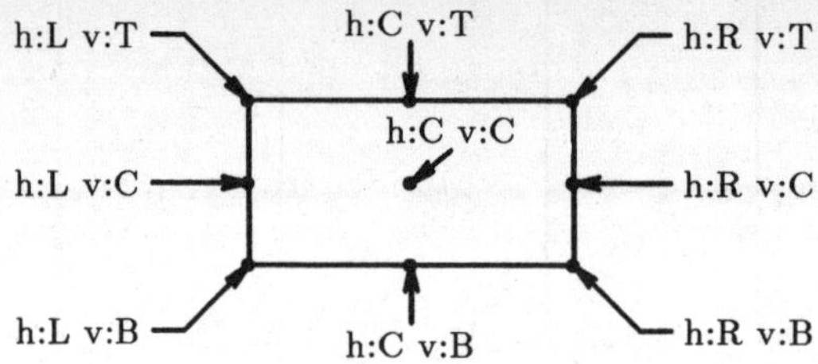

The existence of these nine choices greatly facilitate the user placement of text in graphics.

The commands for producing this diagram will be found in Appendix A.

5.5 Circles, Arcs and Fills

TEXGraph uses the circle, arc, and fill commands of the QMS Laser printer produce curves. The commands are

```
\lcir r:<radius>  % the <radius> is in the default dimensions
\larc r:<radius> sd:<starting degrees> ed:<ending degrees>
                 % the starting and ending degrees are INTEGERS
\fill p:<number>  % <number> between 0 and 24 ... each different
```

An example of a use of arcs and fill is given below. The fill pattern is purposely chosen so that the underlying lines would show.

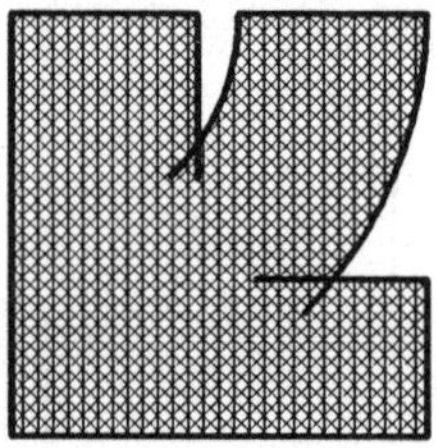

The version with the black fill is given below. Note that the "sloppy" arcs have disappeared.

This logo is given by

$$

```
\centergraph{\btg
             \unitscale .2  % reduces the scale
             \larc r:2.8 sd:0 ed:45  % two arcs
             \larc r:5.1 sd:0 ed:45  % note degrees not critical
             \move h:0 v:0
             \lvec h:2.3 v:0
             \lvec h:2.3 v:2
             \move h:3 v:3.2
             \lvec h:5.1 v:3.2
             \lvec h:5.1 v:5.1
             \lvec h:0 v:5.1
             \lvec h:0 v:0
             \move h:2.8 v:0
             \lvec h:5.1 v:0
             \move h:1 v:1
             \fill p:20 % black fill
            \etg}
$$
```

5.6 Advanced TEXGraphics and Segments

The most important advanced feature of TEXGraph is the graphical segment. These are delimited by `\beginsegment`... `\endsegment` pairs and are used to create graphical items that can be placed at any specific location in a graph. This capability, combined with TEX's ability to create definitions allows for the creation of libraries of symbols. The following is a list of some of the important points concerning segments:

- A segment is a group and is defined by a `\beginsegment`... `\endsegment` pair.
- Each segment has a *segment reference point.* This is the location in the enclosing segment or `\btg \etg`, which is really just a special segment.
- `\unitscale` <number> affects the present segment and all enclosed segments unless they have their own `\unitscale`. A `\unitscale` may be changed at any time within a segment.
- `\segmentscale` <number> affects the present segment and all enclosed segments unless that segment is protected by an `\absolutescale`. The segment scales accumulate.
- The actual scale used for interpreting position numbers is the product of all of the enclosing segmentscales times the presently active unitscale.

- The *segment reference position* is the location when the the `\beginsegment` is executed. Absolute positions within a segment are relative to the *segment reference position*. Relative positions are relative.

5.7 Comments on TEXGraph

TEXGraph is very powerful, and creates magnificent looking output. With the increased capabilities of a `PostScript` printer it will probably do anything that is required. The major difficulty is that it is just not very much fun to use. What is needed is an nice graphics interface that allows for interactive building of graphics much like MacDraw [7] but with the ability to better control text placement and to use TEX fonts. In most instances a "rough sketch" to "finished form" capability is what is really wanted. TEXGraph is a long way from that. However its output is of such high quality that it is used in preference to MacDraw by fussy people.

6. Some Observations

From some perspectives, both INRSTEX and LATEX are severely lacking. Under no circumstances can it be said that TEX is fun. Users need a TEX/Graphics enviroment that allows quick feedback so that they have confidence that what they are doing is correct. The document preparation features of INRSTEX or LATEX must not be dropped by the wayside when designing such a visual interface. Although they may not be terribly important to a typist, they are very important for an author. It is incredibly reassuring that a reference to an equation is not suddenly going to become incorrect just because of some textual permutation. These are the features that are at the heart of INRSTEX and must be retained.

A second area of grave concern is error messages. Most users, other than TEXperts tend to ignore them because they can make no sense out of them. It is not that they are without sense. It is rather that they require a degree of knowledge that is probably only available to the macro designer. Perhaps faster visual feedback will reduce the distance before detection of an error and enhance extrication.

This paper has given a slice of INRSTEX as used at INRS-Télécommunications. This slice was meant to give a flavor of the system and its capabilities rather than be an exhaustive description. For such a description it is necessary to consult various technical reports [3, 5, 8]. Better yet, play with it.

References

1. L. Lamport, **LATEX**, Addison Wesley, New York, 1985.

2. M.J. Ferguson, "Table Making with INRSTEX", TUGboat, Vol. 7, No. 2, July 1986.

3. M.J. Ferguson "The INRSTEX Reference Manual", INRS Technical Report No. 84-19, 1984

4. Adobe Systems Inc. **PostScript Langauge Reference Manual**, Addison Wesley, New York, 1985.

5. M.J. Ferguson, "A Multilingual TEX", Tech. Report No. 85-14, INRS-Télécommunications, April 1985.

6. QMS Inc., **QUIC Programming Language, Version 3**, Publication No. 1720460.0100, QMS Inc, Mobile, Alabama, Oct. 1984.

7. Apple Computer Inc. **MacDraw**, Apple Product No. M1509, Apple Computer Inc., Cupertino, Calif., 1984.

8. M.J. Ferguson, "An Introduction to TEXGraph", Tech. Report No. 85-07, INRS-Télécommunications, Feb. 1985.

Appendix A. Commands for the Text Reference Box

This appendix give the commands used to produce the text reference box in Section 5.4.

```
\def\bl{\htext {$\bullet$} }
\def\tref{\beginsegment
           \textref h:C v:C
           \lvec h:1 v:0 \bl
           \lvec h:2 v:0 \bl
           \lvec h:2 v:.5 \bl
           \lvec h:2 v:1 \bl
           \lvec h:1 v:1 \bl
           \lvec h:0 v:1 \bl
           \lvec h:0 v:.5 \bl
           \lvec h:0 v:0 \bl
           \move h:1 v:.5 \bl
          \endsegment}
\def\tlabels{\textref h:R v:C %left hand labels
             \htext{ h:L v:T } \lvec h:.2 v:0 \avec h:.6 v:.4
             \move h:0 v:.9 \htext{ h:L v:C } \avec h:.6 v:.9
             \move h:0 v:1.8 \htext{ h:L v:B } \lvec h:.2 v:1.8
                             \avec h:.6 v:1.4
             \textref h:L v:C %right hand labels
             \move h:3.2 v:0 \htext{ h:R v:T } \lvec h:3 v:0
                             \avec h:2.6 v:.4
             \move h:3.2 v:.9 \htext{ h:R v:C } \avec h:2.6 v:.9
             \move h:3.2 v:1.8 \htext{ h:R v:B } \lvec h:3 v:1.8
```

```
                          \avec h:2.6 v:1.4
          \textref h:C v:B % Center Top
          \move h:1.6 v:0 \htext{ h:C v:T } \move h:1.6 v:.05
            \avec h:1.6 v:.4
          \textref h:L v:C % Center Center
          \move h:2.0 v:.7 \htext{ h:C v:C } \lvec h:1.85 v:.7
                      \avec h:1.6 v:.9
          \textref h:C v:T % Center Bottom
          \move h:1.6 v:1.8 \htext{ h:C v:B } \move h:1.6 v:1.75
                       \avec h:1.6 v:1.4
         }
$$
\centergraph{\btg
          \arrowheadsize l:.08 w:.02 \arrowheadtype t:0
          \tlabels
          \move h:.6 v:.4 \tref
          \etg}
$$
```

AsHTEX: An Interactive Previewer for TEX or The Marvellous World of AsHTEX

Laurence GALLOT
INRIA SOPHIA-ANTIPOLIS
Route des Lucioles
06560 Valbonne, France

Abstract

This paper describes an interactive multi-window previewer for TEX. This tool is built on a screen handler called ASH, that is part of Brown Workstation Environment developed at Brown University. Today, AsHTEX runs on SM90 with the Numelec Bitmap screen and on SPS9.

1. Introduction

Using TEX for typesetting all our documents, we have required tools to help us in this work. We have adapted to our computers the Brown Workstation Environment, BWE, which makes it possible to design graphical applications easily. With BWE we have realized an interactive multi-window previewer for TEX that we present in this paper.

We first explain what a previewer is and why we need such a tool for displaying documents typeset with TEX. Then we describe the specific functionalities that are desirable. Next we give the details of the implementation of our previewer, that we have named AsHTEX, and finally we describe the problems we have encountered, and how they were solved when possible.

2. Description of a Previewer

2.1. What is a previewer and why does a TEX user need such a tool?

When you prepare a document using a typesetting system, such as TEX, the initial work consists in typing a correct source file on a standard alphanumeric terminal. Next the TEX program is run on this file to obtain an intermediate file called a *dvi file*, and finally by interpreting this dvi file with a driver output is generated. Notice that the driver used depends on the type of the output device.

While the source file consists of the text and of command strings for the typesetting, one doesn't see very precisely what the final document will look like. Thus very quickly, one wants to see output. The most usual and simplest way of looking at the result consists of outputting the document on paper. Unfortunately this method is often slow and may be expensive. For instance, there is often only one printer for several workstations; to use the printer files must be transfered to the appropriate machine and then wait for the output. If there are many users for the printer, this may take awhile. Futhermore pages on such a (laser or electrostatic) printer are very expensive — we have computed that a page on our laser printer is about one Franc, which is at least three times more expensive than photocopying. It is expensive and cumbersome to output 10 draft copies before getting the output just right.

One often wants to look only at a part of a page. For example, for designing complicated equations or arrays, it may take many tries before the output is correct, or sometimes the page layout is to be checked. While it is not reasonable to get hardcopy output for each modification on the source file, it would be nice to be able to look at the document quickly without outputting it on paper.

Since personal workstations with high resolution display have recently become widely available, one would like to view the TEX output directly on the screen. This method makes the preparation of a document easier and less expensive. A tool that enables the user to look at his document without outputting it on paper is called a previewer. A previewer allows the user to look at *what he will get* on the paper. The layout on the screen is exactly the same as on paper. The only difference comes from the resolution of the display device, and the result on the screen may look less beautiful than the hardcopy version. Although the lower resolution of the display (around 100 dots per inch for the Numelec display against 300 dots per inch or more for a laser printer) results in the characters being less beautiful, it seems very sufficient for preparing a document. The user can quickly see the results and make modifications.

2.2. What does the user want from a previewer?

Clearly the user wants to look at any page in the document and does not necessarily want to view the pages in sequential order. However, when viewing a page it is often the case that the next or previous page of the document is the one the user wants to look at next. Thus the previewer should provide facilities to get the next or the previous page easily while still providing the freedom to see any arbitrary page. Also he may want to look at more than one page at the same time on the screen — for side-by-side comparison. Perhaps the pages to be compared even come from different documents. Thus, the previewer must handle requests for multiple pages and multiple dvi files.

Depending on the output device and the size of the pages in the user's document, it may not be possible to fit the whole page on the bitmap screen at once.

Thus, the user must be able to "scroll" through the page, both in the horizontal and vertical directions. That is, if the page is too tall and cannot appear totally on the screen, the user needs to be able to move the page up or down quickly to see a different portion of the page.

A multi-window system makes it possible to realize these needs. Each page viewed is in a window (a portion of the screen delimited by a border). If there are several windows (pages) on the screen, they may overlap one another. If the multi-window system used is powerful enough, the pages can be moved around. If there are many pages (windows) on the screen, it is necessary to quickly move the page to be viewed to the forefront so that it is no longer obscured by the others. It should be possible to change the size of a window: if one wants to keep visible only a small part of a page, one can resize the corresponding window and move it in a corner of the screen where it remains visible. The user can also choose the number of pages that he wants to see on the screen at the same time. For example, he may choose to only have one or two windows; pages to be viewed are put in one of these windows. However, he may have a window on the screen for each page he views — perhaps a bit cluttered for a 15-page paper. But the user has control of creating and destroying windows.

3. Implementation of AsHTEX

We now examine how we have implemented the previewer facilities of the previous section. To realize our previewer we needed a multi-window system. We used the Brown Workstation Environment (BWE) that we have adapted for use on the SM90 workstation with Numelec bitmap screen and on Bull SPS9.

3.1. Presentation of BWE

BWE is a workstation environment developed at Brown University, for the design of interactive graphical applications. This environment consists of different libraries, and provides facilities for using powerful hardware components such as high-resolution bitmapped displays and locator devices (e.g. a mouse) with a minimum amount of effort. In particular, it allows input management (using both the standard keyboard and a locator device), sophisticated graphical output to multiple overlapping windows, and text and graphics editing.

The main feature of this system is its portability; it can be adapted to machines running a Unix system and including a high-resolution output device (monochrome or color) and any locator device (mouse, light pen, data tablet, etc.) Portability is obtained by coding in the C language for Unix and by carefully isolating all the machine dependencies in virtual device interfaces for input and for output. Adapting BWE to a machine requires only writing these interfaces.

At Brown the system has been developed on Apollo workstations, and then adapted to the Sun workstation. At INRIA Sophia, we adapted it for SM90 workstation with the Numelec bitmap display and SMX system, and for SPS9 computer running Unix. Our objective here is not to describe in detail each component of the BWE system (for more information refer to the BWE documentation [1].) However we present here the ASH library which makes it possible to implement our previewer for TEX.

3.2. Presentation of ASH

ASH is a low-level screen handler completely independent of the machine and of the output device used. It allows the user to create, modify, and manipulate bitmaps and representations of these bitmaps on the display. The main data structure manipulated by ASH is the window. An ASH window is a virtual bitmap on which the application draws and outputs text. A window can be displayed on the screen in full, in part, or not at all.

The main part of the work of the screen handler ASH consists in computing the visible area associated with each window and displaying the border that delimits the visible part of each window. Windows are maintained by ASH in two ways. First, they are maintained in a tree-hierarchy as they are created. The screen is the window associated with the root of the tree-hierarchy, and each window is the child of the current window at the time when it was created. For each window, its visible part is entirely contained in the visible part of its parent. The second way ASH maintains the windows is to have for each a list of its children ordered for the display. The ordering of the children is such that any window above a given one may obscure this window, however, no window below it in the list may obscure any portion of the given window.

For drawing and outputting text, each window has its own set of graphic attributes: current color, text color, background color, combination rule (mode for combining bits: or, xor, etc.), fill pattern, line style, and font. These attributes can be changed at any moment during the execution of the application program.

3.3. Description of the output screen

The screen of an ASHTEX session consists of windows for outputting the pages, menus, and a dialog window for the output of messages and keyboard input.

3.3.1. The output windows

As we have seen before, pages are almost never fully displayed on the screen because of their size. In fact, once a page as been computed (as an array of bits), it is stored in a virtual bitmap, and partly displayed on the screen in a window.

The windows we have implemented look like *MacIntosh* windows. They have a header, in which the dvi file's name and the number of the associated page are written. The user can move the window by clicking in the header. At this time a ghost (rectangular box) appears around the window and follows the moves of the mouse until the mouse button is released. The last position of the ghost indicates the new position of the window. In the left corner of the header there is a small black square that allows the window to be destroyed.

The windows have two scrollbars. One scrollbar is vertical, on the right border of the window, and it permits vertical scrolling of the corresponding page in the window. The second scrollbar is horizontal, on the bottom border of the window, and permits horizontal scrolling. The fact that the entire page exists somewhere in memory (in a virtual bitmap) makes it possible to scroll very quickly and makes the scrollbar very useful.

A scrollbar consists of a rectangular area, with a square button at each end. In each button there is an arrow indicating a scrolling direction, and clicking in one of these buttons allows for a step by step (incremental) scrolling. In a scrollbar, there is also a small rectangular area (called a thumb) representing the part of the page that is visible in the window; the size of the thumb is proportional to the visible part of the page and the position of the thumb in the scrollbar represents the position of this visible part within the total page. To jump to another part of the page, one clicks on the thumb and then positions it (actually an outline or "ghost" version of the thumb moves) within the scrollbar; releasing the mouse button results in moving the thumb over the ghost and the corresponding portion of the page appears in the window. Depressing a mouse button in the scrollbar but not on the thumb results in the thumb moving by a given step and the page scrolling accordingly until the button is released or the designated point lies within the thumb.

A small square area, in the right bottom corner of the windows allows the resizing of the windows. When a button of the mouse is depressed in this area, a ghost appears around the window and grows (or shrinks) following the moves of the mouse until the button is released. The last size of the ghost becomes the new size of the window. When the window is resized, the header, scrollbars, thumbs, and the visible part of the page are resized accordingly.

3.3.2. The menus

In AsHTEX we use two kinds of menus: a permanent one and two pull-down menus. The pull-down menus are accessed through the permanent menu. The permanent menu has an horizontal format and lies in the top left corner of the screen; it has five buttons named *stop*, *refresh*, *new dvi*, *new frame*, and *new page*.

The first button is used for stopping the program. Click this button and a three-button pull-down menu appears. These give three choices *clear* (to stop and clear the screen), *leave* (to stop and leave the screen as it is), and *cancel* (to remain inside AsHTEX). Note that when the *stop* button is chosen if the mouse button is released outside of the pull-down menu, the command is also cancelled.

The button named *refresh* is used to refresh the screen. This is useful, for example, to remove parasitic messages from the system or from another user.

The third button of the permanent menu, named *new dvi*, is used to load a new dvi file. When this button is chosen the program asks for the name of the dvi file to load, and for the number of the page that one wants to see first. If the user asks for loading the same dvi file (with the same name), the program asks him if he really wants to reload the same file. Note that pages can only be selected from the current dvi file. Thus alternating between pages from different dvi files requires that the dvi file be loaded at each switch. This is because ASHTEX uses a very simple driver for dvi files. Thus information is only maintained about the "current" dvi file. Switching between dvi files requires some start-up overhead to load the information from the dvi file and read the corresponding fonts.

The next button, named *new frame*, is used to get a new window on the screen. The user has to give a point on the screen, where the top left corner of the new window will appear, and the number of the page that he wants to see in this new window. By default, we have chosen to create two windows at the beginning of the program. The user can destroy one window if he desires, or he can create some windows (with the *new frame*) button if he wants to works with more than two windows. In this (default) setup the user would see each new page requested appear alternating in the two windows; thus the screen always has the last two pages asked for.

Finally, the last button, named *new page*, is used to change the current page. When this button is clicked, an other three-button pull-down menu appears. The content of the header of this menu is the name of the dvi file and the number of the current page. The three choices offered by the menu are: *next* (page following the current one), *previous* (the previous one), and *other* (to get any page from the document). Clicking the *other* button, the user is asked to give the number of the page he wants. If the chosen page is not already in a window on the screen, it is computed using the current dvi file and written in some window. The window whose contents is the requested page is moved to the top of the screen, and this page becomes the current one. This implies in particular that the number of this page will appear in the header of the pull-down menu, when calling *new page*.

3.3.3. The dialog window

The last component of the output screen of ASHTEX is the dialog window. It is a rather small window that appears in the right top corner of the screen when keyboard input is needed. It is used for communicating with the user, for example, sending error messages or requesting the name of a dvi file or what page to show.

3.4. Computing and displaying the pages.

When a page that isn't already in a window on the screen is requested this page has to be computed and then copied in a window. The width of the window is determined by the width of the page in the dvi file, while the height is computed so as to be in the "golden ratio" with the width. Computing a page is obtained by using a driver that interprets the dvi file and generates an array of bits. For AsHTEX we use the same driver as for our Canon printer. Because of the different resolutions of the printer and of the bitmap, the fonts used differ but the main part of the computation of a page is the same. When the called page is computed, the program has to choose which window of the screen will be associated with the new page. For that purpose we use a *virtual memory managing* technique: the chosen window is the least recently-used one. The program maintains a list of the windows displayed on the screen, when a window becomes the current window, it becomes the first element of the list and pushes the other windows behind it in the list; the window chosen to show a new computed page is the last of the list. If there is only one window on the screen, for each page computed, the contents of this window is overwritten.

4. The problems and our solutions

In this section we describe the various problems that we have encountered in developing AsHTEX. The main problem was one of speed because a tool such as a previewer has to be fast if it is going to be used at all. The second one was a problem of input management because using mouse input is rather difficult; the programs quickly become complex and hard to maintain. The third problem was a fonts problem because of the unusual resolution of the Numelec bitmap.

4.1. Speed

The previewer has to run quickly in two ways: first the modifications to the screen such as moving a window, scrolling, or popping a window have to be done just when they are requested by the user. Likewise ghosts and thumbs must move smoothly. Pages should not seem to be built from small rectangles. Secondly the pages have to be computed by the driver quickly enough, so that the user doesn't wait too long when asking for a new page.

The first point is handled through ASH which is a very powerful screen handler. It uses a lot of memory (keeping a copy of each virtual bitmap) but makes it possible to modify the screen very quickly. For the second point we had to improve the performance of the driver, particularly the part of the driver computing the pages. To start with, the driver was only used for outputting on the printer, where speed wasn't so important. But when the user asks for a new page in an interactive previewer, it is not possible to let him wait more than a few seconds before the page appears on the screen. By modifying crucial parts of the code the computation time of a page on the SM90 was decreased from more than 14 seconds to approximately 4 seconds. On a more powerful workstation, incorporating a

68020 rather than a 68010 microprocessor, it is clear that this time will drop below 1 second. This work was performed by J. Incerpi and F. Montagnac and will be reported elsewhere.

4.2. Input management

To resolve the problem of input management in a graphical user interface, some languages exist that can help the programmer to describe interactions using a mouse and that generate C code which can be integrated in the graphical application. The language that we have chosen to help us for managing input in AsHTEX, is a general synchronous programming language named *ESTEREL*, developed by G. Berry [2,3] at CMA in Sophia Antipolis. We haven't used ESTEREL for the entire input management of AsHTEX, but for a complex part of it: the scrollbars. Berry has described the behavior of a scrollbar in ESTEREL and his system has generated a C automaton that we have integrated in AsHTEX. This method has been useful in many ways. First of all the C code generated is compact and optimized. There is only one ESTEREL program for both the vertical and horizontal scrollbars. This method also provides modularity: the input management is completely separated from the rest of the program. And finally, to modify the behavior of the scrollbar, it is much easier to modify the ESTEREL program that more closely reflects the real behavior than to modify a big automaton implemented in a conventional language.

4.3. Missing Fonts

Using AsHTEX, we have quickly encountered the problem of missing fonts. For the resolution corresponding to the Numelec bitmap (around 100 dots per inch) we have a library of 118 dots per inch fonts but it is not very complete. This library contains all the fonts for TEX without magnification but if a document has a magnification command then some fonts may be missing and the driver will not be able to compute some pages of the document. If the magnification commands are removed from the TEX source file, the document can be displayed on the screen through AsHTEX. However this is not a satisfactory solution because removing the magnification commands from the TEX file changes the layout of the paragraphs and pages. The output of the document in AsHTEX will be very different than the output on paper. Not to mention that the document would have to be run through TEX another time to put back in the magnification desired before outputting on paper. Clearly having a full set of fonts for the device is the best solution but barring this we would like to see output that is as close to that on paper as possible. Retexing the file with and without magnification is not the solution. Thus our previewer offers an option to take the dvi file generated from a TEX source file with some overall magnification, and display it using the default (non-magnified) fonts. This works in general since if a font exists at all it is in this non-magnified size. This seems to be a reasonable solution since the page layout and line breaks are those that will appear in the hardcopy version, it is just that the characters are smaller. Note the spacing within the lines is proportional to the fonts used so that proofreading and checking layout is not hindered.

5. Conclusion

At this time ASHTEX runs and is used on SM90 workstation and Ridge computer. We are planning to move it to a Sun workstation in the near future. To move ASHTEX to a different environment first requires that ASH be adapted to this new machine. We've already mentioned that ASH's design makes this rather easy to do. As well, the code for the mouse management, which is very machine dependent, would have to be adjusted. ASHTEX is written, however, in a very modular way. Our previewer consists of modules for computing pages from the dvi file, for the scrollbars, for the graphical layout of the screen, and for handling keyboard and mouse input. This not only makes porting ASHTEX to another machine easy but could allow using the previewer environment for manipulating different objects. That is, rather than displaying pages of TEX output, we could manipulate digital pictures using most of the components of our system.

Many people have used ASHTEX in a daily fashion to prepare documents. The user-community that helped in defining its functionalities seems satisfied with the current compromises. The performance is considered acceptable, although improvements in this area are always welcome.

The cycle for writing documents typeset with TEX still has three separate steps: writing source file, then running TEX, and finally displaying the document. This is not entirely satisfactory. There is actually no interaction between the output on the screen and the source file. From the source file to the displayed output, one has to run TEX to get the dvi file and while previewing a part of the output (a word, a line, an equation, or a page) there is no way to get the corresponding string in the source file. Using an multi-window previewer such as ASHTEX, the user ideally wants to pick something on the screen and from within another window modify the corresponding string and see the newly adjusted output without leaving ASHTEX. We aren't as yet able to create such a powerful tool for the TEX user. Although we can see very well how desirable it would be.

Bibliography

1. The Brown Workstation Environment Documentation, Brown University, October 1984.
2. Gérard Berry, *Programming a Digital Watch in ESTEREL,* CMA ENSMP, Sophia-Antipolis, February 1986.
3. Georges Gonthier, The ESTEREL v2.1 Language Reference Manual, CMA ENSMP, Sophia-Antipolis, March 1986.

A LANGUAGE TO DESCRIBE FORMATTING DIRECTIVES FOR SGML DOCUMENTS.

Huu LE VAN – Elisa TERRENI

Department of Computer Science
University of Milan
Via Moretto da Brescia, 9 Milano - Italy

Abstract

SGML is a standard proposed by ISO for documents description based on generalized markup technique. The formatting process of a SGML document could consist in singling out markup elements and inserting formatting directives into the document in accordance with the class of the markup elements themselves, using a suitable map table.

This paper will present an implementation of an environment of SGML documents production, emphasizing a special language, METAFORM, for the map table construction.

1. Introduction.

For several years now authors have usually been submitting their manuscripts to publishing houses in hard copy form. Publishers, if provided with some electronic systems able to format and to print out the document, had to retype the manuscripts in the input form of the formatting program.

The continual increase of personal computers with their own user-friendly word processors lead authors to prefer generating their manuscripts eletronically. This on one hand makes the publishers' typing job easier; however, on the other, it gives them new problems to resolve. One of the principal problems is related to the physical form of manuscript disks or magnetic tapes, which requires a conversion in readable form for the destination machine. Usually it is resolved by means of interface software or devices [FER85].

Another problem that deserves particular attention regards information contained in the file transferred. This information could be of different types: the textual part of the manuscript without formatting codes; the DVI file for some typesetting system; the output format of some word processor ...

In the case of the DVI file it is necessary, on one hand, that the publisher has a specific driver able to understand it and that, on the other, the author has a specific formatter able to produce the DVI file itself. This means publishers must have on hand different drivers if they want to accept different types of DVI.

In other cases it requires a reformatting process of the manuscript. This could consist of inserting formatting codes and typesetting information in the manuscript in accordance with the formatter system avalaible to the publishers. In this process it is not easy to recognize from the manuscript file the text portion belonging to the specific object class (e.g. title of document, paragraph, title of appendix ...) to which to associate the formatting functions.

This difficulty could be diminished if the manuscript has been described using some kind of generic coding. Generic coding is a data management technique capable of describing the logical structure of text data file. It uses generalized markup, which identify each element of the document associating with it a logical class. A document described with generic coding could assume the following aspect:

```
: section
    This is the first section. It contains:
: list
: item
    1) The introduction ...
: item
    2) The description of ...
: endsection
```

where lines representing codes are started by ":".

Using generic coding, processing and formatting instructions are external to the text, which therefore is not dependent on any particular application [GCC78].

Generic coding, in various forms, is already in use today. There are implementations of generic coding for particular environments, such as the Langton Company for technical documentation production [WES85] the UK Government Printer and Publisher for the UK Government Legislation [HMS85], as well as more general-purpose ones, such as GML of IBM [IBM76a] and GenCode of GCCA [GCC78].

Recently, generic coding has become argument of international organizations for standardization work. ANSI began to define a generic coding based on IBM's DCF GML. Then the work is continued by ISO, which named the proposal standard as "Information Processing Systems – Programming Languages – Text Interchange and Processing – Standard Generalized Mark–up Language", for short "SGML". It is a draft international standard and as such is waiting for approval by member bodies [SMI85], [GOL81].

For a publisher who has on hand a particular formatter the reformatting process of a manuscript described using generic coding consists in singling out text elements by means of markup and in inserting formatting command sequences into the file in accordance with the class of the markup itself.

It is natural to think of performing this step automatically. An approach could be to use a map table containing the correspondences between markup and control sequences of the formatter itself. Then the step could consist in:

1) Recognizing generic codes from the manuscript file.
2) Retrieving the corresponding control sequences from the map table.
3) Generating the output file with these control sequences and text portions of the manuscript file.
4) Submitting the output file to the formatter system, which will yield the final layout.

Naturally, we can create different map tables for different formatter systems.

The approach considered determines a rigid association between generic codes and control sequences of formatters. In some situations we need a flexible association between them. For example, what happens if we need to associate with the same code two different sets of control sequences, one for the "title" of the book, the other for the "title" of the appendix ? From this situation we note that the action to undertake for a generic code depends on its position in the document; in other words it depends on the current status of the document. Therefore, rather than a rigid association, the mapping elements should be described by means of some sort of more flexible language.

This paper will present a current implementation of a system for the preparation of documents conforming to the generalized markup technique proposed by the standard SGML. The presentation puts emphasis on a language for the construction of the map table in an attempt to resolve the above mentioned problems. The language is capable of expressing, by means of statements and control structures, the processing to associate with various SGML markup elements present in a manuscript, in relation of its current status.

2. SGML.

SGML [ISO85] is a standard language proposed for text description. It considers a document as an element composed of others elements. The relationships among these elements constitutes the document structure. SGML provides a coherent and unambiguous syntax for describing that structure; in other words it is a formal expression of document markup.

One of the main objectives of the standard is to render the marked document both usable by humans and processable by the full range of word processor and text processing equipment. Consequently, the standard does not depend on application systems or devices [ADL85].

SGML describes documents using markup called generic identifiers (GIs). They are inserted among portions of text identifying them. Moreover, every element can be described, not only by GI, but also by attribute values. In this way two text portions can be considered different, even if identified with the same GI, when they have two different attribute values.

We report an example of a document described using SGML

```
1 <!ELEMENT article (title, author, paragraph * )>
2 <!ELEMENT (title | paragraph) (#CHARS)>
3 <!ELEMENT author (#CHARS) type (principal | co-author)>
4 <article>
5 <title>
6         The SGML standard proposed by ISO.
7 <author type = "principal">
8         Le van Huu
9 <paragraph>
10              This is the first paragraph ...
11 </paragraph>
12 </article>
```

Leaving out the syntax of SGML, we emphasize some significant aspects of the above document. Lines 1, 2, 3 establish the logical document structure; i.e., they define the model of every GI (the GI "article" can contain "title", followed by the GI "author", which in turn is followed by "paragraph", repeated 0 or more times, etc ...). They are known as "markup declaration".

The remaining lines identify text elements, marking them by using GI (e.g. article, author ...) and possibly also attribute values (type="principal"). They are known as "markup descriptive".

From the example we note that describing a document using SGML consists of two phases:

a) Definition of the document type, i.e., its logical structure

b) Markup of the text according to the structure defined above, creating a physical structure of the document.

But these steps are not enough to provide us with the final page out. It is necessary to submit the document to some formatting process. To achieve it one approach could be to create various "profiles" for various document types. Every profile contains the association between the GIs and the formatting procedures. This approach, similar to that used by the SCRIBE system [REI80], and GML di IBM forces publishers to build programs with these particular formatting procedures. But generally every publisher has his own formatting system and tends not to want to change. On the other hand, one of SGML's objectives is to permit every formatting system to process document described with SGML elements.

Therefore, a second approach could be considered. It consists in transforming the SGML document into a source file for every formatter wanted, then to submit it to the formatter itself. In this way, publishers could use again their own formatting system to procure the final layout of manuscripts. [LEV85a]

In the next section we will present the proposal for a system of SGML document production based on the second approach mentioned.

3. The proposed system.

The system comprehends: [LEV85b]

- A SGML parser that processes documents containing SGML markup. These documents can be generated by an ordinary text editor or come from a specifically designed interactive document input system based on manipulation of windows to represent document elements [LEV85c].

  The parser produces an intermediate file containing different information relating to the physical structure of the document. The main pieces of information contained in the intermediate file for every GI of the document are:

  a) name of GI
  b) name and value of attributes associated
  c) pointers to the relating text portion in the SGML source file

  Other information is not so important and we do not report in this paper.

- A parser module of a special language, called METAFORM, defined purposely for the map table specification. The map table contains, for every formatter and for every GI, a set of METAFORM statements. They specify processing to undertake when the corresponding GI is matched in the intermediate file. The output of the parser is a set of pseudo codes (p_codes) which simulate the functioning of a hypothetical stack machine [WIR81].

- An interpreter module which subsequently executes these p_codes. It generates as output the source file for the formatter to which the METAFORM program refers, in accordance with the order of GI present in the intermediate file.

3.1 The language METAFORM.

As previously mentioned, processing to be associated with each GI is specified in the map table, using a suitable language. METAFORM is a special-purpose language, defined purposely to describe formatting directives to be inserted in a document. From this comes its name: METAlanguage for FORMatting problems. The syntax of the language to some extent draws inspiration from language C [KER78] and from the standard STPL (Part Five – Formatting and Compositions Functions) [ISO84].

In this section we will briefly describe some relevant aspects of the METAFORM language.

Logically a METAFORM program can be organized following this structure:

```
BEGIN_GI gi_name_1
   BEGIN_ATT attribute_name_1
        block of statements associated with the attribute attribute_name_1
        of the generic identifier gi_name_1
   END_ATT

   BEGIN_ATT attribute_name_2
        block of statements associated with the attribute attribute_name_2
        of the generic identifier gi_name_1
   END_ATT
   ...................
   ...................
END_GI
BEGIN_GI gi_name_2
   BEGIN_ATT attribute_name_1
        block of statements associated with the attribute attribute_name_1
        of the generic identifier gi_name_2
   END_ATT

   BEGIN_ATT attribute_name_2
        block of statements associated with the attribute attribute_name_2
        of the generic identifier gi_name_2
   END_ATT
   ...................
```

As we can see, METAFORM instructions for a GI are included between the keywords BEGIN_GI and END_GI. These instructions are divided in different blocks in accordance with the different types of its attributes.

In using the BNF formalism, the structure of a METAFORM program is the following:

<program> ::= {<macro definition>} {<generic id block>}.
<generic id block> ::= BEGIN_GI <gi name>
{<attribute block>} END_GI
<attribute block> ::= BEGIN_ATT <atttribute name>
<statements> END_ATT
<gi name> ::= <identifier>
<attribute name> ::= <identifier>
<identifier> ::= <letter> {<letter>} | {_} | {<number>}

The first section of the program is reserved to the macro definition. Every macro can have parameters and its body can contain every type of METAFORM statements.

The constructs "attribute name" and "gi name" represent names of attributes and generic identifiers. The construct "statements" represents all statements of METAFORM. This will be presented in greater detail later on.

In comparison to a structured programming language, the couple BEGIN_GI and END_GI could be considered a procedure at level 0. We will call it "GI procedure". Consequently, statements between every couple of BEGIN_ATT and END_ATT constitutes a procedure just one level below. We will call it "attribute procedure".

Not always does a GI have attributes; therefore, there would be no "attribute procedures" associated with it. To avoid this, every "GI procedure" always contains a standard "attribute procedure", called "SYS.ATT", to be executed at the end of the execution of all other ones.

Every METAFORM program refers to a specific formatter. It must be compiled by a parser, which produces a set of p_codes, ready to be interpreted by the interpreter module. Using it, the formatting process of a SGML document could take place in the following way.

Once decided which formatter will process the document and, consequently, which METAFORM program to be executed, the intermediate file is scanned by the interpreter. When a GI occurs, the interpreter searches forward for the related attributes. For every attribute matched, the set of the corresponding METAFORM instructions, (or, better yet, the p_codes generated), is executed, just as the in the case of a procedure call. METAFORM I/O instructions usually access to the SGML source document, by means of pointers present in the intermediate file, to retrieve texts which are to be worked on. Execution of METAFORM instructions for an attribute will produce as output a part of the source file for the formatter selected.

At the end of the intermediate file scanning, the entire source file is generated. Then it is submitted to the formatter, which will compose it generating the final pages out. To better explain the above concepts we will show an example of the use of METAFORM language, even if many of its elements are still unknown.

Let us suppose to select TEX as formatter and to define every document in the most sample way as follows:

```
 1 \input basic
 2 \hsize 3in
 3 \vskip 1in
 4 \centerline { title of document }
 5 \vskip 30pt
 6 \centerline {\sl author name }
 7 \vskip 2.30cm
 8 \parindent 10pt
 9     paragraph text
10 \par\bye
```

From this we can single out some formatting elements to associate with logical elements of the document, such as the head part (lines 1, 2, 3) that specifies the format of the document, the title to be centered (line 4), the author name to be centered and written in the slanted 10–point font (line 6), the paragraph to be indented with 10 points (line 8). These elements could be represented by SGML GIs as "document", "title", "author", "paragraph". Moreover, the GI "document" could have an attribute "type" with two possible values: "sample" and "complex". On the basis of them we can decide to select the format, for example, "basic" or "math".

A METAFORM program which is able to generate the above TEX document from a SGML one could be:

```
BEGIN_GI document
    BEGIN_ATT type
        IF $ATTVAL == "sample" THEN
        BEGIN
            WRITE ("\input basic");
            WRITE ("\hsize 3in");
            WRITE ("\vskip 1in");
        END
        ELSE
        BEGIN
            WRITE ("\input math");
            WRITE ("\hsize 3in");
            WRITE ("\vskip 1in");
        END
    END_ATT
END_GI
```

```
BEGIN_GI title
     BEGIN_ATT SYS.ATT
          WRITE ("\centerline {");
          READTRANSFER (); -- title
          WRITE ("}");
          WRITE ("\vskip 30pt");
     END_ATT
END_GI
BEGIN_GI author
     BEGIN_ATT SYS.ATT
          WRITE ("\centerline {\sl");
          READTRANSFER (); -- author name
          WRITE ("}");
          WRITE ("\vskip 2.30pt");
     END_ATT
END_GI
BEGIN_GI paragraph
     BEGIN_ATT SYS.ATT
          WRITE ("\parindent 10pt");
          READTRANSFER (); -- paragraph text
          WRITE ("\par \bye");
     END_ATT
END_GI
.
```

On the other hand the processing of the following SGML document

```
<document type="sample">
<title>
   An example of METAFORM
<author>
   Le van Huu
<paragraph>
   This is a very sample example.
</document>
```

by the SGML parser will cause the production of an intermediate file containing, as mentioned, information about elements of the document, such as name of GIs, name and value of attributes, pointers to text portions present in SGML source file. Precisely, the content of that file is the following:

document, type = sample, title 35/22, author 69/10, paragraph 95/30, where the couples of numbers 35/22, 69/10, and 95/30 refer to SGML source document. They represent respectively the start position and the number of characters contained in the text portions of "title", "author", and "paragraph" elements.

The interpreter module, scanning it, will produce TEX document as reported above. In fact it begins to recognize the GI "document" and its attribute value from the intermediate file. This causes the activation of the attribute procedure "type" of the GI procedure "document" of the METAFORM program. The condition of the IF statement is true because the current value of the attribute ($ATTVAL) is "sample", therefore the lines

```
\input basic
\hsize 3in
\vskip 1in
```

are written in output (see instructions 5, 6, 7).

Then the recognition of the GI "title" from the intermediate file causes the execution of the attribute procedure SYS.ATT of the GI title (because title has no attribute value). This, first of all, writes the line (see instruction 19)

```
centerline {
```

into the output. Now it is necessary to add the title of the document. This is performed by the procedure READTRANSFER, which accesses to the SGML document by the pointers specified in the intermediate file (value 35), reads the text portion and transfers it into the output file, generating the line

```
An example of METAFORM
```

Then instructions 21, 22 of the METAFORM program cause the final lines

```
}
\vskip 30pt
```

to be generated.

The processing of the remaining statements of the METAFORM program follows the same scheme.

Now we will describe some main elements of the language.

3.1.1 Variable.

Variable of a METAFORM program can assume either string or real type. There is no declaration instruction. In fact, a variable is implicitly declared when it is referred for the first time, precisely when it appears on the left hand of an assignment statement. Moreover, the type of a variable can be changed during the execution of the program, in accordance with its current value.

There are two principal categories of variable:

1) user variables, the names of which are defined by the user (METAFORM programmer). They are local variables of an "attribute procedure".

2) system variables, the names of which are defined in advance by the language. They are recognizable by the character "$" in front of their name. System variables are divided, in turn, in two categories:

2a) document status variables: they represent the status of the document being examined. In fact, they refer to information about:

- the GI contained in the intermediate file. For example:

– GINAME: the name of the GI just matched in the intermediate file.
– GIPARENT: the name of the GI that contains the current one.
– GIOCCUR: the number of occurrences of the current GI in the text.

- the attribute of the current GI. For example:

– ATTNAME: the name of the attribute just matched in the intermediate file.
– ATTVAL: the value of the current attribute.

- the current line of the document. For example:

– LNLENGTH: length of the line.
– LNWORDS: number of words contained in the line.

- the current word. For example:

– WDLENGTH: length of the word
– WDCUR: the word just read from the text.

The last two types of variables mentioned allow the programmer to examine the current word and line of the document. The need to use them comes from the fact that some formatters use insert control sequences among particular characters of a word or among particular words of a line.

The values of document status variables are usually updated automatically by the interpreter. For example, every time that a GI is read from the intermediate file, the new value is assigned to the variable GINAME.

Statements of an attribute procedure can refer to them to know the values. These statements can also assign to them new values, even if this could cause incongruencies among document status variables.

2b) formatting variables: They represent parameters for the formatting process. Principal variables of this category concern the page. For example:

- PGHEIGHT: the height dimension of the page
- LEFTMARGIN: the value of the left margin
- RIGHTMARGIN: the value of the right margin
- CURINDENT: the current indentation

Formatting variables are managed by the programmer. They are useful to prepare the formatting directives to be written into the output file.

3.1.2 IF statement.

The structure of the IF statement can be expressed by the following BNF construction:

<if statement> ::= IF <conditional_expression> THEN
BEGIN {<statements>} END
| IF <conditional_expression> THEN
BEGIN {<statements>} END
ELSE BEGIN {<statements>} END
<conditional_expression> ::= <relational condition>
| <logical condition>
| <inclusion condition>
| <belonging condition>

The relational condition and the logical condition do not differ much from those of an ordinary programming language. They are expressions linked by relational operators, such as <, <=, >, >=, <>, ==, and by logical operators such as AND (&), OR (|), NOT.

The last two conditions deserve, instead, more attention. They can be expressed by:

<inclusion condition> ::= <string>IN<variable> | <variable>IN<variable>
<belonging condition> ::= <gi value> OF <gi value>
<gi value> ::= <string> | <variable>
<variable> ::= <identifier> | $ <identifier>
<string> ::= " <character> {<character>} " |
' <character> {<character>} '

The inclusion condition allows the test of the presence of a substring in a word.

For example, the statement

IF “oe” IN $WDCUR THEN ...

searches the string “oe” in the current word of the text (stored in $WDCUR). This could be useful when the formatter reserves some particular processing to the characters “oe”. For example, let’s suppose that the formatter selected is TEX. If it is necessary to specify “\oe” to produce the French ligature “œ” the substitution of the string “oe” by “\oe” can be expressed by the following METAFORM statements:

```
IF “oe” IN $WDCUR THEN
BEGIN
   WRITE (“\oe”);
END
```

that will write into the output file the string “\oe” in place of “oe”. As we will see shortly the same result can be achieved by using a standard procedure which performs the same substitution for the entire text.

The belonging condition regards the status of the document; precisely, the condition of the current GI. It tests the relation of that GI, respecting the others matched up till then. Particularly, it tests if the current GI belongs to some other GI. The need to have this type of condition arises when it must associate different processes with the same GI, depending on which GIs it belongs to. Let’s examine the following SGML document:

```
<document>
<cover>
<title>
   TEX and METAFONT – New Directions in Typesetting
</title>
<chapter>
   This is the first chapter.
</chapter>
<appendix>
<title>
APPENDIX A
</title>
```

We can note that the GI “title” belongs both to the “cover” element and to the “appendix” element. Therefore, if we want to process the title of the cover in a different way, respecting the title of the appendix, we can specify the alternative directives using:

```
IF $GINAME OF "cover" THEN
BEGIN
   statements 1
END
ELSE
IF $GINAME OF "appendix" THEN
BEGIN
   statements 2
END
```

3.1.3 WHILE statement.

The BNF construct of the while statement are:

```
<while statement> ::= WHILE <loop condition>
                                BEGIN {<statement>} END
<loop condition> ::= <relational condition>
                                <logical condition>
```

The loop condition is evaluated before every loop; as long as the loop condition is true, statements of the WHILE body are executed.

3.1.4 Assignment statement.

As previously mentioned, variables of the program take on the type of their current value. In fact, in the following example

```
A = 10;
B = "This is a string";
A = B;
```

the variable A changes its type from integer to string, after the assignment of the third line. Naturally, values of variables which constitute operands of an expression must be integer or real. The control of the type congruency of operands in an expression is performed during the execution of the program, not at its compiler time.

3.1.5 Functions.

It is not possible to define new functions in a METAFORM program. In compensation the language is provided with a set of useful standard functions.

A function call follows these constructs:

```
<function call> ::= <function name>
                         ({parameter} {, parameter})
<parameter> ::= <variable> | <string> | <numbers>
<function name> ::= <identifier>
```

Standard functions regard primarily:

- The current word of the text, such as:
  - SUCC: it returns the following word of the current one
  - PRED: it returns the preceding word of the current one

- The status of the text. In this context we intend "text" as the text portion of the document associated with a GI. These functions are:
  - EOT: it is a boolean function to test the end of the text.
  - EOL and EOW: they refer to the end of the current line and word.

- The status of a GI, in relation to another one which contains it. For this purpose, the language is provided with the following function

  OCC (gi_1, gi_2);

  which calculates occurrences of the GI gi_1 within the text portion of the GI gi_2. For example, let's consider the following SGML document structure:

  <!ELEMENT section (paragraph * , note)>

  which allows the "section" element to contain zero or more "paragraph" elements. The aspect of a document which respects that structure could be

  <section>
  <paragraph>
  This is the first paragraph
  </paragraph> -- end of the first paragraph (*)
  <paragraph>
  This is the second paragraph
  </paragraph> -- end of the second paragraph
  <paragraph>
  This is the third paragraph
  </paragraph> -- end of the third paragraph
  </section>
  The function OCC, called in the following way:

  OCC ("paragraph", "section");

(*) characters "--" is a SGML notation which marks the beginning of a comment line.

when the second GI "paragraph" is matched in the document, will return the value 2. It indicates that up till that point two paragraphs are specified in the section. This allows us to distinguish one paragraph from another, so that it is possible to associate a different set of processing with every paragraph , following the order in which it appears in the section.

- The status of the attributes. Sometimes we need to verify if an attribute associated with a GI has been specified in the current document. The boolean function ACTIVE takes care of resolving this necessity. In fact, using

  ACTIVE (attribute_name);

  it is possible to verify if the attribute "attribute_name" is present in the text portion of the current GI.

- Auxiliary functions. Such as: ISODD, to test if the value of an integer variable is odd; TOUPPER function, to transform lower characters of a string to upper ones; CHAR to obtain a sequence of characters extracting them from a string; etc ...

3.1.6 Procedures.

As in the case of functions, a METAFORM program cannot define new procedures. It is possible to use only standard procedures provided by the language. All of them, except the SUBSTITUTE procedure, regard I/O operations. We remember that a METAFORM program can read data only from the file containing the text portion of GIs; i.e., the SGML source document. Moreover, it can write only on the file that constitutes the source file for the formatter. Consequently, I/O procedures do not need to know the name of the file on which they work. Let's examine them in detail, together with the SUBSTITUTE procedure.

1) READ: The READ procedure call follows this syntax:

<read call>	::=	READ (" <control> ", <argument>)
<control>	::=	%c | %b | %p
<argument>	::=	<variable>

The procedure reads data from the SGML source document according to the format specified by the "control" parameter, depositing the result in a variable indicated by the "argument". For every call the READ procedure gets a character from the text if the control parameter is "%c", otherwise it selects a word. In this context a word is intended as a sequence of characters bound by blanks, if the control parameter is "%b", otherwise, by punctation

characters and blanks.
Some examples of the use of the READ procedure are:

```
READ ("%b", A);
READ ("%p", B);
```

If the line to read is

i.e. this is an example.

then the first instruction will read entire string "i.e." storing it in A, while the second one will stop at the first punctuation character. Therefore, it assigns to B only the character "i".

2) READTRANSFER: In some cases the text portion of a particular GI does not need to be examined but only written just as it is on the output file. The READTRANSFER procedure performs this function. It copies the whole text portion of the GI on the output file without making any modifications.

3) WRITE: It is considered the most important procedure because it permits the correct production of the source file for the formatter selected. Its syntax is described as follows:

< write call> ::= WRITE (" <control> "
{ , <argument>})

The procedure writes values of various "argument" parameters on the output file under the control of the "control" parameter. This parameter, bound by quotation marks, is of several types, such as:

a) Constant string: It constitutes the value to be written.
b) Format specifications: Each of them refers to an element of the argument list and indicates the writing modality of the argument itself. The format specifications are:

%s: whole value of the corresponding argument is written

%c: a next successive character of the corresponding argument is written. For example, in the following program:

```
A = "Text";
WRITE ("%c", A);
WRITE ("%c", A);
```

the two write instructions produce, respectively, characters "T" and "e". This type of format control is useful when it is necessary to manipulate characters of a word before writing them in output.

4) SUSPEND and RESUME: Sometimes, for some formatters, a command line contains parameters which refer to information about the text portion which it will process. For example, to obtain n centered lines of text using NROFF formatter [OSS76] we must specify the command ".ce n", where the parameter n indicates the number of lines to be centered, before the n lines themselves. In this case, the person who is generating the source text for NROFF can behave in the following way. He/She writes the line ".ce n" with the value of n undefined. Then he/she writes all lines of the text he/she wants to make centered, counts them and comes back to update the value of n. These same steps could be executed by a METAFORM program, as we will see shortly, using the SUSPEND and RESUME procedures.
The SUSPEND procedure call, with the following syntax:
<suspend call> ::= SUSPEND (<identifier>)
produces an undefined value for the variable specified as parameter and writes it in the output file. Subsequently, when the value of that variable becomes known, the RESUME procedure call, with the following syntax:
<resume call> ::= RESUME (<identifier>)
can be specified. The procedure will come back to the point of the output file where the variable has been suspended and will update it with its current value.

In this way, the METAFORM program to resolve the problem of centered lines in NROFF could be:

```
linecount = 0;
WRITE (".ce ") ;      -- The procedure writes string ".ce"
SUSPEND (N) ;         -- The procedure writes an undefined
                            value for N and re-marks that
                            point in the output file.
WHILE NOT EOT         -- For all characters of the text
                      --    portion of GI.
   BEGIN
    READ ("%c", charoftext);
                      -- Reads a character and stores it
                      --    in charoftext.
    IF (charoftext == EOL)
    BEGIN
     linecount = linecount+1;
                      -- Update count of lines.
    END
```

```
    WRITE ("%c", charoftext);
                         -- Writes a character stored in
                         --    charoftext;
END                      -- End of text portion. The variable
                         --    linecount indicates the number
                         --    of its lines.
N = linecount;           -- N is updated.
RESUME (N);
```

In this case the RESUME procedure comes back searching for the point where N is suspended in the output file (the line ".ce") and updates the line with the current value of N, i.e., the line count.

5) SUBSTITUTE: Sometimes a specific word of the document should be treated in a particular way by the formatter; for example, when it represents a logo to be printed with a special font. Then it is necessary to substitute that word with the name of the font, for the entire document. This operation is performed using the procedure

```
SUBSTITUTE (from, to);
```

which replaces all strings corresponding to the parameter "from" with the string contained in "to".

3.1.7 Macros.

It is possible to define macros with formal parameter to be called later in any point of the program. Macro definition must be inserted at the head of the METAFORM program. It follows this syntax:

```
<macro definition> ::= DEFINE <macro name> <parameter part>
                        <macro body>
<parameter part> ::= () | ( <formal parameter>
                        {, <formal parameter>} )
<macro body> ::= BEGIN_MACRO {<statement>} END_MACRO
<formal parameter> ::= $1 | $2 | $3 | $4 | $5 | $6 | $7 | $8 | $9
<macro name> ::= <identifier>
```

There are at most nine formal parameters for a macro. Statements of macro body can contain these parameters, which will be updated during the macro expansion. These statements can be of any type, including, a macro call instruction.

The syntax of a macro call is the same of the procedure call. When a macro is called, its body gets expanded with formal parameters replaced by actual parameters, according to the order of their specification.

4. Conclusions.

The system for SGML document production described in this paper offers some advantages for authors and publishers. In regard to the authors, they are relieved from typesetting problems; therefore they are able to concentrate their attention on the content of their manuscript. These advantages derive from SGML features. In the environment proposed authors could transmit to publishers the SGML source documents, or, as more probable, the intermediate file, if they have on hand a SGML parser.

These files could be transmitted to all publishers, independently of the kind of formatter program they have on hand. Publishers have only to execute the interpreter module to process the intermediate file received and to generate the source file for their formatter. If the document that they receive does not correspond to any structure of GIs present in the map table, the work of the publishers increases somewhat: they have to add processing instructions in the map table using METAFORM language.

From what we have described about METAFORM, it seems that the definition of formatting directives for a document is a long and complicated process. This is true. But we must not forget that this work is performed just once for all possible SGML documents. Once the map table is constructed, the METAFORM executable codes are able to interpret whatever document the user desires.

Despite the fact that METAFORM is a programming language, it is not oriented to expert programmers. It is designed for persons who construct the map table defining the output format of documents. These persons, experts in composing and typesetting problems, are not necessarily familiar with all programming technique. Therefore, the language tries to be as easy to use and natural as possible, even if this makes the language not very powerful. For this reason, METAFORM is provided with a very small set of statements. Instead, we prefer to define several useful standard procedures and functions and system variables so as to make the work of the programmer easier.

The language is at the initial stage of development, even if the construction of its parser and interpreter has already began. We admit that the language needs to be completed with many other features. Probably in some situations METAFORM language is not able to describe the intention of the user. In fact, the more powerful the formatter, the more sophisticated become the needs of the user. Moreover, the difficulties in describing formulas, tables, graphics elements only increase these concerns.

These considerations will be object of our future considerations.

References:

[ADL85] Sharon Adler, Bill Davis: *"SGML tutorial"* GenCode/SGML Orientation Tutorial (Heidelberg, Germany 3 June 1985).

[FER85] Peter Ferris, Geeti Granger: *"Apollo"* in Proc. of the Second Intern. Conference on Text Processing Systems (Dublin, Ireland 23-25 Oct 1985). Ed. J.H. Miller Boole Press Ltd. Ireland.

[GCC78] GRAPHIC COMMUNICATIONS COMPUTER ASSOCIATION: *"GenCode Primer: A method of Generic Text Markup"* ISO/TC 97/SC 18/WG3 N. 157 (1978).

[GOL81] C.F. Goldfarb: *"A generalized approach to document markup"* in Proc. ACM SIGPLAN/SIGOA Conference Text Manipulation (Portland, Ore., June 8-10 1981), ACM, NY, 1981.

[HMS85] Her Majesty's Stationery Office: *"The use of Generic Coding for UK Government Legislation"* in Proc. of Mark-up '85, the Third Intern. Conference on Electronic Manuscript Preparation and SGML (Heidelberg, Germany 4-6 June 1985).

[IBM76a] INTERNATIONAL BUSINESS MACHINES: *"IBM SCRIPT/370 User's Guide"* IBM Data Processing Division, White Plains, NY, 1976. Order N. SH20-1857-0.

[IBM76b] INTERNATIONAL BUSINESS MACHINES: *"Document Composition Facility: GML Quit Reference Summary"* IBM Data Processing Division, White Plains, NY, 1976. Order N. SX26-3719-0.

[ISO84] ISO TC97/SC5 WG12: *"Information Processing Systems – Programming Languages – Text Interchange and Processing"* Eighth Working Draft, ISO TC97/SC5 WG12 N. 100 (1984 Sept. 01).

[ISO85] ISO TC97/SC18/WG8: *"Generic Document Representation Specification (SGML)"* Draft Proposal Intern. Standard ISO/DP 8879/6, January 1985.

[KER78] Brian W. Kernighan, Dennis M. Ritchie: "The C programming language", Prentice-Hall, Englewood Cliffs, N.J. 1978.

[KNU79] D.E. Knuth: *"TEX and METAFONT: New Directions in Typesetting"*, Digital Press and the American Mathematical Society, Bedford, mass, and Providence, R.I. 1979.

[LEV85a] Le van Huu: *"TEX and ISO/STPL Standard"* in Proc. of the First European Conference on TEX for Scientific Documentation (Como, Italy 16-17 May 1985). Ed. D. Lucarella, Addison-Wesley Publishing, August 1985.

[LEV85b] Le van Huu: *"SGML: A standard language for text description"* in Proc. of the Second Intern. Conference on Text Processing Systems (Dublin, Ireland 23-25 Oct 1985). Ed. J.H. Miller Boole Press Ltd. Ireland.

[LEV85c] Le van Huu: *"SGML: features, applications and implementation"* in Proc. of Mark-up '85, the Third Intern. Conference on Electronic Manuscript Preparation and SGML (Heidelberg, Germany 4-6 June 1985).

[OSS76] J.F. Ossanna: *"NROFF/TROFF user's manual"* Computer Science Tech. Rep. 54, Bell Laboratories, Murray Hill, N.J., Oct. 1976.

[REI80] B.K. Reid : *"SCRIBE: A document specification language and its compiler"*, Ph. D. dissertation, Computer Science Dep. Carnegie-Mellon Univ., Pittsburgh, Pa., Oct 1980.

[SMI85] Joan M. Smith: *"The computer and Publishing: an oppurtunity for new methodology"* in Proc. of the Second Intern. Conference on Text Processing Systems (Dublin, Ireland 23-25 Oct 1985). Ed. J.H. Miller Boole Press Ltd. Ireland.

[WES85] A.M. Western: *"Multimedia Publication and Generalized Text Markup"* in Proc. of Mark-up '85, the Third Intern. Conference on Electronic Manuscript Preparation and SGML (Heidelberg, Germany 4-6 June 1985).

[WIR81] N. Wirth: *"Pascal-S: A subset and its implementation"* in Pascal-The language and its implementation. Ed. D.W. Barron, John Wiley & Sons, Ltd 1981.

RETRIEVING MATHEMATICAL FORMULAE

Dario Lucarella
Dipartimento di Scienze dell'Informazione
Università degli Studi di Milano

Abstract

This paper describes a prototype system for storing, retrieving and accessing mathematical formulae. The proposed environment combines information retrieval capabilities with a composition system used to provide formulae representation and to improve readability of the retrieved objects. Peculiar problems concerning manipulation and searching of formulae material are discussed while, on the other hand, some design issues are proposed for a generalized information retrieval environment based on concept browsing and structured query processing.

1.Introduction

This paper presents some results and perspectives of a continuing research [Luc84] experimenting with the problems of retrieving and accessing mathematical formulae.

In a previous paper [Luc85] we have already discussed the compilation of mathematical formulae dictionaries and the relevance that such tools may cover both in mathematical research and education. Related works and experiments can be found with reference to Chemical formulae [Wel83] as well as in the field of genetic sequences manipulation as reported in [Nan86] where a formulae data base is searched with artificial intelligence techniques and made available through a document preparation system conceived as a mediator.

The variable nature of the formulae leads to considerable problems in information retrieval both in terms of representing such formulae and searching them for desired structural features. Three areas have been addressed in this context. These are the facilities for loading formulae to the system, the internal representation of this information and the searching through files of such representations, given a query represented in similar manner. The aim is to provide the theoretical and practical basis for implementing a system comparable in use and performance with those which deal with textual documents [Sal83].

Over the last few years Don Knuth has devised a language capable of defining every kind of complicated formulae in a linearized way and has embodied it into the TEX composition system [Knu79].

The TEX language has been adopted to provide an input medium from which a complete and unambiguous representation can be generated. The ability to specify the graphical two dimensional structure of mathematical formulae by means of a linearized language creates the opportunity of loading, manipulating and accessing formulae as ordinary text strings. Items logically related may be retrieved, viewed and eventually printed after being processed by the TEX system so that the pictorial layout of the formulae is reproduced. From this point of view, the current project may be regarded just as en experiment in order to integrate a composition system with an information retrieval system.

In the following, after a brief remark about the description language, design issues for the information retrieval envioronment are proposed. Search strategies are analyzed with reference to the supported facilities: browsing through the information structure and query formulation with the involved algorithms for sequence comparison and similarity evaluation. Hence the features are sketched of an advanced end user interface under development.

2.Representing and filing formulae

Advances in text processing and essentially in the area of document preparation systems have enabled the composition of texts including mathematical notations. Mathematical formulae are text in the sense that they are written in lines, using a set of characters closely related to classical alphabets but, at the same time, they differ for the frequent use made of the vertical dimension to express elements such as subscripts, exponents and fractions and so on. Even if this usage is certainly not indispensable as it is shown by the linear representation of formulae used in programming languages, a two dimensional approach becomes advisable if we want to present the item in a familiar and easily comprehensible way. Obviously, a pictorial presentation is far more relevant than a written sequence.

Thus the solution to the problem of mathematics typesetting is to design a language for specifying unambiguosly mathematical notations taking into account typographical details and notions of typographical aesthetics [Ker75] [Knu79]. Two dimensional formulae must be represented as a one dimensional sequence of instructions that can be entered easily from every Ascii terminal and then processed to reproduce the pictorial layout.

In the TEX system, a model has been introduced based on *box* and *glue* primitives to define textual and mathematical objects. Within this framework every formula may be regarded as a set of boxes pieced and nested together in various ways. The description language is well known and widespread, so we assume the reader's knowledge. As a basic source [Knu84] can be referred to. Some details about the loading of formulae are discussed in [Luc85] where an excerpt is presented drawn by an implemented formulae dictionary.

Once the problem has been solved of representing formulae as character strings, the task of searching formulae files can be assimilated to that of searching textual items [Cro82]. With the previous assumption, we define formulae in analogy with textual documents as composed of a header and a body. The header contains formatted data representing attributes $A_0, A_1, \ldots A_n$ where A_0 is a special attribute which contains a unique system-wide identifier for the formula and others A_i attributes denote concepts to which the formula can be related. The body is a text string providing the internal representation in terms of TEX language. The implementation of the prototype, here discussed, accommodates two types of retrieval strategies:

- *Access based on concepts*

A concept network is managed whose structure will be shown in the next paragraph. It can be conceived as a generalized tool for helping users to retrieve, view, classify and interconnect information via trials of association. Facilities are provided to both users with specific requests and users who have only a vague idea of what they are looking for. In the latter case, a browsing facility enables the user to navigate on the concept network and to inspect the formulae appended to the network nodes. In many cases, such a browsing facility could help to locate directly the requested formulae without supplying a formal query.

Access based on formulae

This can be conceived as a filtering capability. The user specifies a filter and the retrieval procedure locates all formulae relevant to the user query and arranges them according to a rank order. It would be nice to retain the properties of a sequential scan where formulae are retrieved one at a time. Formulae which do not qualify according to the filter are skipped while those which qualify are retrieved and presented to the user in a familiar format so that he can visually check the objects retrieved. The specified filter restricts the attention to a manageable subset and formulae within the subset are obtained sequentially.

While the specification of values for formatted attributes can make use of standard indexes for their evaluation, the specification and evaluation of patterns is more complicated. We could, however, make use of indexing methods for special symbols in order to restrict the size of searchable set. The organization is based on the file structure already reported in [Luc85]. Essentially it is a structure of multiple indexes on the formulae file where index entries contain the reference to the identifiers A_0 of associated formulae stored in fixed length random blocks. With this canonical organization, it is possible to get access from multiple views, as required, considering that the same formula may be related to different semantic contexts [Bar83].

During the loading phase, the user selects the concepts to which the formula must be logically attached while the formula body is processed in order to identify significant mathematical symbols. Such symbols and their location are respectively used to update the related index.

In the proposed environment, the user can approach the location of the relevant material either travelling on the concept network or entering the query facility. In the latter case, the system displays an appropriate template. Optionally, the user specifies some values for fixed attributes A_i, that is concepts, and a pattern P for the required formula by partially filling the template. Values entered for A_i are interpreted as selection conditions. The pattern P may be any kind of complicated expression of math symbols and linear strings. Formulae that satisfy the query are those that satisfy the conjunction of all selections and whose structure is similar to the one proposed with the pattern P.

In the following these two approaches to formulae retrieval are discussed in further detail.

3.Concept Network

An emerging paradigm in the most innovative information retrieval systems is the management of *concepts* as entities that enable the users to better qualify their requests as well as to disclose new associations. This can suggest inspecting new paths into the information web and locating relevant items [Sho81]. The attempt is to provide a tool favouring the typical human approach of *thinking by associations* [Fre83].

The problem of the structure, presentation and access to a concept base has been addressed in the field of document management as well as in artificial intelligence applications. In the latter case, however, the attention is on reasoning techniques starting from the contents of the built up knowledge base. As remarked in [Fin79], the concept base could be organized in graphs with a connecting structure independent from the knowledge domain and generalized navigation tools. So offering a versatile and friendly interface that allows the user to follow some paths or to jump from an item to the other as soon as this is suggested by the proposed travelling links.

Thus, the main component becomes a *concept network*. A concept is denoted by a natural language expression and represents the entity to which a stored object, in our case a formula, is related. Such a knowledge organization requires the definition of semantic links among concepts to relate different hierarchical levels for any given subject and links to relate concepts showing some analogy.

During the interactive phase of query, the aim is to map the submitted request to the appropriate concept set and to propose it to the user who can inspect the attached information items or can start an interactive travelling on the network. With this goal, a dictionary is maintained which contains the keywords occurring in the expressions denoting the concepts.

The resulting network has a structure very close to the one proposed in [Bar84]. It presents concepts as nodes and three types of relations as edges: broader concept, narrower concept, related concept. The first two links are used to handle semantic inheritance associations. A class of concepts inheriting properties from a superior one is linked to that and vice versa. The third type of link associates concepts exhibiting some relation with each other. Analyzing the terms present in a query, the system is capable, if the terms belong to the dictionary, to identify a set of concepts. Essentially this facility allows the user to select a concept and to enter the network at an appropriate entry point.

3.1.Browsing

The idea of *browsing* has strongly influenced our present approach toward interacting with knowledge [Lec82]. In fact, we want to emphasize the navigation through a neighborhood of information referencing items by *pointing* and *recognizing* instead of accessing items directly using a known name. We think of the network nodes as providing choices for the user to select a path through the stored information.

In the actual implementation a menu driven interface supports the user, starting from the *current* concept node, to move either to broader, narrower, related nodes or to inspect attached items. For every concept the surrounding edges are shown and the first level linked concepts are presented. When the user picks up a new concept through the listed alternatives, the system switches to the other semantic region, the new node becomes current and its context is presented highlighting the provenience node. This refinement process goes on until the user is satisfied by the precision of the retrieved concept and he requires the appended objects. They are presented in a sequential fashion and the last node remains current. The current node is the only node presented on the screen and it gives the actual position within the semantic network. Successive movements are stacked in order to retain a trace of the followed path and to allow a sort of *undo* feature that lets us go back and forth easily or come back immediatly to the mainstream after having explored a semantically related region.

The same facility is available during the loading phase with the aim of locating the appropriate set of concepts to which the item must be appended.

Further improvements will be achieved by the introduction of graphical presentation facilities that are planned in future extensions on the model depicted in the *Caliban* system [Fre83].

It is worth while remarking that the previous description has been given without any reference to the particular kind of stored objects. In fact the presented concept network and browser have been proposed and implemented as a generalized tool to be used in conjunction with text retrieval applications disregarding the information nature.

In this specific application, as we have discussed in the previous paragraph, it represents one way for the user to identify and access a class of formulae of his interest. In our prototype dealing with a collection of formulae in the field of functional analysis, the concept network and the keyword dictionary have been initialized with AMS subject classification entries.

4.Filtering Facility

The ability to locate formulae guided by the concepts to which they are related highlights the semantic context but fails to retrieve formulae which exibit a structure very close to the searched one. Such considerations led us to implement a facility for specifying, by means of a template, a pattern of precoordinated TEX control sequences not completely refined. So underlining only some structural constraints on the features that the retrieved objects have to present.

This task is concerned with the organization of a collection of mathematical formulae, normalized with regard to representation rules and vocabulary and with the implementation of a procudere executing the *approximate match* of an input pattern against the whole collection. Usually current techniques in string matching use algorithms without any regard to the global organization of the data collection. The proposed approach uses a hierarchical indexing scheme of the formulae files so that it is possible to reject most of the sequences in the data collection by first accessing the small index table.

The attention in this paragraph is on the design and the implementation of such a filtering capability. We assume that the user will seldom be able to specify an absolutely tight filter. His specification will reflect his partial knowledge and will allow more formulae to qualify in addition to the ones he is really looking for. By a visual check he will finally reach the desired objects. So, if the specification of the filter is not exact, the implementation need not be exact. It means that, if the specification of the filter allows a certain percentage of non relevant formulae, the user will not care if the filter implementation will add some other non relevant item. The objective is to execute a rapid and less expansive search in order to eliminate from further consideration those structures which fail to comply with the structural characteristics of the search query.

The user specifies the pattern with relevant attributes. *Attributes* are elementary items used to emphasize the structure of a sequence. The proposed pattern can be considered as an expression indicating the co-occurance of some attributes in some precise position within the sequence. In particular we are interested in discovering that two mathematical formulae expressed with the corresponding TeX sequence *almost match*. The implemented algorithm matches a given sequence against the collection and finds all formulae that exibit a certain degree of *similarity* returning a list of pointers.

4.1.Sequence Comparison

Given the sequences S and T representing linearized formulae, we define a *similarity function* σ which produces a real number $\sigma(S,T)$ in the interval $[0.0\ldots1.0]$ such as an high value implies an high degree of resemblance [Hal80]. Thus the similarity problem can be formulated in the following way: given S, find all the formulae T such that $\sigma(S,T) \geq k$ where k is a predefined threshold or, also, given S, find the N formulae $T_1,\ldots T_N$ such that their $\sigma(S,T_i)$ have the N largest values. With retrieval based on *similarity* and a *threshold* the trade-off can be controlled varying the threshold in proper way.

In the following we define a sequence as a string that can be divided into a number of discrete units according to a set of rules. We consider the matching of two sequences S comprising the units $s_1, s_2, \ldots s_m$ and T comprising the units $t_1, t_2, \ldots t_n$. Assuming that the sequences have different lengths, the appropriate correspondence to use is not known in advance but it must be selected over possible corrispondences that satisfy suitable conditions, such as preserving the order of the elements in the sequence. Within this framework [Pai85], the overall resemblance can be computed as:

$$\sigma(S,T) = \frac{1}{\max(m,n)} \sum_{x=1}^{m} R(s_x, t_{J(x)}) \qquad \sigma \in [0.0 \ldots 1.1]$$

The function R computes the matching between two string units and the function $J(x)$ is a mapping function such that $t_{J(x)}$ denotes the unit of T which is mapped on the unit s_x of S with the following assumptions:

1) $J(x) = 0$ if s_x is unmapped. In which case $R(s_x, t_0) = 0$.

2) All values $J(x) \neq 0$ are distinct. It means that each unit of T can only be mapped onto one unit of S.

3) $J(x+1) \geq J(x) + 1$. This condition preserves the sequence order.

This latter assumption reflects also the fact we are dealing with a problem of partial knowledge. Hence the search clue may be not completely refined but the units which are present in it must be present in the retrieved items. With reference to the theory of sequence comparison [San83], this choice has reduced considerably the complexity of the problem. In fact, if the distance between two sequences is computed as the smallest number of elementary operations that must be applied to transform the first one into the second one, here such operations are reduced only to insertions and do not include deletions and replacements. So the problem of selecting the mapping becomes easier.

Given a similarity computation algorithm, we need a file organaization which restricts our attention to the set of appropriate items. Formulae are indexed on the basis of the primary TEX control sequences appearing in the body and an inverted index is maintained. The query string is processed by the same indexing procedure and the extracted keywords are used to look up the inverted file. A manipulation of the index entries leads to locate a reduced set of items that are candidates for successive inspection. An exaustive matching is carried out on this set with the evaluation of the corresponding similarity weight for each element.

The more the structure is refined by the user the more the search will be fast and selective improving the system precision.

Two problems concerning the formulae description language have been faced. The first is created by the presence of many TEX control sequences which produce a typographical effect and, obviously, have no meaning from a mathematical point of view. Such commands have been conceived to improve the aesthetics of the final layout and affect the size of special symbols, the spacing rules and so forth. With analogy to an usual approach in the indexing of textual objects, such commands have been included into a negative dictionary of so called *stopwords* and they are checked and stripped away from strings while being processed.

The second encountered problem concerns the association rules for some operators within the TEX language. An example can better clarify the problem: in order to specify exponents and deponents, no precedence is required and so the same expression a_i^n can be indifferently produced both by the notation $a \uparrow n \downarrow i$ and $a \downarrow i \uparrow n$. Such alternative notations can be clearly source of failure during the matching procedure. The problem has been solved considering them as *istances* of the same equivalence class. Even in this case, the analogy can be underlined with the textual environment: different flection forms for the same word belong to the same equivalence class with canonical form being the word stem. A very close approach is adopted here. Starting from the query string supplied by the user, equivalent configurations are automatically generated and searched.

5.End User Interface

The combination of available devices such as high resolution screens and current trends towards object oriented languages are leading to new models for man-machine communication. The objective seems to be the elimination of traditional written command languages to control the applications. With the new interface technology, windowing, direct popping up into menus, selecting objects, symbols, alphabets and moving them on the screen with the mouse should be the basic operating style.

As discussed beforehand, this research activity also focuses interest on the use of a composition tool as a presentation layer for an information retrieval application. Mathematical formulae are observed in this framework as generalized documents. So, it is possible to associate convenient and more readable visual representation to the abstract aspects of mathematical notations. However, the internal form is always available so that a formula can be displayed either at its poorest level as a string of ascii chars or riproducing its pictorial layout [Nan86].

The same considerations apply to the imput phase. A pure editor capable of manipulating formulae as ordinary text strings has less interst here. The main aspect is to design a tool able to support and guide the mathematician to compose his formulae. The user should always operate on a visual graphical representation and never have to deal with their internal description. The objective is to transform this step from an *encoding* task to a *descriptive* task [And85].

With this goal the integration is in progress with the EasyTeX system and particularly with its *formula processor* module. EasyTeX is an interactive document preparation system presenting an integrated environment to manipulate texts, formulae and pictures [Cri85]. With reference to our requirements it presents two attractive features: on one hand it allows the creation of formulae directly on the screen according to the fashion of *wyswyg* while, on the other, produces as output the TEX language linearized representation. Within this environment the formula is described naturally in the same way in which it would be dictated. Constant guidance is supplied with the machine prompting and aiding the user as necessary and with the cursor movement which indicates the element to be entered into the formula being generated. Mathematical symbols are entered by means of a virtual keyboard displayable on the screen and commands are supplied by pressing function keys or selecting them from a menu. EasyTeX uses the wide spread personal computer IBM/XT with graphic card. The station can be used locally as well as in conjunction with large main frames.

It is remarkable to notice that the information retrieval application has no direct access to the physical device. The results are displayed through the formatter and the imput data come from the EasyTeX editor.

6.Concluding Remarks

In the previous pages we have presented the main aspects of a continuing research aimed at solving the problems of organizing, searching and accessing a formulae collection. Some innovative ideas in the field of information retrieval systems have been reported and the role of document manipulation tools has been rivisited as interface layers in order to improve the man-machine communication.

TEX has been proposed as a basic language for compilation, typesetting and searching of formulae.

A new end user interface based on the reported guidelines is under development. It will include graphical presentation services for interactive viewing of the concept base and the integration with the EasyTeX editor to provide facilities for entering formulae in a friendly, easy to use, environment.

Further research is needed to refine searching algorithms and to relate threshold values of the similarity function to performance parameters like *recall* and *precision*.

In a long term vision, this may be conceived as the first step towards advanced interaction techniques with formulae bases as required in many fields of scientific knowledge.

Aknowledgments

Thanks are due to Prof. DegliAntoni from the Information Science Department for discussions about the formulae retrieval facilities and to Prof. Montaldi from the Physics Department for his suggestions about the user requirements in accessing a formulae base.

This work has been partially supported with funds from The Ministry of Public Education with reference to the research program titled *Scientific Communication Systems*

References

[And85] J.Andre, Y.Grundt, V.Quint: *Towards an Interactive Math Mode in TEX* TEX for Scientific Documentation Ed. D.Lucarella Addison-Wesley Pub. Comp. (1985).

[Bar83] M.Bartaschi, H.P.Frei: *Adapting a Data Organization to the Structure of Stored Information* Research and Development in Information Retrieval Ed. G.Salton Springer-Verlag (1983).

[Bar84] E.Barbi, alii: *A Conceptual Approach to Document Retrieval* Proceedings ACM SIGOA Conference (1984).

[Cri85] E.Crisanti, alii: *EasyTeX: An Integrated Environment for Scientific Document Preparation and a TEXFront End* Protext II Proceedings Ed. J.H.Miller Boole Press (1985).

[Cro82] W.B.Croft:*The Implematation of a Document Retrieval System* Research and Development in Information Retrieval Ed. G.Salton Springer-Verlag (1983).

[Fin79] N.V.Findler: *Associative Networks. Representation and use of Knowledge by Computers* Academic Press (1979).

[Fre83] H.P.Frei, J.F.Jauslin: *Graphical Presentation of Information and Services: An User Oriented Interface* Information Technology: Research and Development Vol.2, (1983).

[Hal80] P.A.Hall, G.R.Dowling: *Approximate String Matching* ACM Computing Surveys, Vol.12, n.4, Dec.80.

[Ker75] B.W.Kernighan, L.Cerry:*A system for Typesetting Mathematics* ACM Comm. Vol.18, n.3, Mar.75.

[Knu79] D.E.Knuth:*TEX and METAFONT: New directions in Typesetting* Digital Press (1979).

[Knu84] D.E.Knuth:*The TEXbook* Addison-Wesley Pub. Comp. (1984).

[Lec82] Y.Leclerc, alii: *A Browsing Approach to Documentation* IEEE Computer, Jun.82.

[Luc84] D.Lucarella:*TEX Document Retrieval* Protext I Proceedings Ed. J.Miller Boole Press (1984).

[Luc85] D.Lucarella:*TEX Formulae Dictionary* TEX for Scientific Documentation Ed. D.Lucarella Addison-Wesley Pub. Comp. (1985).

[Nan86] M.Nanard, alii: *Semantic Guided Editing. A Case Study on Genetic Manipulation* (to appear in) Text Processing and Document Manipulation Ed. J.C.van Vliet Cambridge University Press (1986).

[Pai85] C.D.Paice, V.Aragon-Ramirez: *The Calculation of Similarities between Multiword Strings using a Thesaurus* Proc. RIAO 85, 18-20 Mar.85 Grenoble, France

[Sal83] G.Salton, J.McGill:*Introduction to Modern Information Retrieval* McGraw Hill (1983).

[San83] D.Sankoff, J.B.Kruskal: *The Teory and Practice of Sequence Comparison* Addison-Wesley Pub. Comp. (1983).

[Sho81] P.Shoval: *Expert/Consultation System for a Retrieval Data Base with Semantic Network of Concepts* Proceedings ACM SIGIR Conference (1981).

[Wel83] S.M.Welford,alii:*Towards Simplified Access to Chemical Information in Patent Literature* Journal Inf.Science n.6 (1983) North-Holland

INTEGRATING TEX IN AN EDDS WITH VERY HIGH RESOLUTION CAPABILITIES

Philippe PENNY

Centre National d'Etude
des Télécommunications
38-40 rue du Général Leclerc
92131 Issy-les-Moulineaux, France

Jean-Louis HENRIOT

MYFRA
83 bd Aristide Briand
92120 Montrouge, France

Abstract

We present the integration of TEX on a very high resolution bitmap display workstation used by the SARDE project at **cnet**. *The characteristics of this subsystem will allow to propose a computer aided publishing (CAP) environment as one function in a distributed electronic document delivery system (EDDS).*

1. The SARDE project

The aim of the SARDE project (standing for *Electronic Document Archival and Retrieval System*) is to automate entirely the management and the consultation of the whole technical documentation related to the maintenance of the French telephone network. Started in 1983 at **cnet** (the French National Research Center for Telecommunications), the SARDE project [4] conducted feasibility studies until 1984. An experimentation was launched early this year, and its evaluation should lead to the specifications of the full-scale system (one national server and 2000 workstations). Technological transfers have already been achieved in several fields, some of them with MYFRA concerning the architecture of a commercial EDDS (SMDOC) and specialized hardware subsystems.

The SARDE project developed an architecture for scanning, indexing, storing, transmitting and displaying large amounts of documents (five millions eventually) all over the national territory. Document acquisition is achieved through a massive process involving scanners with a resolution ranging from 200 to 400 dots/inch (dpi) for documents on paper (A4 format), microforms or films on aperture cards for large plans. The indexation is already available from an existing database for the most part, with a certain percentage of discrepencies inherent to the volume of data and to the heterogeneity of document producers (the manufacturers of telephone equipment).

Images are stored on WORM optical discs after compression with facsimile standard techniques or through an original hybrid method combining vector construction, pseudo pattern recognition and facsimile coding [3]. The images of documents can be accessed locally or from remote workstations through the best network facility available *in situ* (the 64 kbps throughput of the future national ISN and of the Telecom1 satellite wherever applicable, or the 9.6 to 48 kbps of Transpac in the worst cases).

Documents are retrieved in the database from workstations having very high resolution capabilities and powerful document manipulation facilities. The characteristics of these machines were very attractive for document preparation also, which corresponds to the next natural step after the all-scanning approach of the exploratory SARDE experiments. Indeed, in our application most technical documents are currently produced with word-processors but there is not yet an infrastructure for communicating and consulting them in their primary electronic form, and only the paper could be dispatched till now. It is expected that a distributed electronic document delivery system (EDDS) like SARDE [5] will be used as the unique support for documents from creation to consultation, and even to annotations, corrections and formation.

In this context, TEX was introduced in the SARDE project for evaluation on the workstations described in the next section, and it should be proposed later as the main processor of a computer aided publishing (CAP) environment within a consistent commercial EDDS line.

2. The very high resolution Orion workstations

In the case of the SARDE project, the technical documents on paper scanned at 200 dpi are not originals but already copies of copies, and their facsimile images are not in good shape, to the point that misinterpretations could occur (is it a dashed or a partially erased line on this electronic schema?) if usual 1 million pixels screens were used by maintenance staff. This led to the development of several bitmap displays by concurrent manufacturers following the specifications of the SARDE project, *i.e.* the possibility (1) to display a 200 dpi A4 format document (corresponding exactly to a 512 kb—or 4million pixels— facsimile image) on a very stable monitor, (2) to manipulate this image with simple procedures involving icons and a pointing device, and (3) to run a bibliographical application dialog on windows superimposed to document images.

MYFRA was the first company to fulfill these requirements with an A4 portrait version of its Orion display subsystem, and with a 19" landscape monitor. This preliminary version includes one bitmap accessed through a specialized vector-oriented interface, a wired character generator (each character can be turned on or off above the bitmap), a reconfigurable keyboard and a mouse. It was proposed for a general-purpose 32-bits multiprocessor (the sm90 designed at **cnet** and running Unix), which is already used at each functional level of the SARDE experiments.

A second and more powerful version of the Orion terminal has been introduced recently. It comprises two 4 million pixels bitmaps which can be accessed as R/W memory, or through an interface capable of vector to raster mapping and of raster inclusion from another memory into any one of the two bitmaps. These two separate bitmaps can be displayed according to several modes involving a programmable, virtual grid which allows to show individually in each element of the grid any one of the two raster memories; in case of superimposition of the two bitmaps within one element of the grid, boolean operations can be applied. The images are displayed on a 19" screen, and a completely programmable keyboard and mouse interface is connected to a serial line of the computer.

Essentially, this new version of Orion is dedicated to tasks involving the simultaneous manipulations of several documents:

- windows of text for dialog with a database server, displayed above images of the selected documents,
- computer aided drawing, as projecting high voltage electrical lines on top of geographical maps,
- document preparation ...

3. Integrating TEX on Orion (first version)

During the evaluation of TEX within the SARDE project, we intended to integrate three activities:

- entering and updating texts with a 'TEX-mode' editor,
- analyzing text by TEX and being able to fix problems synchronously in the source,
- reviewing the displayed output and simultaneously editing the source for enhancements.

This evaluation started with the first version of the workstation decribed above (one 4 million pixels bitmap and a wired character generator) and it used the implementation of the TEX processor conducted by FOATA and ROY at the Université Louis Pasteur in Strasbourg [2]. It consisted essentially in the developement of two 'preview' drivers for:

- the A4 portrait version of the monitor (with a 200 dpi resolution),
- the 19" landscape version (corresponding to a true 132 dpi resolution).

This 'landscape' version allows, using 150 dpi fonts, to display two full A4 pages side by side alternatively. Thus the end user prepares a text in very comfortable conditions, thanks to the progressive exploration of a very high quality output.

At the same time we were working at the integration of Winnie, an emacs-like editor written in C at the Université d'Orsay [1]. This multiwindow, multibuffer and multimode text editor proved to be very efficient on the character generator of the first version of the Orion terminal, displaying 54 lines of 143 fixed size characters. Thanks to specific extensions, it gave us the possibility to propose a first TEX environment integrated on the same terminal with the following functions:

- since any process can run 'in' a window of Winnie, TEX can be started to analyze a text in one window while the text is available for fixing bugs in another window as they are detected by TEX; it can be noticed that only 'semantic' errors should occur since the text is edited using a 'TEX-mode' which deals with common syntactic verifications (balanced braces, predefined macros and aliases, ...).

- The components of a source text are edited in typically 71-character wide windows which can be turned on/off at will or moved according to vertical of horizontal symetries; then the user can visualize editor windows on one side of the screen and one of the two pages output with the bitmap on the other side, or two pages of output if necessary; in all cases, the presentation of the output is controlled by the corresponding driver which runs as a process in a dedicated text window of the editor, and under the final control of the user.

Eventually we got the desired functionalities with relatively small efforts, most of our activity having been spent in the creation of TEX macro sets for internal use (technical documentation, administrative notes, articles, even a thesis of linguistics).

It must be noticed that we decided not to offer the required functions through general bitmap multi-window managers, as it is done on most computers with raster displays. One reason was the actual definition (4 million pixels) of the screen and the absence of wired operators for raster manipulations in the interface of the Orion terminal. The second was that the end user spends most of his time editing source text, and not playing around windows. In these conditions, it is completely useless to overload the main processor with raster operations on such a large bitmap, when the available combination of the character generator and of the bitmap display (driven by the TEX-extended Winnie editor and by the TEX output driver respectively) were enough to fulfill our first requirements.

4. A CAP environment within an EDDS

The next step consists in building a computer aided publishing environment considered as the major document production source within EDDS applications like SARDE. Compared to the facilities integrated until now, it must include enhancements in data entry and indexation, typeset interactivity and multiple inputs manipulation.

In large organizations issuing standardized notes, reports, brochures, ..., the TEX-mode editing process must be specialized for each kind of document produced, in order to encapsulate TEX with the adequate set of macros (mainly related to the structure of the document and to indexes), plus some typographical possibilities. Such macros could output essential data ready to be entered in reference databases of the EDDS where the document will be archived. In this scheme of automatic index construction, both quantity and quality of index entries should be considerably enhanced compared to present documentation systems, since the authors are still at the best place to indicate how to index their documents.

As a text is keyed in by a typist, it seems possible to give an immediate feedback of textual typesetting: font changes can be interpreted by the text editor, as in STRATEC [2], and a paragraph can be typeset and output as soon as it is completely entered [6] (without page 'shipout' however). But interactivity in the other way is more difficult (pointing a mistyped word on the output in order to be automatically positioned on the same word in the source text); it could be achieved on the basis of pages however, since the large editor windows are able to contain most of the source text output on the same page by TeX.

In an EDDS like SARDE where all kinds of documents are stored, it is already possible to create new documents from parts of others, manipulating facsimile bitmaps and adding personal annotations. Now multiple inputs manipulations will take advantage of the new functionalities of the Orion terminal. With two bitmaps which can be selectively displayed through a programmable grid and boolean combinations, it is easy to integrate drawings, figures, even ordinary text within a TeX output, and to arrange a final document from different sources, according to traditional publishing manipulations.

5. TeX in distributed EDDSs

An EDDS distributed all over a large organization becomes the backbone of applications for document manipulations involving remote partners. For instance a technical manual issued by a manufacturer must be validated by an evaluation team, then broadcasted to end users who are expected to indicate inconsistencies between its contents and the reality. Such a large EDDS would include heterogeneous computer systems (from micros to mainframes) and it is probable that TeX can run on most machines, as it is the case at **cnet**.

In these circumstances, source and even '.dvi' files can be used as a *de facto* standard for communicating documents throughout the whole network, since the same outputs will be produced everywhere, while the reference database of the EDDS records the semantic structure of each document and its links with others. Such an exciting perspective, along with the high resolution capabilities of the Orion terminal, urge us to enhance the existing integration of TeX in distributed EDDSs.

References

1 AMAR Patrick, FILOTTI Ion. — *WINNIE,* LRI Univ. Orsay, 1985.

2 FOATA Dominique *et al.* — *STRATEC,* Publ. IRMA Strasbourg, 1984.

3 JOLY Pascale, ROMÉO Fraçoise. — *A high compression coding method for facsimile documents,* Proc. 2nd Int. Tech. Symp. on Optical and Electro-Optical Applied Science and Engineering, Cannes, 1985.

4 PENNY Philippe, PICARD Michel. — *Application of novel technologies to the management of a very large data base,* Proc. 9th Int. Conf. on VLDB, Florence, 1983.

5 PENNY Philippe. — *Technical Documentation Storage and Retrieval,* Invited paper to be published in Proc. of the 86 IFIP Congress, Dublin, 1986.

6 ROY Yves *et al.* — *TeX et son environnement,* Proc. Jour. sm90, ADI, 1985.

THE TEX - BASED DOCUMENT FACTORY IN A UNIVERSITY ENVIRONMENT: PROCESS MODEL, IMPLEMENTATION STEPS, EXPERIENCES

Heinz W. PETERSEN
RWTH AACHEN
Computing Centre
5100 Aachen, Germany

Abstract

The importance of document processing is briefly described by some examples and an overlook of the idea of a "document factory" and the individual requirements of an university environment is given. The system complexity and implementation characteristics make it necessary to develop and use a processing model which allows to describe all functions and interfaces in a satisfying resolution. The model is used as a basis for local standards, makes it easier to discuss and include international recommendations and gives the organisational structure for the complete implementation work. Conclusions and configuration examples close the presented paper.

1. Introduction

During the last five years the ideas of computer assisted document preparation systems have claimed more and more publicity. One central reason seems to be, that these systems are of great interest in different application areas—such as inhouse publishing, publishers of printed media, the printing industry, the universities and research centres representing the authors of scientific and technical papers. Therefore we understand a document as a combination of different information types, such as character strings, formulas, graphics, tables etc. Analysing the needs and requirements of the university people, we find that document processing tools and methods have more application aspects than especially automatic typesetting and printing. Although it is as much the primary goal to help the scientific authors performing the production and publishing process, it seems to be usefull to investigate some general ideas with respect to this process and to watch some quickly arising environment depending problems. Regarding the variety of now available tools for electronic document processing (TEX for typesetting purposes, data bases, laser printers, laser typesetters etc.) we can state that:

- basically, a complete set of tools can support the publishing process from the author's part of the game to the distributor of readable material,
- the university administration discovers its interest to publish information for students and the scientific staff (curriculum, forms, inhouse messages, teaching materials, correspondence courses) as well as to improve the universities general public representation,
- the interfacing of literature supply by libraries and external data bases to support the scientific work can be integrated,
- the further development of document processing systems leads to a strict separation of information content, logical and layout structure, a better understanding of knowledge handling and the process of knowledge representation, i.e. the basic university business.

2. The idea of the "Document Factory"

We understand the so called document factory as the set of available or desirable tools, methods and add ons for document storage, processing, presentation etc. The name was chosen, because everybody, who began to use text processing systems and later on TEX to produce his documents, found, that after having done the first step, a variety of additional services and tools could be helpful. On the other side, investments in hardware and software for such services should give benefits to a considerably large number of users (e.g. campus licences for software, protocol converting to other systems, inhouse software development).

Some of the goals which should be reached by implementing and combining these tools are the following:

- the scope of the authors should be separated from the scope of the production people (scanner operators, typesetting specialists, programmers, font designers etc.). This, in many cases, causes different workstations, soft- and hardware-tools.
- the service should be available for each member of the university, that is students, scientists, secretaries, administration employees etc. This implies different application fields and different user interfaces (in case of TEX different user oriented macro packages).
- the document processing has to be embedded in the existing environment. This requires tools for input, storage and processing of already existing documents, interfaces to typesetting or printing facilities and the implementation of formats for the interchange of documents.
- library services and the usage of external data bases have to be integrated.

- central services as font conversion and support, definition of document classes, delivery and test of special application programs, device drivers and error handling have to be installed.
- the existence and development of international and national standards have to be taken into account.
- document editing software for text, formulas and graphics should be available on simple PCs for any author and licenced by the university.
- since central functions are necessary by organizing or financial reasons, they should be offered as a network service.
- a central institution should be responsible for the document processing service.
- special efforts have to be made for education and user support by competent persons.

3. The Document Processing Model

The most important of all the experiences, which were made during the first steps into the document processing world, was the fact, that the complexity of the proposed system would at first require an abstract model. This model is needed to define functions, data objects and interfaces between them. In addition it is used to incorporate existing software packages by translating different input and output formats if necessary. It gives an orientation and a frame for all the work that has to be coordinated. A very rough overlook of the system parts is given in *fig.1*.

Part 1 is called the document preprocessing module. This part is necessary mainly for the input of existing printed documents. These documents are read by a scanner and have to be converted to a processable form. The processable form in this case is called the "manuscript" and consists of a description of the documents logical structure and the content portions. The content portions are different types of information as text, formulas, composite graphics, tables, raster images etc. Since the system functions in general are very different, depending on the type of information, part 1 works as a "split function" where these types of information have to be separated. Hence, the following functions on manuscripts and the presentation process can be shown in three dimensions, where the third dimension describes the different processes of handling different types of information. Immediately before the physically recognizable document occurs, the different data objects, representing text, formulas, graphics etc., must be assembled and integrated. That's what we call the assembly function.

Part 2 contains the manuscript as data object and two classes of functions: the editors, which are the basic software tools for authors and the manipulation functions for data, represented by the description of their content and logical markers, describing the information structure.

Part 3 shows the presentation process, that is the mapping of manuscripts to a certain output device. The main function of this part, the formatting process, is performed by TeX . Without any doubt, TeX is the most powerful available typesetting program for scientific applications, although there should be some necessary attachements and upgradings. In spite of these, all the presently known needs of harmonization between TeX and the user requirements can be achieved, as including graphics and raster images, application oriented user interfaces, the compatibility of non-TeX fonts etc.

The model is now shown in further details by *fig.2.* In this figure, data objects are shown as squares, functions as arrows and the user interfaces, which represent the interactive system paths, are marked with "U"s.

This graphic representation of the complete process (without the manuscript handling part) must be thought again as three-dimensional, where the third dimension is built by the different information types as text, graphics, formulas etc. It shall be stated at this point, that the structure of the process and the basic requirements concerning data objects, functions and user interfaces are identical, although some of them are not sufficiently described and implemented (e.g. the logical markup of graphics and the transformation to a layout structure). We understand the meaning of the model elements (from left to right) as follows:

Beginning with the document preprocessing part as an input function into the system for existing printed documents or the input of sketched graphics, we find each document as a set of pixels. Therefore we call this the uncoded, unstructured state of the document, or shortly "the sketch". To get the next state, the coded but unstructured form, we can use character recognizers for text recognition resp. coding and vectorizers to do the same with graphics. Since these functions—represented as the leftmost arrow in the model—cannot work completely satisfying in all cases, the interactive path for support by the user is very important. Anyhow, to get the coded state named "text", we have to work on some unusual software tools and interactive techniques. The text (the meaning of this word is not restricted to character strings!) can then be marked up with (in our case) SGML-based markers and the resulting state of the document is the so called "manuscript". The manuscript is understood as containing the content of the document and the description of its logical structure. No information about layout, design, physical representation etc. is contained in this state.

A second way to get manuscripts into the system is, that the author uses a manuscript editor to interactively generate this state of his document. The work on those editors, which use the document type definition (or document class representation), is still in progress, but we believe, that these editors will give a powerful tool and help for the authors.

The third way of getting manuscripts—reading external text with logical markup—makes it necessary to use an SGML-parser in order to verify the syntactical correctness of the specific document. By any method, the manuscript is the input for the formatting process. This process starts by replacing the logical markers by typographic commands. These commands express, how the user wants to get his document designed. The transformation from manuscript to "typoscript" is performed with respect to the "layout directives" which are offered by the system and edited by those people, who are trained in typographics. The typoscript is the processible document state and is transformed by TEX into the "printscript 1", the device-independant formatted state of the document (or DVI-file). The formatting process is influenced by "aesthetic functions", in case of TEX realizable by macros. The macro parameters, such as individual letter spacing, line spacing, positioning of mathematical symbols, etc. should be editable by means of an editor with an adequate user shell.

The device driver now produces the "printscript 2", that is the document's device dependant presentation. Generally, the driver has to integrate the different information types and to calculate the correct positioning and mapping of graphics, pictures etc. In special applications we want to edit this P2-file, for example the pixel-file of a scanned or generated logo.

After these short illustrations of the model elements, three points ought to be highlighted: Looking at the model makes clear, that there exists a straight forward batch oriented function of the complete process in vertical orientation. This holds for a lot of documents to be processed, but it is useful and necessary to find the principal points of human interaction. These points require paths to a certain user interface, which have basically the same structure as the batch process, i.e. translation of an entire manuscript to a visible form. These entire manuscripts are the different states of the documents which are processed automatically and the related data. This fact leads to some general implementation characteristics.

Real systems often require mixed procedures, i.e. the batch process is to be supported by interactive means. We believe, that future system developments either in the university or the industry area will lead to complete systems in the sense, that all horizontal and vertical paths are available and the combination of system functions which are in use, depends only on the document type, resp. the necessary production process.

It is possible to classify the existing text and document processing systems by comparing their properties with the data objects, functions and interfaces of the model. The result is the definition and implementation of protocol converting procedures (or to understand why this could be impossible) between systems of different manufacturers and different application areas, e.g. phototypesetters, typesetting systems, computer and text processing equipment. Our experiences showed, that one of the most important problems in most cases is the incompatibility of fonts.

It is obvious, that the usage of this model requires the detailed definition of interfaces and data structures. Unfortunately the international standardisation work (e.g. SGML, ODA, ODIF) has just been set up—so far the de facto standard of TeX is very helpful.

4. Organizational Remarks

The document factory is organized in "departments", which are responsible for the following working areas (*fig.3*):

1. production environment
2. storage and transmission functions
3. device drivers
4. TeX application
5. user interfaces
6. SGML-processor and manuscript editing tools
7. document preprocessing

Possibly the most important department deals with the production environment, i.e. the operational aids for interfacing the document preparation process to the users, the network services, font preparation, delivery of documents over the campus, accounting system etc. Presently one main interest is, to solve the font compatibility problem together with the interface to professional document processing in the graphic industry.

5. Implementation steps

Naturally, the first experiences in the field of scientific publishing were made by TeX and different mainframe installations. Since (in our case) PCTeX is available, the number of users grows fairly fast. *Fig.4* shows an example of the *experimental* implementation at the University of Aachen, i.e. the service is not yet in public use. The DVI-file processing for different devices and the integration of graphics (preferably produced by an interactive tool named uniCAD) is performed by a TeX-server based on IBM AT hardware. The manuscript editing is done by PCs or typewriters in simpler cases—therefore the input into the system is organized by an OCR-reader or an interface converter for different floppy disc formats. The connection to professional typesetting systems is just in preparation.

From our point of view we can state, that the usage of document processing tools for scientific and technical applications shows a new quality with respect to software, hardware and the requirements to the professional market. We expect a very dynamic development for the near future. But our main experience is, that TeX—together with the appropriate environment and some education efforts—is a very successful instrument to upgrade the efficiency of scientific work.

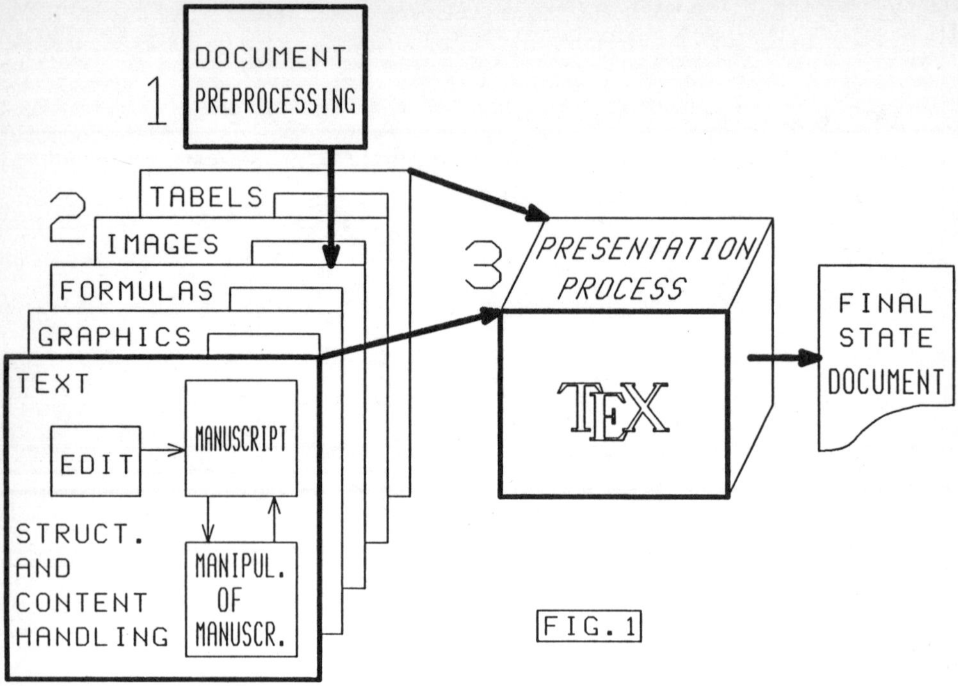
DOCUMENT
PREPROCESSING
1
2
TABELS
IMAGES
FORMULAS
GRAPHICS
TEXT
EDIT
MANUSCRIPT
STRUCT.
AND
CONTENT
HANDLING
MANIPUL.
OF
MANUSCR.
3
PRESENTATION
PROCESS
TEX
FINAL
STATE
DOCUMENT

FIG. 1

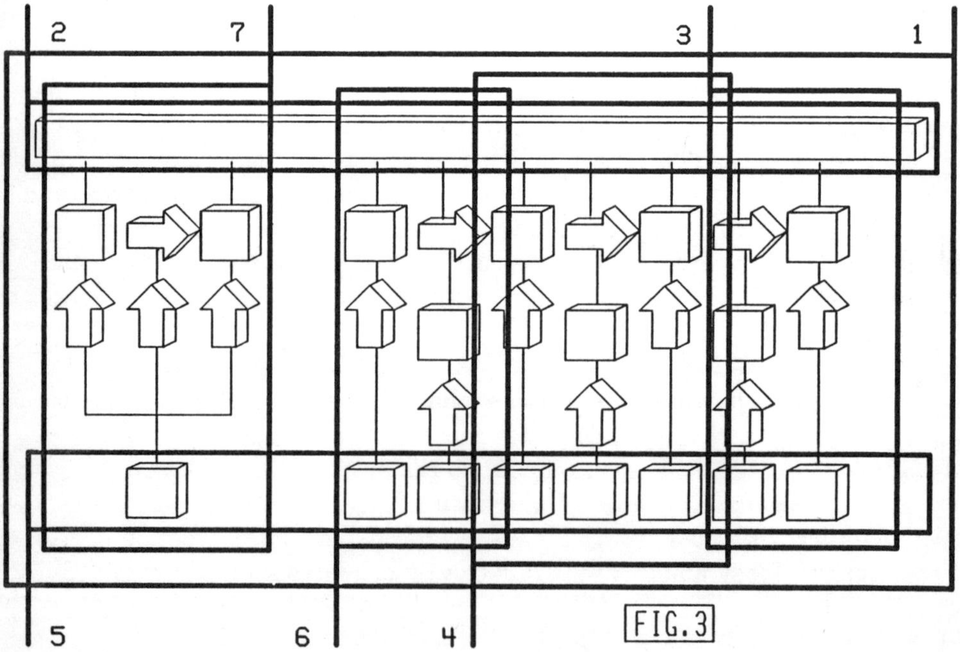
2
7
3
1
5
6
4

FIG. 3

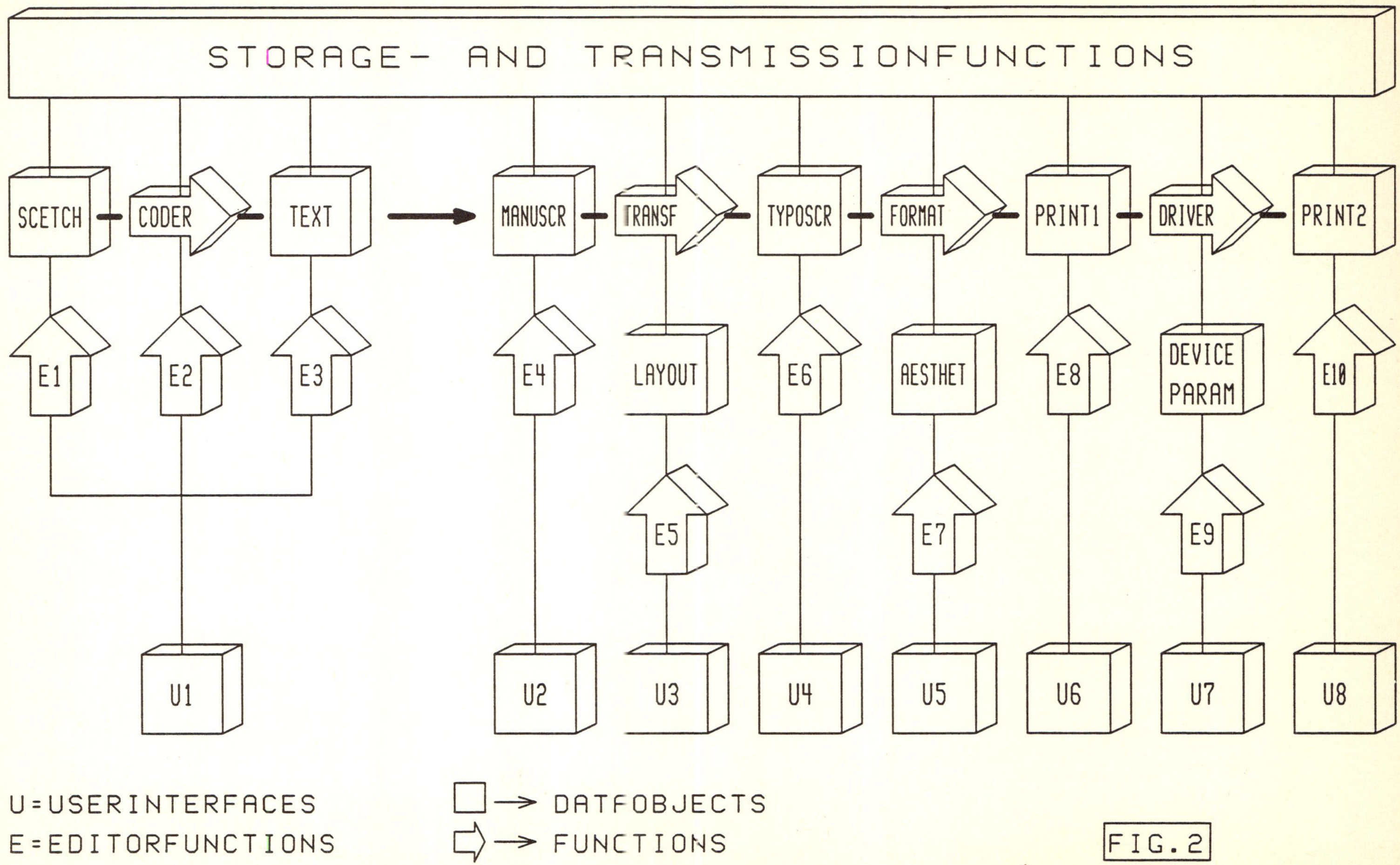
STORAGE- AND TRANSMISSIONFUNCTIONS
SCETCH
CODER
TEXT
MANUSCR
TRANSF
TYPOSCR
FORMAT
PRINT1
DRIVER
PRINT2
E1
E2
E3
E4
LAYOUT
E6
AESTHET
E8
DEVICE PARAM
E10
E5
E7
E9
U1
U2
U3
U4
U5
U6
U7
U8
U=USERINTERFACES
E=EDITORFUNCTIONS
→ DATFOBJECTS
→ FUNCTIONS

FIG.2

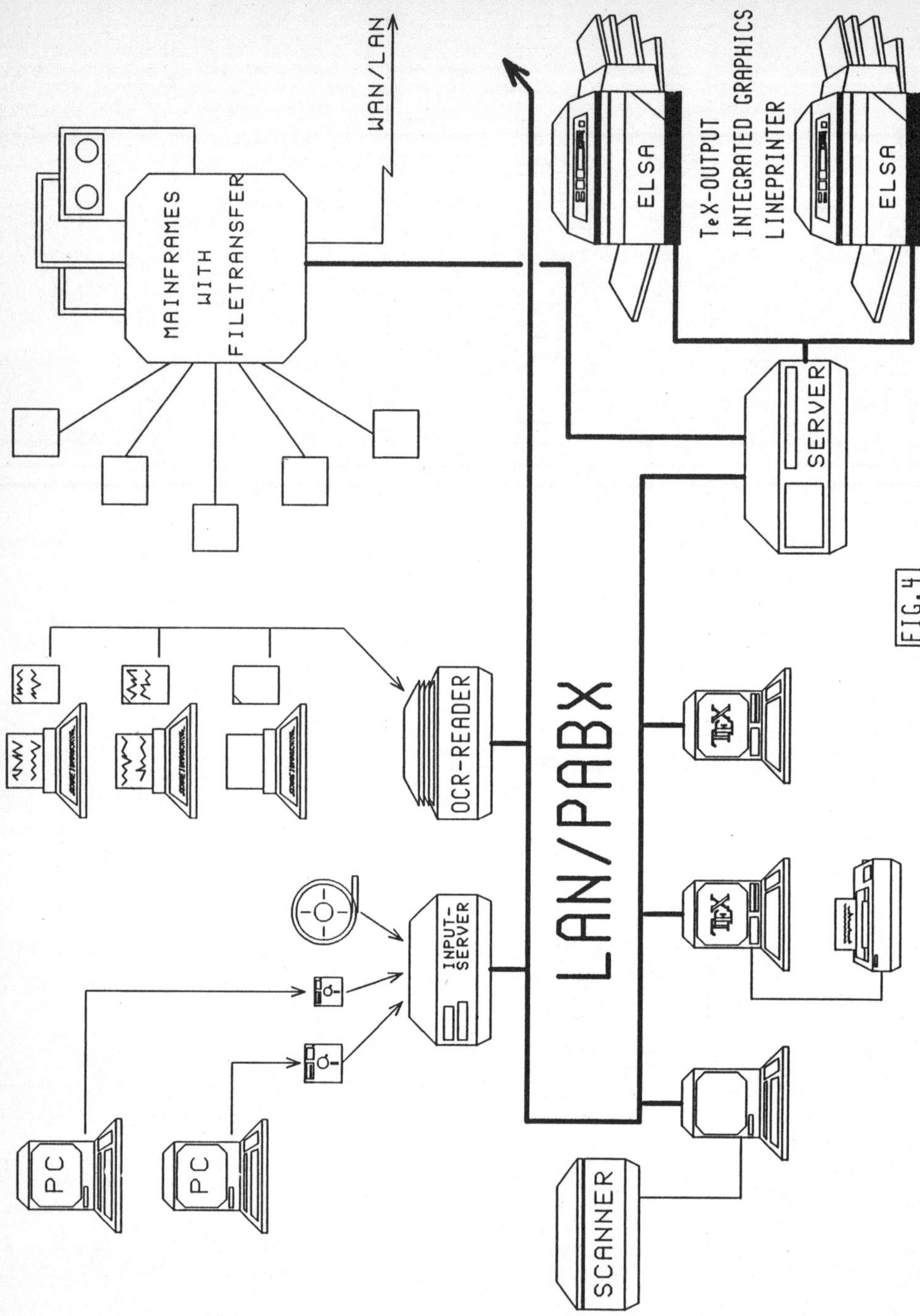
MAINFRAMES
WITH
FILETRANSFER
WAN/LAN
TeX-OUTPUT
INTEGRATED GRAPHICS
LINEPRINTER
ELSA
ELSA
SERVER
LAN/PABX
OCR-READER
INPUT-
SERVER
PC
PC
SCANNER

FIG.4

GRIF: AN INTERACTIVE ENVIRONMENT FOR TEX

Vincent QUINT
Irène VATTON
Hassan BEDOR
Laboratoire de Génie Informatique
Université de Grenoble
BP 68, 38402 St Martin d'Hères, France

Abstract

Several attempts have been made for making TEX more user-friendly by providing specific tools for preview or input of documents. We propose a different approach which uses an interactive system for editing the documents intended to be formatted by TEX. This system, Grif, is based on a structured model of documents and allows the user to define the structure and presentation of documents edited. We present how it may be used for efficiently preparing documents to be printed by TEX.

1. Presentation

TEX [6] is well known for the typesetting quality of the documents it produces, but it is also known for its input language, which is not so user-friendly. A number of solutions have been proposed for making TEX more convivial (see [1], [2], [3], [4], [5]). All these projects intend to help the user to input TEX documents. Other tools have been developed for displaying an image of the final form of the document on the workstation screen; these preview systems are used for shortening the cycle input, formatting, proof-reading, correction.

In these systems, the trend is to make TEX more or less interactive. Our approach is to use a true interactive system in conjunction with TEX. The system we use is Grif [9], an editor for manipulating structured documents. We take advantage of the openness and flexibility of Grif for adapting it to the TEX requirements.

In the next sections we present the document model on which Grif is based and the main principles of the interactive editor. The way documents are printed is then described and finally we present two different view-points for using TEX in such an interactive environement.

2. The document model

As with many high-level formatters, Grif is based on a *logical* model of documents. A document is seen as an organised collection of elements. The organisation describes the logical structure of the document, with elements like chapters, sections, sub-sections, paragraphs, notes, titles, etc. Each element has a type and a document contains several elements with the same type. Each type is built with other types: a chapter is built with a title and a sequence of sections, a section is built with a title and a sequence of paragraphs, and so on. This way of building an element with others defines a *generic structure*, a model after which the *specific structure* of each document is built.

In order to be able to manipulate a wide variety of documents, we do not define a unique generic structure for all kinds of documents. We rather define several generic structures, each one describing the organisation of a set (we say a *class*) of similar documents. So, we can define a class "letter", or a class "technical report", or a class "contract", each class having an adapted generic structure with its own types of elements: there is no chapter in a letter, but there is an address and a signature, which are not present in a report.

Even if each class has a different generic structure, many classes use such common types of elements as paragraphs or notes. Therefore a generic structure may use other generic structures, in order to share this kind of structure of general use. This sharing of structures is not only used for textual elements, but also for elements like tables, or mathematical formulae. Thus we define classes of non-textual objects, for these objects may be structured in the same way as documents. This leads to an homogeneous model which encompasses whole documents of various kinds as well as the objects they contain.

In fact our model is a meta-model which allows models of documents and objects to be described. This approach is very flexible as it allows new models to be defined according to the needs and it ensures that each model is well adapted to the documents or objects it is supposed to represent. For example, we can have several classes of tables, each one with a different kind of organisation.

Structures built according to such a model are trees. The main structure is a tree representing the whole document, and most objects included in the document are sub-trees of that tree. Each node of the tree has a type (title, chapter, fraction, numerator...) and may have *attributes* which add semantics to the element. Examples of attributes are the language in which a part of the document is written, or the importance of a fragment of text (keyword or index). These attributes are useful for several different applications and especially for printing the document: a formatter hyphenates words according to the language; it prints them with typographical attributes corresponding to their importance.

In addition to the main tree structure, there are *references* which represent non-hierarchical relationships between elements; this allows one element to be referenced from another independently of their relative levels in the tree. It is thus possible from any paragraph to refer to a chapter ("As seen in chapter

..."), a figure or a bibliographic quotation. The system may then substitute the number of the referenced element or its title or any other of its sub-elements for the reference.

Using this kind of structure, an editor or a formatter can display or print the document with very little additional information from the author. The presentation of a document or object may be automatically generated from the structure. For example, a fraction is displayed with the numerator centered over the denominator and with a horizontal bar between both expressions; the title of a report is printed with large letters and centered in the page.

If an editor knows about the structure of the objects it manipulates and if it has rules for presenting these structures, then the user does not have to worry about presentation: when the title of a report is entered, the editor can automatically change the character size and center the text.

Another advantage of this automatic presentation is that it leads to a homogeneous presentation for all documents belonging to the same class. All reports will have their title centered and written with the same size, if the system uses the same presentation rules for the class "report". The presentation is not intermixed with the structure or the content of the document; it is described outside the document, within the set of presentation rules associated with the class. This set of rules is called a *presentation schema.*

Several presentation schemas can be defined for the same class of documents, allowing the user to display the document in different ways according to the task to be performed. It is thus possible to use a simple presentation schema for editing and a more sophisticated one for previewing, without modifying the document itself, just by changing the presentation schema used by the system.

The presentation schema defines how each type of element defined in the structure schema is to be displayed by the editor. There are presentation rules for elements of the structure and for attributes. Presentation rules use the same model of boxes as in TEX. To each element of the structure corresponds a box; the presentation rules define relative positions and dimensions for boxes according to their types and relation in the document structure. This model allows text to be presented as well as formulae or tables or other types of objects.

In a presentation schema, several views may be defined. A *view* is a partial representation of a document. So, a table of contents is a view which collects together all section titles. The presentation schema allows any number of views to be defined, specifying for each type of element in which views the element is visible and how it is to be presented in those views. While editing, the user can create the views he requires, being able to destroy any view at any time. He can then use these views for editing or moving across the document.

As the layout of the document can be built from its structure and from a presentation schema, a document is stored with only its specific structure and its content, but without any presentation information. This representation is called the *external representation* of the document.

3. The Grif editor

Grif is based on the above notion of document model. The whole system comprises several programs: three compilers, an editor and a converter (see figure 1). Generic structures are described with a dedicated declarative language, called S. Similarly, presentation schemas are written with a specific language, called P. With these two languages it is possible to specify new classes of documents or objects as well as new presentations for documents and objects. Languages S and P are compiled and the compilers produce tables which are used by the editor.

The editor itself is split into two main components for separating the user interface functions handled by the Mediator from the processing functions handled by the Editor. The Editor checks the specific structures of documents; it elaborates them according to their generic structures and prepares their display. The Mediator takes full responsibility for the physical support; it produces pictures on the screen and manages all physical interactions with the user. The Editor defines the set of commands it is able to interpret and the Mediator builds forms and menus to present these commands to the user and returns the user's answers to the Editor.

The Editor uses the generic structures of document and objects for generating the *abstract tree* of a document which represents the specific structure of the whole document being edited. Using the presentation rules in accordance with the structure of the document, the Editor produces an *abstract picture* of the document. An abstract picture gives the logical layout of what the Mediator has to show. It is in fact a tree describing the arrangement of several types of units: texts, pictures, graphics and symbols, which are the leaves of the tree. A node of an abstract picture corresponds to a node of an abstract tree. The Mediator analyses each abstract picture and, by taking into account the physical characteristics of the device (character size, window size, etc) it constructs a set of boxes making up the *real picture*, which is finally displayed.

A node of an abstract picture gathers together information and presentation constraints which define how the associated information is to be presented. The Mediator builds a box for each node of an abstract picture; presentation constraints permitting the calculation of the width, height and positioning of the boxes, the bodysize and style of the characters and the construction of lines.

In all cases, presentation constraints are completely device independent. For example the choice of font style and size is performed by the Mediator by deduction from two logical constraints: the highlight level and the relative pointsize. In the same way, the horizontal and vertical units used are converted into physical units according to the associated relative pointsize. This allows the presentation schemas to be completely device-independent. The construction of lines is performed by the Mediator, by interpreting constraints set by the Editor: mode of adjustment, centering, indentation, line length, line spacing, etc.

Finally, the set of boxes is organized into a connected graph which represents all relationships between boxes (relative positions and dimensions). This connected

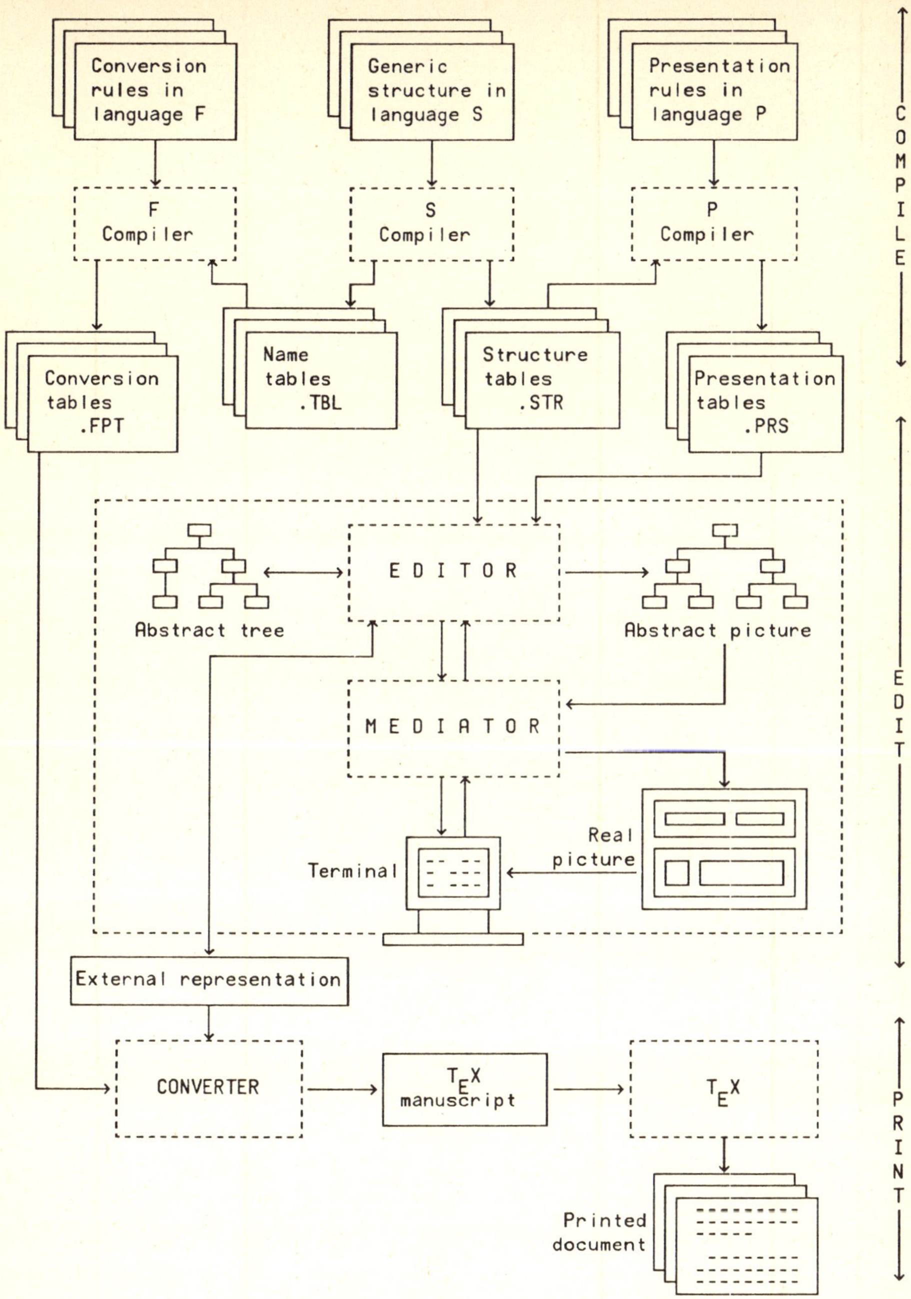

Figure 1: Grif architecture.

graph allows the Mediator to update the real picture as soon as the document content is modified by the user.

Until now, interactive structure-oriented systems have mainly been used for manipulating programs. Therefore they have been designed to be used by computer oriented people. In those systems, the structure of the program being edited is represented by a tree and the user is supposed to have a good knowledge of this structure as commands are often expressed by reference to that tree. This approach cannot be used in a document manipulation system where the user is unfamiliar with such concepts. Although a rich structure is necessary for powerful processing, it is not desirable to use it systematically in the dialogue between the user and the system.

Grif is an interactive system: every user action immediately reacts on the document content and every document change is directly visible to the user. Of course, the Editor takes advantage of its knowledge of the documents being handled. It knows their generic structure and so can guide the user in the elaboration and modification of the document. As with syntactic editors used in programming environments, it offers powerful commands based on structure, especially for movement, selection and creation.

Whereas structural organisation of documents permits efficient manipulations, it complicates normal text manipulation. In Grif, structure manipulation does not inhibit text manipulation. The user can select a part of the document by searching for character strings, extend this selection by pointing to a character as well as by invoking a structure selection command. When the user deletes, copies, or inserts within a part of the displayed picture, Grif ensures that the right choice is made between manipulations made on the structure and those made on the text, and that this is transparent to the user. The Mediator manipulates the text part of the document and calls the Editor for updating the structure part.

4. Printing documents

While editing, Grif produces a picture of the document from its specific structure and from the presentation rules chosen by the user. The same principle could be used for generating the picture of the document on paper, but we took another approach.

The displayed picture and the printed picture of documents have different functions. The displayed picture is produced to allow the user to quickly see the result of the actions he makes by giving him immediate feedback. The user needs to see clearly in what way the editor interprets the commands he issues, in order to be able to react in case of mistake. For this purpose the presentation rules may emphasize some visual effects that would not be so evident in a printed document. The second function of the editor's picture is to allow the user to directly designate on the screen the part of the document on which he wants to act. In order to make selection easier, presentation rules may increase some spaces within the document.

Response time is also an important point for the editor. Even with an incremental redisplay policy and optimized algorithms, it is not possible to attain the best typographical quality on the screen of an interactive editor; the user would have to wait too long on each occasion that the screen needs reformatting. Therefore, although it is well adapted for editing, the displayed picture cannot be printed identically.

As it is not necessary (nor possible) when editing, to use the most sophisticated formatting algorithms (like those used by TEX), we did not implement them in Grif. Obviously we need them for producing beautiful papers, but fortunately formatters have them. Hence we use formatters for printing the documents produced by our interactive editor.

Keeping in line with the editor, the produced documents are printed in a flexible way. Grif does not impose a formatter for printing documents but proposes instead a general mechanism for converting the external representation of a document into a description of that document in the language of a formatter like TEX. This conversion is performed by the *converter*, which is driven by conversion tables.

4.1. The Converter

The conversion processes is independent of the data contained in the document. As shown in fig. 1, this process is carried out in two phases. In the first phase we write conversion rules for the generic structures of different document classes to print them using a certain formatter. These conversion rules are written in a dedicated language called F and are compiled once to produce the corresponding conversion tables. In the second phase, for each document, the converter uses the appropriate conversion tables for guiding it in generating the formatter source.

The conversion rules are determined by three factors: the document structure, the used formatter, and the desired layout. In the conversion table associated with a generic structure, there is a set of conversion rules for each type of element, which is applied when the converter finds an element of that type in the document being handled. For each generic structure there is a conversion table to be applied for a given formatter. In LaTEX for example, we have conversion tables for papers, formulae, etc.

As the formatting commands are different from one formatter to another, we have different conversion tables for different formatters. For example we have two conversion tables for the class Paper; one is used with TEX and the other is used with LaTEX. Finally it is obvious that if the desired layout is changed we need to use other conversion tables.

4.2. The language F

The language F which is used to write the conversion rules is very simple. F programs contain two divisions: the declaration division and the presentation division.

The declaration division consists of several parts. It essentially contains the name of the conversion table and the name of the associated generic structure. It also specifies the maximum length of the lines to be produced, the constants, the counters and the variables. A constant is simply a name given to a string of characters. A variable is a name given to a sequence of strings, constants and counters. Counters are used to number elements by counting the occurences of certain types of elements in the document. There are three types of counters: the first type counts the occurence of the element from the beginning of the document, the second type counts the occurence of the element within a certain part of the document (for example counting figures within chapters) and the third type counts the level of the recursive elements (i.e. elements which contain elements of a same type).

The second division is the presentation division and consists of two parts. In the first part we define sets of rules which are applied to different attribute-value pairs. For example there are a set of rules applied when the used language (attribute) is English (value) and another set if it is French (value). This is useful when treating multi-language documents.

The second presentation part is constructed as follows: for each type of element declared in the corresponding generic structure we may write one or more conversion rules. We have six types of rules: If, Get, Call, Translate, Create, and Remove.

With the If rule we can apply a group of rules on any given element conditionally: if it is first, last, not first, not last, within a given element or not, etc. For example the first line of the paragraph is indented if it is not the first paragraph of the section, and is not indented if it is within the abstract.

The Call rule allows us to use another conversion table for certain types of structured elements. For example the same conversion table may be used for all formulae whatever the type of the document wherein they appear: reports, articles, books, etc. It is important to note that the conversion table called is not recompiled with the program which calls it, but that the call statement is performed at conversion time only.

The Remove rule permits any element that is not considered by the formatter to be removed. Such an element is totally removed together with its contents.

The Get rule permits the order of elements in the document to be changed. For example if Grif produces the elements **A,B,C,D** in this order and the formatter accepts them in the order **B,C,A,D**, we write in the set of rules of element **A**:

GET B;
GET C;

The Create rule allows strings of characters to be written before an element, after it, at the beginning of the produced file, at the end of the file or when referencing this element. The created string may contain any single 8 bit character. The characters that cannot be inputted by the terminal are written using their codes.

Finally the Translate rule helps us to translate certain sequences of characters or even to remove them. For example the accented letters are treated in different ways from one formatter to another. Translate rules are used to produce the suitable sequence of characters for generating these letters. As another example, the integration symbol in formulae is represented in different ways from one formatter to another; the Translate rule being used to generate the most suitable presentation of such symbols.

At compilation time the F compiler uses the name tables (.TBL) to guide it in compiling and producing the conversion tables (.FPT). At generation time the converter uses these tables to guide it in generating the formatter input-source from the external representation of the document.

5. TEX as a postprocessor

A first way to use TEX with Grif is to consider TEX as a postprocessor of Grif. With this point of view, generic structures for documents and objects are defined independently of TEX, just taking into account their logical structure and the operations that can be performed on them, for a document is not only edited, formatted and printed, but can also be used in applications such as information retrieval systems, data bases, software engineering, etc. Each kind of application may have some specific requirements on the document structure, in order to be able to process it efficiently.

When document structures are designed independently of the way documents will be printed, several formatters may be used. The user may choose one or the other according to the results he wants to achieve, or to the adequation of the formatting commands to the structure of the documents. TEX would then be mainly used for documents requiring the finest typographical quality, and especially when they contain mathematics. For that kind of usage, the basic commands offered by plain TEX are sufficient. It is not necessary to use the macro facility or any macro package, since the conversion rules play this role: they transform the logical entities defined in the generic structures into sequences of basic formatting commands.

With this approach, some problems may arise when entities of the generic structure have no equivalent in TEX. This type of problem was pointed out by [3], when converting mathematical formulae from Edimath into TEX.

6. Grif as a preprocessor

This kind of problem may be avoided by taking the opposite point of view, which consists in considering Grif as a preprocessor for TEX. The idea is to take full advantage of TEX features and to use Grif as an interactive tool specifically adapted for producing documents to be formatted by TEX. With this approach, generic structures are defined according to the structures manipulated by TEX.

As plain TEX does not use a structured model of documents other than for formulae, it is not well suited, but LaTEX [7] with its logical structure of documents is. Thus we define generic structures which correspond to the document styles of LaTeX. We also define a generic structure in accordance with the structure of mathematical formulae of TeX. With these generic structures Grif produces documents that can be very simply converted into LaTeX.

We define presentation rules for these generic structures and try to give to the picture produced by the editor an aspect close to what will be produced by LaTeX when formatting the document. The aim is not a WYSIWYG system, but to present the user with a picture in which he can easily associate with what is on a previous version of his document printed by LaTeX. So line breaks are different on the screen and on the paper, page breaks are not visible on the screen, but character sizes and styles, indentations, spaces, centerings, and so on are approximately the same. Footnotes are not displayed at the bottom of the pages (there being no notion of page on the screen...), but in a different window; however the reference is clearly visible in the text.

Formulae are displayed in two dimensions and it is really easy to edit them, like with Edimath [8]. Again, the pictures of formulae are not strictly the same as those produced by TeX, but they are sufficiently precise for editing and for avoiding most errors done when typing the TeX language directly. The result is an agreeable interactive TeX environment, with a WYSIWYG style of interface, but also with all the possibilities of TeX concerning high quality typography.

7. An example

The following example shows how to manipulate a document in a Grif-LaTeX environment. It explains the production of a Paper in this environment. First the Paper is edited using the Grif editor. During this phase the user sees the picture shown on fig.2. The editor uses the following generic structure:

```
Paper = BEGIN
        Title= Text;
        Authors= LIST OF (Author= Text);
        Address= LIST OF (Address_Line= Text);
        Abstract= Text;
        Sections= LIST OF (Section=
                     BEGIN
                     Section_Title= Text;
                     Section_Body= LIST OF (Sect_Elem=
                            CASE OF
                            Paragraph= Text;
                            Displayed_Formula= Math;
                            END);
                     END);
      END;
```

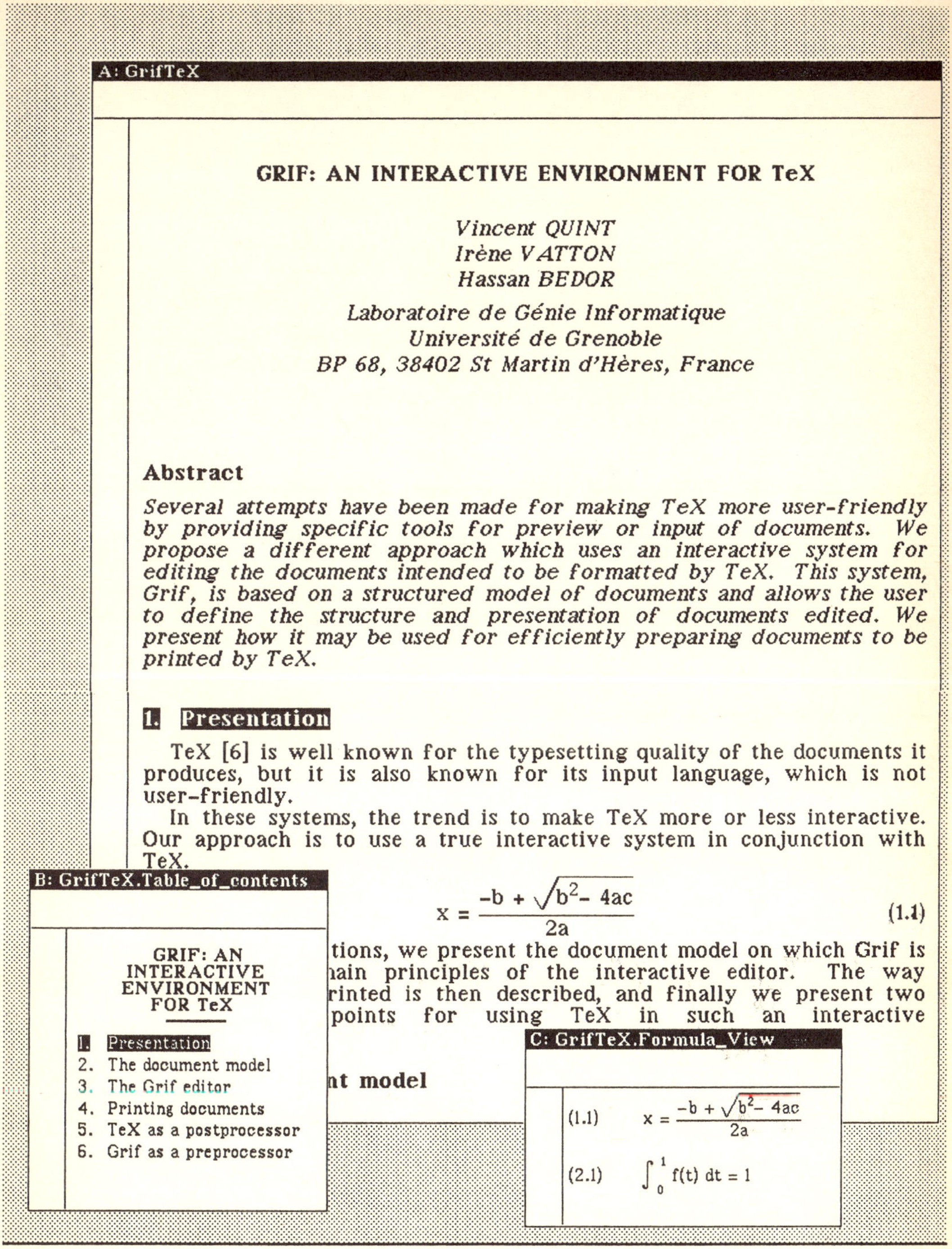

Figure 2: A Grif screen.

As declared in this generic structure, a Paper consists of a Title which is a simple text (a character string), Authors which may be one or more (each Author is a simple text), the Address (a sequence of Address_Lines), the Abstract, which is a simple text and finally the Sections, which are one Section or more. Each Section consists of a Section_Title, which is a simple text and the Section_Body, which is a list of Sect_Elem's. A Sect_Elem may be a Paragraph, which is a simple text, or a Displayed_Formula, which is another structure called Math (generic structure for formulae).

The structure compiler produces a table of names which is used by the F compiler to produce the corresponding conversion table. For the class Paper we use the following conversion rules (\12 represents a new line and \134 represents a back slash):

```
Paper : BEGIN
        CREATE '\documentstyle{article}\12' HEAD;
        CREATE '\begin{document}\12';
        CREATE '\12\end{document}\12' TAIL;
        END;
Title : BEGIN
        CREATE '\title{';
        CREATE '}\12' AFTER;
        END;
Authors : CREATE '\author{';
Author : IF NOT LAST CREATE '\134\134\12\and\12' AFTER;
Address_Line : CREATE '\134\134\12' BEFORE;
Address : CREATE '}\12' AFTER;
Abstract : BEGIN
        CREATE '\maketitle\12\begin{abstract}\12';
        CREATE '\12\end{abstract}\12' AFTER;
        END;
Displayed_Formula :
        BEGIN
        CREATE '\12\begin{equation}\12';
        CALL MathTex FOR Math;
        CREATE '\12\end{equation}\12' AFTER;
        END;
TEXT_UNIT : TTRANSLATE
        BEGIN
        'TeX' : '\TeX';
        '\11' : '\`{e}';
        '\37' : '\"{e}';
        END;
```

As we can see, the set of rules associated with the element Paper creates three LaTeX commands:

`\documentstyle{article}` at the head of the file,

`\begin{document}` before the Paper contents and

`\end{document}` at the tail of the file.

The rules for element Title creates `\title{` before and `}` after and so on. We can also see the condition `IF NOT LAST` which is used within the rule for the Author element.

In Displayed_Formula we find the CALL statement which has two arguments. The first argument (MathTex) is the name of the conversion table that will be used for the generation of formulae. The second (Math) is the name of the generic structure of formulae.

As we can see the TEXT_UNIT (or Text as indicated in the structure) is a basic element of the structure. There are other basic elements such as SYMBOL_UNIT, GRAPHIC_UNIT and PICTURE_UNIT. The rule associated with the TEXT_UNIT is Text Translation by which we translate three strings from their Grif representation to their LaTeX meaning.

Later on, for any paper generated by Grif, the conversion will produce the following LaTeX source:

```
\documentstyle{article}
\begin{document}
\title{GRIF: AN INTERACTIVE ENVIRONMENT FOR \TeX}
\author{Vincent QUINT\\
\and
Ir\`{e}ne VATTON\\
\and
Hassan BEDOR\\
Laboratoire de G\'{e}nie Informatique\\
Universit\'{e} de Grenoble\\
BP 68, 38402 St Martin d'H\`{e}res}
\maketitle
\begin{abstract}
Several attempts have been made for making \TeX\ more ...
the structure and presentation of documents edited.
\end{abstract}
\section{Presentation}
\TeX\ [6] is well known for the typesetting quality of ...
system in conjunction with \TeX.
\begin{equation}
x=\frac{-b+\sqrt{b^{2}-4ac}}{2a}
\end{equation}
...
```

8. Conclusion

This project has been made possible due to the rich model upon which Grif is based. The high level document model allows it to be readily adaptable to any kind of document and to several formatters.

Prior to the project presented in this paper we had performed an analogous experiment with a Troff-like formatter, but due to the low level of that formatter only the first approach presented above has been taken. We are now planning to do the same kind of work for Mint, with the same objective: to take advantage of all functions of a formatter through Grif, so making the user-interface convivial. This should be easily done, for the design of both Mint and LaTeX, have been inspired by the same model: Scribe [10].

Bibliography

[1] M. Agostini, V. Matano, M. Schaerf, M. Vascotto, "An Interactive User-Friendly TeX in VM/CMS Environment". *TeX for Scientific Documentation*, D. Lucarella ed., Addison-Wesley, 1985, pp. 117-132.

[2] L. Aiello, S. Pavan, "Towards a friendly workstation for TeX". *Internationaler Kongress fur Datenverarbeitung um Informations Technologie*, Berlin, 1982.

[3] J. André, Y. Grundt, V. Quint, "Toward an Interactive Math Mode in TeX". *TeX for Scientific Documentation*, D. Lucarella ed., Addison-Wesley, 1985, pp. 79-92.

[4] G. Canzii, G Degli Antoni, S. Mussi, G. Rosci, "SDDS: Scientific Document Delivery System". *TeX for Scientific Documentation*, D. Lucarella ed., Addison-Wesley, 1985, pp. 15-25.

[5] D. Foata, J.-J. Pansiot, Y. Roy, "Stratec and a Rationalized Keyboard for Inputting TeX". *TeX for Scientific Documentation*, D. Lucarella ed., Addison-Wesley, 1985, pp. 105-116.

[6] D.E. Knuth, *The TeXbook*, Addison-Wesley, Reading, Massachusetts, 1984.

[7] L. Lamport, *LaTeX: A Document Preparation System*, Addison-Wesley, Reading, Massachusetts, 1986.

[8] V. Quint, "Interactive Editing of Mathematics". *PROTEXT I*, Proceedings of the First International Conference on Text Processing Systems, J.J.H. Miller ed., Boole Press, Dublin, 1984, pp. 55-68.

[9] V. Quint, I. Vatton, "Grif: An Interactive System for Structured Document Manipulation". *Proceedings of EP'86*, J.C. van Vliet ed., Cambridge University Press, 1986.

[10] B. Reid, "A High Level Approach to Computer Document Formatting". *Proc. 7th Annual ACM Symposium on the Principles of Programming Languages*, January 1980, pp. 24-31.

ABSTRACT MARKUP IN TEX

Johannes RÖHRICH
Universität Karlsruhe
D-7500 Karlsruhe 1, FRG

Extended Abstract

The purpose of abstraction in document markup schemes and languages is discussed. Many abstraction concepts found in modern software engineering may also be useful in document markup, e.g. abstraction from (1) machines and devices, (2) data representations, (3) procedural aspects, (4) concurrency—which occurs in documents in the form of several interleaved streams of text—and (5) *small* vs. *large* concepts such as document architecture and the managing of large amounts of related documents.

However, while there is a common understanding of programming language semantics today, the semantics of markup languages are not yet well defined. We discuss semantic models for documents and alternatives to formally define the semantics of markup languages, based on what we would like to call a documents' *meaning*. We argue that—at least in the area of scientific publication—there is no really strong interaction between the meaning of a document and its (typo)graphical representation. This enables us to specify a scheme of five layers of abstraction: (1) device abstraction, (2) size abstraction, (3) font family abstraction, (4) style abstraction and, (5) abstraction from the layout of a document on paper or CRT displays. The last layer only preserves the structured document *contents* which we consider its meaning.

Unfortunately, TEX markup only provides device abstraction. The other four layers are mixed together instead of being supported by corresponding syntactic *and* semantic language concepts. Examples of this as well as of the mixing between imperative vs. declarative, implicit vs. explicit, and procedural vs. declarative markup styles in TEX and LaTEX are given.

The second part of the contribution deals with the MAX system that has been developed at the University of Karlsruhe. MAX is a declarative, SGML-like markup language, and a document compiler bearing the same name. The objective of the development of MAX has been to provide what may be called "grey" documents, i.e. documents that can be visualized and printed on a wide variety of *distibuted* devices using almost arbitrary formatters—namely TEX, Troff under UNIX, Runoff under VMS, Reuf under BS2000, etc. MAX markup is easy to learn and to use, it frees the user from the burden of learning a new markup language every year, but gives him/her the opportunity to produce high quality output with TEX or similar composing systems. On the other hand, the user may visualize the contents of a MAX document on locally available equipment.

One of the major problems that must be solved in such a distributed setting is that of providing essentially the same family of typefaces in the formats required by each of the available document formatting systems. Therefore, we are developing tools that convert between METAFONT, UNIX vfont, Imagen and Impress font formats. A facility to interactively manipulate glyphs is also provided.

We are now addressing the problem of providing essentially the same, multilingual hyphenation mechanism in all of the available formatters.

Designing a new typeface with METAFONT

Richard Southall

Laboratoire de typographie informatique
Université Louis-Pasteur
67084 Strasbourg, France

Abstract

This paper summarizes the conclusions reached as a consequence of two years' work on the design of an original typeface using METAFONT. While being in one sense unsuccessful, in that the design of the typeface is still far from complete, the experience has been instructive in pointing up a number of discrepancies between the underlying assumptions about the design process that professional type designers bring to their work and those current in the TEX world.

These discrepancies, and what appear to be the reasons for them, are discussed.

1 Terminology

The computer science literature on document preparation has traditionally been bedevilled by the misuse of terms carelessly borrowed from the existing technologies of typography and type manufacture. The word *font*, for example, is used indifferently in the literature to refer to three or four fundamentally distinct entities: this leads to a good deal of confusion in discussions about typefaces, type design and similar subjects. So the first thing we need to do is to define a useful and consistent terminology[1].

1.1 Typefaces and character images

A *document* is an assembly of mechanically-produced marks on a substrate. The marks that make up the verbal components of the document are *character images*, and it is these images that the reader sees. We need to define terms that allow us

[1] This terminology is a shortened form of the fully-worked-out version proposed in *Designing new typefaces with METAFONT* (Southall, 1985b).

to discuss how character images are produced, and what part the type designer plays in deciding on their appearance.

A *script* is a set of characters used to write one or more languages.

A *typeface* is a set of distinctive, visually related shapes that represent some or all of the characters of a script and are intended for mechanical reproduction.

Each of the character shapes in a typeface has an *identity*, which is that of the character it represents. The typeface as a whole – the set of shapes with different identities – has a number of *visual attributes*. It is the visual attributes of a typeface that distinguish it from other typefaces.

The visual attributes of a typeface are of two kinds: *stylistic* and *functional*. Stylistic visual attributes are such things as *seriffedness* and *cursiveness*; functional visual attributes are such things as *boldness* and *condensedness*. Typeface classification schemes such as DIN 16 518 : 1964, and aesthetic criticism of the traditional kind, deal with the stylistic visual attributes of typefaces. The functional visual attributes of typefaces are those that make different typefaces useful in differentiating the components of complex text.

A *family of typefaces* is a set of typefaces with similar stylistic visual attributes and differing functional visual attributes[2].

The character images in a document have *graphic attributes* that give them their *appearance*. The appearance of character images realizes the visual attributes of the typeface the images represent.

1.2 Fonts

The character images (as well as the other marks) in a mechanically-produced document are made by a *marking device*. This contains a *marking engine*[3] that uses a *marking process*. Thus the character images in the document that constituted the camera-ready copy for this paper were made by a Canon CX-2000 laser marking engine. This was inside a Canon LBP-8 A1 laser printer driven by a Telmat SM90 minicomputer: these two machines together made up the marking device. The marking process was the familiar electrographic one, in which a laser writes on the surface of an electrically-charged semiconducting drum which then transfers toner to the surface of plain paper.

---

[2] On this definition, the Computer Modern family of typefaces (Knuth, 1980) is a long way from being the traditional nuclear family of roman, italic and bold. The stylistic attributes that relate the sanserif or the `typewriter face` to Computer Modern Roman are not at all easy to recognize, except in some features of certain characters.

[3] The term *marking engine*, like much else that has helped to clarify thinking in this field, is due to Brian Reid.

An engine like the Canon CX-2000 has no knowledge of its own about the shapes of character images. Somewhere inside the marking device there need to be sets of instructions to the marking engine that tell it how to make the images that realize the character shapes of a typeface in a particular size or range of sizes. These sets of instructions are the *fonts*.

Thus, in the TeX–METAFONT system, there is the Computer Modern family of typefaces, of which `cmr10` is a member. The character shapes of `cmr10` are described in `cmr10.mf` and its associated METAFONT programs. Running these programs with `mode=imagen` and `mag=1` produces a 'generic font file' `cmr10.300gf`: this is not a font, but an intermediate in the font production process. Running `gftopxl` on `cmr10.300gf` produces the pixel file `cmr10.1500pxl`. This *is* a font: it contains instructions to the Canon printer (which uses the same marking engine as the Imagen printer for which the font was developed) about how to produce character images that realize the visual attributes of the typeface `cmr10`.

Notice that the font is *device-specific*: not only is it made for a particular writing resolution (300 dots per inch in this case: the fact that the extension of the font file name is `.1500pxl` is a peculiarity of the system) but the `mode` information that the programs read assigns values to the METAFONT variables `blacker`, `fillin` and `o_correction` that are appropriate for the Canon engine. These variables would be assigned different values if the font were being made for the Xerox 1200 marking engine, which has the same writing resolution of 300 dots per inch as the Canon but very different marking characteristics.

2 What is design?

In order to be able to evaluate METAFONT's usefulness as a typeface design tool, we need to find out what is involved in designing a typeface. Before doing this, it is important to get a clear idea of what the word 'design' implies in this context.

Design, like *font*, is a word whose meaning in the vocabulary of computer science tends to be rather different from the meaning it carries in everyday life. In normal use, at least among designers, *designing* means making something new: in the case of a typeface, a new set of shapes for the characters of a script, that are not the same as any set of shapes for the same characters that have existed before. Used in relation to computer-produced documents, the word often appears to mean more or less exactly the opposite: the design activity seems to be intended to produce something that resembles an existing object or set of objects as closely as possible.

In this paper, I use *adaptation* for the second of these two meanings, and keep *design* for the first. Thus I would consider Computer Modern Roman to be an *adaptation* of the Lanston Monotype Company's Modern Series 8A (Knuth, 1980, p. 2), and the letters in the METAFONT logo to be an original *design*.

The important difference between design and adaptation, in the context of a discussion about type production, is that in the second case the typeface already exists: the adapter does not have to decide what shapes the characters ought to be. Nor is this all: character images exist as well, that arise from fonts that have been fully developed to be technically satisfactory, even if for use in another medium. The results of all the decision-taking that went into the design of the original typeface and the production of the original fonts are available in the material from which the adapter works. It is not surprising that both the nature and the amount of the work involved in type design and font production is misapprehended, if the difference between design and adaptation is misunderstood.

3 Designing a typeface

The end product of type manufacture is a series of fonts.

To be worth making, these fonts must be of good technical quality – that is, they must give rise to sets of character images that are of good technical quality. To be useful, the fonts must give rise to character images that realize the visual attributes of a particular typeface. The type manufacturing process thus has two parts: one in which the visual attributes of the typeface are decided upon, and another in which the fonts that cause these attributes to be realized in character images are produced. What goes on in the first part of the process is *type design*; what goes on in the second part is *font production*.

In traditional type manufacture (which means, in the context of the current discussion, in the era before METAFONT), these two parts of the manufacturing process have usually been the responsibilities of different people. The *type designer* defines the visual attributes the typeface is to have; the *font producer* makes fonts that give rise to character images whose graphic attributes gives them an appearance that realizes the visual attributes of the typeface.

3.1 Type designer and font producer

It is the type designer's task to decide on the appearance of the typeface, and to characterize its appearance by defining its visual attributes. The designer's decisions are almost always expressed in the form of drawings of characters, whose shapes realize the visual attributes the typeface is intended to have.

It is very important to understand the role that the designer's drawings play in the type production process. Except in a very few cases, they are not *patterns* that tell the font producer what shapes the character images ought to *be*: they are *models* that show the producer what the images are intended to *look like*.

This is because the font producer does more than copy the designer's drawings. The font producer's objective is to make fonts that give rise to images of good technical quality that realize the visual attributes of the characters on the designer's drawings. The instructions contained in the font have to take into account the effects of the human visual system on the way the character images are perceived, as well as the effects of the marking process on the shapes of the images themselves.

The effects of the visual system

It is easy to state the criteria for good technical quality in a set of character images: they should be consistent in apparent size, weight and spacing. This consistency is in the *appearance* of the images, not necessarily in their *shape*; in order to appear to be consistent, the actual shapes of the images should allow for the visual effects that occur when they are perceived.

The essential feature of the character images in text is that they are small: one way of looking at the history of type manufacture is to see it as the development of techniques for the rapid multiplication of accurately-defined small shapes. In the perception of small shapes, the human visual system has an effect on what is perceived that is quite different from the effect it has in the perception of large shapes: adjacent parts of a small shape interact with each other on their way through the system. Thus, for example, a square looks larger than a circle whose diameter is the same as the side of the square; parallel-sided strokes that meet at an acute angle look as if they get wider as they approach each other. The effects of these visual phenomena on the perception of small character shapes are discussed by Harry Carter (in footnotes in his edition of Fournier's *Manuel typographique* as well as in his 1937 paper) and by T. L. De Vinne (Carter, 1930, 1937; De Vinne, 1900).

The effects of the marking process

It often seems to be supposed that the effects of the marking process ceased to be important when digital type-composing techniques were introduced. This is far from being the case. One has only to compare output from the Canon CX-2000 and the Xerox 1200 electrographic marking engines, already mentioned, to see how much the differences in present-day marking processes can affect the shapes of the character images they produce. The simple picture that Knuth described in his Gibbs lecture in 1978, of the page of a book as 'a huge matrix of 0's and 1's' (Knuth, 1979: *Mathematical typography*, p.16), omits an important consideration: neighbouring 1's interact with each other, on the physical as well as on the perceptual level[4].

---

[4] Knuth has subsequently advanced from this elementary view (Knuth, 1985).

The font producer's task

Because the marking process has an effect on the shapes of the character images the font gives rise to, the shapes of the images are different from the shapes that are represented in the font. Equally, because they have to take into account the effects of the human visual system, the shapes of the character images (and, *a fortiori*, the shapes represented in the font) are not the same as the shapes of the characters on the designer's drawings. Because the effects that enter into the perception of small and large shapes are different, large shapes change their appearance when they are reduced: a small shape that has the same visual attributes as a large shape will not be simply a smaller version of it. Thus the production of technically satisfactory fonts involves the font producer in *interpreting* the designer's drawings, rather than simply *reproducing* them; and because different marking processes affect the shapes of character images in different ways, this interpretation has to be done differently for each marking process for which fonts are being produced.

The designer's drawings

The shapes on the drawings that the designer gives to the font producer are not made in a single pass, but are themselves the subject of considerable development work (Dwiggins, 1940). It is not until they are consistent in appearance, and express a clear intention on the part of the designer, that the designer's drawings are useful to the producer. (The kind of problems that arise when drawings are given to the font producer before this clarity of intention has been achieved are vividly described in John Dreyfus' account of the production of the Cranach Press italic: Dreyfus, 1966).

In the past, the typeface character shapes on the drawings have been developed empirically, by a process that is also an essential part of font production: iterative testing and modification. Since the shapes are modified by working over them by hand, and the testing usually done in the early stages by putting the drawings up on the wall and looking at them, the designer's activity tends not to look like a process in the usual sense of the word; consequently, the fact that it *is* a process, with certain characteristics that are important in making it effective, is easy to overlook. These characteristics are a high degree of interactivity in the modification phase, and a short cycle time in the testing phase.

3.2 The importance of empirical testing in type manufacture

The knowledge that type designers and font producers have had, both about the effects of marking processes and the characteristics of the human visual system, has mostly been intuitive and qualitative rather than explicit and quantitative. Even though the ways in which marking processes affect the shapes of character images are fairly easy to understand, the extent to which a particular process will affect the shape of a particular image is very hard to predict. Similarly, the kinds of visual effect that occur in the perception of character images are well known, but the way in which they will affect the appearance of a particular shape is difficult to tell without making the shape and looking at it. The development of technically satisfactory fonts for a new typeface, like the development of the designer's drawings, has therefore traditionally been carried out by iterative modification of the font and empirical testing of the character images it produces; and what is tested is essentially the appearance of the images rather than their shapes.

It needs to be made clear, perhaps especially to an audience from the computer science community, that the empirical nature of the type manufacturers' working methods is not due to technical backwardness, or to an anti-technological attitude, on their part. The fact is that not enough is yet known about the human visual system to enable us to construct a theory that will predict exactly, from the shape of a character image, what its appearance will be. Nor is our knowledge of the characteristics of any marking process sufficiently detailed to allow us to predict exactly what shape a particular set of instructions in a font will give rise to. In these circumstances, empirical methods are the only ones that are effective for font development, if the visual quality of the product is to be maintained.

3.3 What does a type manufacturing system need?

The picture we get of type design and font production in the pre-METAFONT era, then, is one in which the subject-matter of the work is the appearance of character images; where communication between designer and producer is carried on by means of exchanges of graphic objects; and in which the desired appearance of both drawings and character images is arrived at by empirical testing and modification, using processes that are at their best when they are most interactive[5].

Since this picture is so unlike the one that METAFONT offers us, we need to ask which of its features are essential to a successful type manufacturing system: that is, one that produces fonts of good technical quality that give rise to character images having the required appearance. It is hard to answer this question by looking at unsuccessful type manufacturing systems from the past, because such systems have not usually survived or been described in published work[6].

What we can say is that type manufacturing systems have produced good results, and have been congenial to the designers working with them, to the extent that the designers have felt themselves to be in control of the appearance of the character images that were the final product of the system. The reservations expressed by the Dutch designer Jan van Krimpen about the success of his work for the

[5] A more extensive justification of this picture is in Section 3 of *Designing new typefaces with METAFONT* (Southall, *op. cit.*).

[6] Oddly enough, the situation with unsuccessful type-composing systems is quite different: these have an extensive and easily accessible literature.

Monotype Corporation are significant in this respect (van Krimpen, 1972). In this respect, too, it is interesting that recently, where electronic systems have allowed designers to work directly on the pixel grid (that is, in our terms, to be their own font producers), the designers have grasped the opportunity with enthusiasm. Examples of the success of this working method are the fonts used for telephone directory composition in France and the United States of America, designed by Ladislas Mandel and Matthew Carter respectively (Cooper Union, 1982).

4 METAFONT as a design tool

4.1 Making type with METAFONT

In a type manufacturing system that uses METAFONT, the shapes of characters are described by programs written in the METAFONT language. The METAFONT interpreter reads these programs and produces a 'generic font file': this is essentially a set of run-length encoded descriptions of character bitmaps at a particular resolution. For each run, the interpreter needs to know the writing resolution of the device for which the output of the run is intended, as well as other information about the device: it finds this out by reading preloaded `mode` information. Fonts are made from the generic font files by the `gftopxl` or `gftopk` programs, which are part of the 'METAFONTware' software.

Knuth's view of his objectives for the METAFONT system seems to have remained essentially unchanged between 1978 and 1985. 'One of my main motivations was the knowledge that the problem would be solved once for all, if I could find a purely mathematical way to define the letter shapes and convert them to discrete raster patterns ... although the precision of the raster may change, the letter shapes can stay the same forever, once they are defined in a machine-independent form' (Knuth, 1979: *Mathematical typography*, p. 17). 'We now have the ability to give a completely precise definition of letter shapes that will produce essentially equivalent results on all raster-based machines' (Knuth, 1986, p. v). The new implementation of METAFONT has solved most of the rasterizing problems that troubled the old system: the technical quality of the new Computer Modern on medium and low resolution marking devices is enormously improved.

In making Computer Modern, METAFONT is playing the role of font producer. Each size of each typeface in the Computer Modern family has a driver program (`cmr10.mf`, for example). This program sets the values of a large number of dimensional parameters for the typeface, and then reads a series of programs (`roman.mf`, `romanu.mf`, `romanl.mf` and so on) that describe the character shapes in terms of the parameters that have been set by the driver program.

This is where the 'meta-ness' comes in: the same programs, read by different driver files, produce characters of very different appearance (from five point roman to **ten point sanserif bold extended**, `typewriter face` and so on) according to the settings of the parameters.

There are a few parameters (`blacker`, `fillin` and `o_correction`) that go some way towards characterizing the marking process used by the marking engine for which the font is intended. The values for these parameters are part of the `mode` information that is read at the beginning of the run.

Knuth does not exclude the possibility of interactive modification of the fonts that METAFONT produces, but sees this only as a 'tidying-up' expedient (Knuth, 1986, p. 195).

4.2 Designing with METAFONT

Knuth's Computer Modern is an example, extraordinarily fully worked out, of the adaptation of a set of existing typeface designs to the METAFONT system. Designs that have been produced with the old version of METAFONT by other workers (Tom Hickey's CHEL, for example, or Georgia Tobin's MF Roman) are also adaptations. To find out about METAFONT's useability as a design tool, we need to find instances of its use for original design.

The designer working with METAFONT has two options. One is to make a set of fully-developed drawings of character shapes in the traditional way; write programs, or cause programs to be written, that describe the shapes on the drawings; and then alter the programs or cause them to be altered until the output they produce is acceptable. While not being exactly the same as the adaptation of an existing design (because fonts derived from the drawings do not yet exist) this way of working is something of a halfway house between design and adaptation. The task of the programmer, or of the designer in the programming phase of the work, is to express in METAFONT's terms the character shapes that already exist on a set of drawings, rather than to develop the shapes using METAFONT itself.

The second option before the designer working with METAFONT is to exploit the characteristics of the system: to use METAFONT itself to help develop the character shapes.

The Euler project

The first of these two options is the one that Hermann Zapf adopted in his design of the Euler typeface for the American Mathematical Society. Zapf made the drawings, and the Digital Typography Group at Stanford wrote the METAFONT programs. In the Euler project, Zapf was treating the Digital Typography Group as a font production team of the traditional kind; the problem that faced the programmers in the group was essentially to teach METAFONT how to do a competent job in its role as font producer.

This turned out not to be particularly easy. The new version of the language had not been conceived when the Euler project began, and the initial phase of describing the character shapes on Zapf's drawings in terms of the virtual pens of the old METAFONT presented great difficulties. The results of the first attempts were rejected by the designer; a program was then developed that allowed the characters' outlines to be described to the computer by means of a digitizing tablet. Writing such a program was a great deal more difficult with the old METAFONT than it would have been with the new, because of the change of emphasis from pen tracks to character outlines in the new version.

The story of the Euler project is told by David Siegel, a member of the Digital Typography Group (Siegel, 1985).

The nmt design

In making the nmt design with METAFONT, I decided to take the second of the two options described above, and work as closely as possible with the computer. This was partly due to the fact that I had just come from using a computer-based font design tool that had many of the virtues (in speed and interactivity) and all the defects (in terms of the lack of generality of the product) of font design systems in general; partly because the studio facilities that would have been needed to make fully-developed character drawings were not easily available in the Computer Science Department at Stanford.

The design was begun in November 1983, using the old version of METAFONT. This early work was abandoned in February 1984; the overall form that the new version of the language would have was becoming clear by that time, and there was evidently no point in struggling to define the outlines of character shapes by means of the tracks of virtual pens whose centres were offset from the outlines, when it would soon be possible to define the outlines directly.

Work on the design was begun again in the summer of 1984, during the METAFONT course at Stanford (Knuth, 1984); suspended between September 1984 and April 1985, while I was in Europe; continued, with a very much developed version of the language, between April and October 1985 at Stanford, and then at Strasbourg until the beginning of June 1986.

It can be seen from this chronology that nmt and the new version of METAFONT have grown up together. This has had its disadvantages. Getting on with the design has tended to take priority over updating the low-level METAFONT routines in the character programs to take advantage of improvements to the language. The consequence is that my programs, on the whole, neglect facilities that have been added to the language and to `plain.mf` since the beginning of August 1985. (It was not until the beginning of June 1986 that version 1.0 of METAFONT was installed at Strasbourg.)

abcdefghijlmnopqrstuvw
nanbncndnenfngnhninjnlnmnnnonpnqnrnsntnunvnwn
oaobocodoeofogohoiojolomonooopoqorosotouovowo
hamburgefons

abcdefghijlmnopqrstuvw
nanbncndnenfngnhninjnlnmnnnonpnqnrnsntnunvnwn
oaobocodoeofogohoiojolomonooopoqorosotouovowo
hamburgefons

abcdefghijlmnopqrstuvw
nanbncndnenfngnhninjnlnmnnnonpnqnrnsntnunvnwn
oaobocodoeofogohoiojolomonooopoqorosotouovowo
hamburgefons

abcdefghijlmnopqrstuvw
nanbncndnenfngnhninjnlnmnnnonpnqnrnsntnunvnwn
oaobocodoeofogohoiojolomonooopoqorosotouovowo
hamburgefons

abcdefghijlmnopqrstuvw
nanbncndnenfngnhninjnlnmnnnonpnqnrnsntnunvnwn
oaobocodoeofogohoiojolomonooopoqorosotouovowo
hamburgefons

abcdefghijlmnopqrstuvw
nanbncndnenfngnhninjnlnmnnnonpnqnrnsntnunvnwn
oaobocodoeofogohoiojolomonooopoqorosotouovowo
hamburgefons

abcdefghijlmnopqrstuvw
nanbncndnenfngnhninjnlnmnnnonpnqnrnsntnunvnwn
oaobocodoeofogohoiojolomonooopoqorosotouovowo
hamburgefons

abcdefghijlmnopqrstuvw
nanbncndnenfngnhninjnlnmnnnonpnqnrnsntnunvnwn
oaobocodoeofogohoiojolomonooopoqorosotouovowo
hamburgefons

Figure 1: nml *in nominal sizes from 8 to 10 pt, reduced from* `\magstep2`.

It should also be pointed out that the nmt programs do not use the pseudo-pens of new METAFONT. Some of the problems I had with getting the stroke-drawing routines to behave well at low resolution would probably have been avoided if I had used these pens; on the other hand, I cannot see at present how to use them to make what I consider to be technically important features of certain characters, particularly small v and w.

The main motive behind the development of nmt has been to make METAFONT do as good a job as possible of font production for actual marking devices. There are two main reasons for this. In the first place, the technical quality of the Computer Modern fonts that were available for medium-resolution devices in 1983, when I began work on the design, left a great deal to be desired. I felt it was important to find out whether it was possible to make a technically satisfactory medium-resolution font with METAFONT, since no-one had succeeded in doing so at that time.

In the second place, I felt that a type design method that was aimed at an ideal marking device ran the risk of giving every user of a real marking device more or less of a bad deal. It seemed to me that the interests of users, in particular those of users of medium-resolution marking devices, were being neglected in favour of an approach to design that ignored the characteristics of marking processes that did exist while aiming at an ideal process that did not exist.

I have also taken the view that one should not impose too high a lower limit on the writing resolution of the devices for which a design is intended. The resolution of a 'high-performance' cathode-ray tube display, in terms of the number of addressable points along the line, is after all no more than that of an Epson FX80 printer in graphics mode. What characters there are in nmt perform reasonably well down to 7 pixels x-height: this corresponds to a nominal size of 2.88 pt or 1.012 mm on the Canon printer, and 5.78 pt or 2.031 mm on the Numelec bitmap terminal.

4.3 Font optimization and 'device-independent' design

In making a technically satisfactory font for a medium-resolution raster-scan marking device, every feature of the character shapes has to be conceived of in terms of the characteristics of the marking process the device uses and the size and shape of the the pixels it produces. The device's pixels are used as building blocks for the character shapes.

With this approach, it is relatively easy to achieve the evenness of apparent weight and spacing of the character images that are important in a technically satisfactory design. On the other hand, though, the character widths become completely device-dependent: there is no device-independent '`tfm` width' that expresses the width of a character in absolute terms.

It is hard to see how device-independent widths for the characters of an original design can be arrived at, if the objective in making the design is to optimize the performance of the fonts it produces. In `plain.mf`, the `beginchar` macro expects the device-independent width and height of a character to be known at the beginning of the program that describes it (Knuth, 1986, p. 275). This seems to me to reflect the conceptual confusion between adaptation and design that I have already mentioned. In adapting an existing typeface, the absolute dimensions of the characters are indeed known before the adaptation is begun, and there is no problem in incorporating them in the programs. In making an original design, on the other hand, where the objective is to optimize font performance, the only way to develop the character shapes is to look at the marks made by particular marking devices. In doing this, it is difficult to describe the characters' dimensions otherwise than in terms of the dimensional units that those devices use. The dimensions of each character become consequences of the way the character is constructed for the marking device in question, and hence are not known at the beginning of the character program.

The question whether or not it is possible to make technically satisfactory fonts for use on medium-resolution devices from designs whose character widths are defined in device-independent terms is an interesting one for the TeX community. The design of every such font has to begin with the definition of a set of device-dependent widths for the characters of the typeface. These widths need to be allocated in such a way that the cumulated differences in character positioning with respect to the device-independent widths amount, over the length of an average word, to less than about a quarter of the average interword space. If this can be done, the characters within a word can be properly spaced without the interword spacing becoming too irregular.

The difficulty is, of course, that both the length of the average word and its composition, in terms of the frequencies of occurrence of different characters, vary between one language and another. A set of character width allocations that produce good results in French text will not work so well in English or in German text. In the German text, also, because the words tend to be longer, the cumulated differences in character positioning will be greater and there will be fewer interword spaces to absorb them.

I cannot see any way out of this difficulty at present.

4.4 Meta-ness in nmt

In the Computer Modern family of typefaces, the specification of each size of each typeface in the family begins with the assignment of explicit values, most of them absolute dimensions, to a large number of variables in the character programs (sixty-two in `cmr10.mf`). This approach is entirely appropriate for a situation of

he eighteenth centur was also something more it was and
above all in rance the nurser of the modern world deas
and social forces the seeds of which were doubtless sown much
earlier can be seen now pushing above the surface not in the
neatl arranged rows of the careful gardener but in the haphaard
tangle of nature et the can be seen and distinguished the
field is no longer a seedbed but it is not et a jungle and a
pattern is discernible

he eighteenth centur was also something more it was and
above all in rance the nurser of the modern world deas
and social forces the seeds of which were doubtless sown much
earlier can be seen now pushing above the surface not in the
neatl arranged rows of the careful gardener but in the haphaard
tangle of nature et the can be seen and distinguished the
field is no longer a seedbed but it is not et a jungle and a
pattern is discernible

he eighteenth centur was also something more it was and
above all in rance the nurser of the modern world deas
and social forces the seeds of which were doubtless sown much
earlier can be seen now pushing above the surface not in the
neatl arranged rows of the careful gardener but in the haphaard
tangle of nature et the can be seen and distinguished the
field is no longer a seedbed but it is not et a jungle and a
pattern is discernible

he eighteenth centur was also something more it was and
above all in rance the nurser of the modern world deas
and social forces the seeds of which were doubtless sown much
earlier can be seen now pushing above the surface not in the
neatl arranged rows of the careful gardener but in the haphaard
tangle of nature et the can be seen and distinguished the
field is no longer a seedbed but it is not et a jungle and a
pattern is discernible

Figure 2: nmt *in 4, 5, 6 and 7 pt, reduced from* `\magstep2`. *The change in 'colour' between the 4 and 5 pt fonts is marked: between 5 and 6 pt or 6 and 7 pt less marked, but still visible.*

a posteriori meta-design, in which the appearance of a large number of existing fonts is to be matched by the output from a single set of METAFONT programs.

I have expressed elsewhere my reservations about the practicability of original meta-design (Southall, 1985a, 1985b). Further experience with nmt has given me little reason to modify my earlier views. The problem is still one of defining, and then testing, the relationships between the parameters that operate at the character level to change the shapes of character images and the typeface-wide parameters that affect the size or the appearance of the typeface.

The nmt programs have three parameters: size, boldness and expansion (the two latter as yet more or less untested). These parameters are intended to be continuously variable between limits. Thus, for example, users can set any character size they like, between upper and lower limits that depend on the writing resolution of the eventual marking device, in increments that likewise depend only on the device resolution. The sort of problems that this approach gives rise to, and that remain to be resolved, are demonstrated by the abrupt steps in typographic 'colour' that occur in the small sizes of nmt when the vertical stroke weight changes by one pixel.

The fact that defects of this kind have survived so long into the development of the design provides a further illustration of my contention about the impracticability of original meta-design. The design of every font involves the designer in a great number of decisions. With METAFONT, these decisions cannot be made and implemented visually, as they can with a font design tool, but have to be incorporated into the character programs. Because there is no theory that allows the correctness or otherwise of such decisions to be predicted in advance of seeing their results, each of the programs that embodies them has to be tested, by the production of actual fonts, over the whole range of parameter settings for the design, for each device for which the design is intended.

Because METAFONT provides no simple way of adding new character shape specifications to an existing font, the whole set of character programs has to be reprocessed every time the effects of a change to one of them need to be assessed. This makes the process of font testing a great deal more time-consuming than it might be.

4.5 METAFONT as a tool for original design

The system described in *The METAFONTbook*, and implemented by METAFONT and the present version of `plain.mf`, embodies a particular model of the type design process. In this model, a set of character shapes are described by METAFONT programs. Character dimensions are expressed in these programs in device-independent units of measurement. Font intermediates (the `.gf` files) are produced by processing the character programs with the METAFONT interpreter, which is given information about the marking device for which the fonts are intended.

The technical quality of the character images the fonts give rise to is assured by correct programming, using the facilities the METAFONT language provides for positioning important parts of characters correctly on the pixel grid.

This model seems to me to reflect a situation like the one that obtained with Computer Modern or Euler, in which fully-developed character shape definitions already existed when the work of METAFONT programming was started. As a model for a process of original design, in which the designer develops a series of technically satisfactory fonts by writing METAFONT programs, it has two serious drawbacks.

The first of these is that the separate problems of defining the typeface character shapes and developing the METAFONT programs that describe them are confounded. It cannot be too strongly emphasised that at the beginning of a design the designer *does not know* what shapes the characters are going to be. The designer necessarily has a clear idea of the appearance of the intended typeface: what is not known is the details of the character shapes that will cause that appearance to be realized. Finding this out, by making sketches, is the first stage in making the design. It is difficult to write a program to describe a shape, if one does not know exactly what that shape is.

The approach to this problem that *The METAFONTbook* seems to recommend is to write a program that produces a shape whose overall features are more or less correct, and then modify the program until the shape it produces is the right one. The difficulty with this approach is that it removes from the shape-development process what to the designer is its most important feature: direct interaction with the shape itself. As Charles Bigelow has said[7] '... the designer thinks with images, not about images'.

The second serious drawback of *The METAFONTbook*'s model of the design process is that it assumes that the technical quality of the fonts the character programs produce can be assured by correct programming. I have argued in section 3.2 above that the theoretical knowledge required to ensure the correctness of the character programs in this respect is not yet available. In the absence of such knowledge, the programs have to be developed by iterative testing and modification. The testing is done by using the programs to make fonts, and looking at the character images the fonts give rise to: as I have suggested, the way the present METAFONT system is configured makes this process a great deal more difficult than it need be. It consequently suffers, even more than the process by which the character shapes are developed, from a lack of the responsiveness that is important to its success.

[7] In an internal discussion paper written for the Digital Typography Group at Stanford in late 1983.

Designer-programmer collaboration in METAFONT design

Knuth suggests that designers and programmers should collaborate in making typefaces with METAFONT (Knuth, 1986, p. v). While perhaps being practicable when programs are being written to describe existing character shapes (though the history of the Euler project suggests some of the possible pitfalls) this approach leaves out of account the fact that in original design work the designer does not know at the time the work is started what shapes the characters should be. The first stage in making a new design is sketching: the responsiveness of the sketching tool to the designer's thoughts, already seriously prejudiced in METAFONT design by the need for shapes to be described as programs, would be further vitiated if the characteristics of the shapes in the sketches had to be explained to another person.

5 Conclusion: font design and the computer science community

In traditional type manufacture, right up to the present day, every advance in marking technology has been followed by the production of new fonts that optimize the rendering of existing typeface designs with the new techniques. This continual revision of their production processes involves the type manufacturers in huge amounts of work. They are obliged to undertake it, because the maintenance of technical quality is the only way to ensure a continued market for their products: bad type won't sell.

The attitude of the computer science community to developments in marking technology is epitomised by Knuth's statement that 'We now have the ability to give a completely precise definition of letter shapes that will produce essentially equivalent results on all raster-based machines' (Knuth, 1986, p. v) and to font design by Eliyezer Kohen's comments in the introduction to his description of the Picor type design system: 'The systems for this purpose are ... too tedious (bitmap editing takes a lot of time)' (Kohen, 1985).

Because of the idealist attitude towards real marking processes expressed in Knuth's statement, consideration of the problems of font design is out of the main current of computer-science thinking: the consequence is that no good computer-based font design tools have yet been built[8]. This in turn has the consequence that the community's attitude towards font design constitutes a self-fulfilling prophecy: it *is* too tedious, because no tools have been built to make it easier, because it is too tedious.

[8] Picor is intended to be a *type* design system, not a *font* design system. The outline description stage that Picor implements is followed by a bitmap editing stage.

In this respect, the approach that the computer science community adopts to the problem of producing fonts (and hence documents) of good technical quality is exactly opposite to the approach adopted by experienced type designers. The designers' approach is exemplified by Hermann Zapf's remarks at the 1983 working seminar of the Association Typographique Internationale at Stanford: 'Today offset printing and electrostatic processes offer some new possibilities in the transfer of letterforms to paper and may automatically require new design solutions. Digitized alphabets therefore should be designed for the bitmap' (Zapf, 1985).

One has to say that the consequence of this difference in views is evident in the appearance of documents produced by computer-based systems. To acknowledge that such documents are much better than they used to be is not to say that they are as good as they should be. The objective of workers in the field should be to produce results with the new technology that are equivalent in quality to those the old technology produced as a matter of course.

References

Carter, H. G.
Fournier on punchcutting: the text of the Manuel Typographique
London: Soncino Press, 1930; New York: Burt Franklin, 1970

—
The optical scale in typefounding
Typography, no. 4, pp. 2–6 (1937)

Matthew Carter: Bell Centennial (Type and technology monograph no. 1)
New York: Cooper Union, 1982

de Vinne, T. L.
Plain printing types
New York: Century, 1900

DIN 16 518
Klassifikation der Schriften
Berlin: Deutschen Normenausschuß, 1964

Dreyfus, J.
Italic quartet
Cambridge: Cambridge University Press (privately printed), 1966

Dwiggins, W.A.
WAD to RR: a letter about designing type
Cambridge, Mass.: Harvard College Library, 1940

Knuth, D. E.
TEX and METAFONT: new directions in typesetting
Bedford, Mass.: Digital, 1979

—

The Computer Modern family of typefaces
Stanford Computer Science Department report STAN-CS-80-780 (1980)

—

A Course on METAFONT Programming
TUGboat, vol. 5 no. 2, pp. 105–118 (1984)

—

Lessons learned from METAFONT
Visible Language, vol. 19 no. 1, pp. 35–53 (1985)

—

The METAFONTbook
Reading, Mass.: Addison-Wesley, 1986

Kohen, E.
An interactive method for middle resolution font design on personal workstations
in Bucci, G., and Valle, G. (eds.), *Computing 85: a broad perspective of current developments.* Amsterdam: North-Holland, 1985

Siegel, D.
The Euler project at Stanford
Stanford, Ca.: Stanford University Department of Computer Science, 1985

Southall, R.
Metafont and the problems of type design
in André, J., and Sallio, P. (eds.), *Typographie et informatique: support du cours INRIA, Rennes, 21–25 Janvier 1985.* Rocquencourt: INRIA, 1985

—

Designing new typefaces with Metafont
Stanford Computer Science Department report STAN-CS-85-1074 (1985)

van Krimpen, J.
A letter to Philip Hofer on certain problems connected with the mechanical cutting of punches
Cambridge, Mass.: Harvard College Library, 1972

Zapf, H.
Future tendencies in type design
Visible Language, vol. 19 no. 1, pp. 23–33 (1985)

"Verheißung und Versprechen"
A THIRD GENERATION APPROACH TO THEOLOGICAL TYPESETTING

Reinhard WONNEBERGER
Alttestamentliches Seminar
Universität Hamburg
2000 Hamburg, FRG

Abstract

The process of producing the monograph "Verheißung und Versprechen" is described both in its relation to previous techniques and as an example for present possibilities. We describe how to produce Greek and Hebrew by means of TEX, say a few words about Gothic and Fraktur, and discuss automatic translation from SCRIPT *into* LATEX. *Indexing using* SCRIPT *is described and leads to a more general discussion of the indexing problem and the rôle of symbols. Further topics are operating considerations and 'manuscript support'.*

1. Three generations of theological typesetting

When we received the first copies of our book "Verheißung und Versprechen"[1] from the publishers, a rather adventurous story of theological text processing and typesetting was closed, part of which shall be discussed here.[2]

To typeset books in theology, and especially books dealing with questions of Biblical exegesis, one usually needs *Greek* and *Hebrew*. If medieval authors are quoted in German, one should also like to have *Gothic*; and uppercase *Fraktur* letters will be needed to deal with textual criticism. These parts of the text often contain entries for the *index*, and other index problems are posed by the conventional sequence of biblical books, which is by no means alphabetical.

In addition to quotations from accented languages like French and languages with special characters, like Scandinavian ones, there are also a few peculiarities in style, such as in-text lists[3] and the abundant use of footnotes to give source

---

[1] R. W. / Hans Peter Hecht: Verheißung und Versprechen. Eine theologische und sprachanalytische Klärung. Göttingen: Vandenhoeck & Ruprecht 1986. xvi, 273 Seiten. ISBN 3-525-60367-3.

[2] The work presented here was mainly done at DESY, *Notkestr.85, D 2000 Hamburg 54, FRG*, and I should like to express my gratitude to this institution and its representatives who helped me in many ways.

[3] Stream lists and related list types for LATEX. TUGboat — The TEX Users Group Newsletter. (Providence, Rhode Island, USA) 6 (1985/3) 156-57. Incidentally, Donald Knuth's description of the WEB system starts with such a list; see also examples in the later parts of this text.

information and side discussions that will often require indexing.[4] While these problems remain unchanged, the solutions offered in electronic data processing have changed a good deal in the last decade.

When my first monograph was published in 1979,[5] I still worked with my own typesetting program SCRIPTOR,[6] written in PL/1, which in its early days read a text and a correction stream of punched cards, and then punched a new text from them, all in uppercase letters, of course. Later on it was extended to handle lowercase and even Greek, and the final output was done on a chain printer. When it came to the final printout, the operator was somewhat puzzled by the request to print twice on the same paper, once with a Latin, and once with a Greek chain. While most features of this program are outdated now, its coding and decoding of Greek is something still of interest, and we shall come back to it in our discussion of Tbl. 2.

The next generation of theological typesetting is represented by my manual on textual criticism,[7] which was produced with SCRIPT Release 2.[8] The problems posed by this book are basically of two kinds: actual typesetting and *document support.*[9] Since it was going to appear in English as well as in German, one of the *document support* problems was to keep the two versions consistent. Conditional processing enabled us to create a single source, containing three layers of material: German, English, and common text, e.g. the Latin symbols and sigla of textual criticism and bibliographic references that remain the same for both editions. This policy also helped with the process of translation. Half a screen of German text was duplicated as a template for English, and while overtyping this text with the translation, the translator could still see the German original. The many cross references between different parts of the book could not easily have been handled manually, and producing the index was rather sophisticated. Expressions from BHS were to be separated from normal keywords and entered differently for upper and lower case first letter, while normal indexing should mix both cases. Biblical books were to appear in their conventional sequence, and chapter and verse numbers were to be sorted according to their numerical order.

As to the typesetting problems, in addition to Greek and Fraktur, Hebrew

---

4 Experts will notice that footnote numbers stay within the height of the notes, while they don't in the text, and that they are preceded and followed by constant space instead of being placed left of some tabbing position.

5 Syntax und Exegese. Eine generative Theorie der griechischen Syntax und ihr Beitrag zur Auslegung des Neuen Testamentes, dargestellt an 2.Korinther 5,2f und Römer 3,21-26. Beiträge zur Exegese und Theologie 13. Frankfurt / Bern / Las Vegas: Lang 1979.

6 Scriptor. Ein Text-Editions-System. Heidelberg: Rechenzentrums der Universität. Skriptum 1976.

7 Understanding BHS. A Manual for the Users of Biblia Hebraica Stuttgartensia. *Subsidia Biblica 8. Rome* 1984. — Leitfaden zur Biblia Hebraica Stuttgartensia. *Göttingen Vandenhoeck & Ruprecht* 1984.

8 International Business Machines Corporation (ed.) Document Composition Facility: User's Guide Program Product (Program Number 5748-XX9 IBM Publication SH20-9161-1) 2nd edition April 1980.

9 'Document support' refers to automatic services like numbering headings, lists, notes, etc., providing tables of content, figures, tables etc., cross referencing, indexing, conditional processing and the like.

was also required. These problems could only be mastered with the aid of two programs by *P. K. Schilling*. CALLIGRA will produce vector fonts, in our case the so-called *Hershey* fonts, on a matrix plotter, and EDITF helps with drawing new fonts, like Hebrew.[10] It should be noted for the discussion to come, that the reverting algorithm for Hebrew was built into CALLIGRA, so that the only task left to SCRIPT was to mark the Hebrew parts of text for later inspection by CALLIGRA.

When TEX[11] became available at DESY in 1984,[12] its outstanding typesetting qualities were tempting, and there was also a fascinating algorithmic approach to some of the problems well known to anybody dealing with text processing.[13] On the other hand, there was not much *document support*, and all the special features that we had developed for theological typesetting were not available. This situation improved with the appearance of LATEX,[14] which contains features similar to GML, the G[eneral] M[arkup] L[anguage] implemented in SCRIPT.[15]

At that time my friend, *Hans Peter Hecht*, and I had done a lot of work exploring the links between *Speech-Act-Theory* and theology, when preparing the book we later called "Verheißung und Versprechen", a book that we wanted to be both scientific and attractive, in short a true pleasure to *read*. So it was quite tempting to express this intention through fine typesetting.

When Temptation approached us in the disguise of TEX, we had already worked hard to put our manuscripts into the computer. Though some of our students helped us in typing, a lot of editing was needed to achieve an acceptable manuscript. I suppose that this decision cost us a lot of time instead of saving it, but, on the other hand, I am convinced that the book would otherwise never have surpassed the state of informal papers. Considering that the book was changed up to the very last moment, before the camera ready copies came off the laser plotter, the decisive gain seems to have been better control over the text. Sometimes, the author is also inspired to develop new features both in style and content. So we used the possibility of floating material to bring independent examples, like a scattered florilegium.

---

10 Details are discussed in my contribution: L'exégèse biblique et l'ordinateur. *Actes du Congrès international informatique et sciences humaines. Liège 18-19-20-21 novembre 1981. (Louis Delatte, ed.). Liège: Laboratoire d'Analyse Statistique des Langes Anciennes* (1983).

11 Donald E. Knuth: The TeXbook. Reading, Massachusetts / Menlo Park, California / London / Amsterdam / Don Mills, Ontario / Sydney: Addison-Wesley. 1984.

12 A survey of the first books printed with TEX is given in: Donald E. Knuth: TeX Incunabula. TUGboat 5 (1984/1) 4-11.

13 See the interview: G. Michael Vose / Gregg Williams (eds.): Computer Science Considerations. Donald Knuth speaks on his involvement with digital typography. Byte 11 (1986/2) 169-172.

14 Rf. Leslie Lamport: LaTeX. A Document Preparation System. Reading, Massachusetts / ... / Amsterdam / Don Mills, Ontario / Sydney / ...: Addison-Wesley. 1985.

15 See Charles F. Goldfarb: A generalized approach to Document Markup. Albert Endres / Jürgen Reetz (eds.): Textverarbeitung und Bürosysteme. IBM-Informatik-Symposion 1981, Bad Neuenahr. Fachberichte und Referate 13. München / Wien: Oldenbourg 1982. P.153-162.

To quote *Oscar Wilde:* "I can resist everything except temptation", and so we decided to move our manuscript from a perfectly working and trustworthy system to an incomplete system full of "dangerous bends". The first step was to write an automatic translation from SCRIPT into LaTeX. For obvious reasons, this had to be done in SCRIPT, and so it need not concern us here. Generally, a manuscript can be run without errors after translation, and manual changes are only required to incorporate new features. In the following sections we shall discuss the main components that were built to fulfil our requirements for theological typesetting in TeX and LaTeX.

2. Poor Man's Greek

To typeset Greek text, one needs Greek characters, a mapping to keys, and accentuation. The obvious way to produce Greek would be to have special Greek fonts. As long as no such fonts are generally available, acceptable results can be produced by simulating them in some way by the existing Greek mathematical symbols.

The problems of mapping, however, are of a more general nature.[16] While the mapping relation of Greek characters to Latin keys is obvious in most cases, at least some letters call for a coding convention. The coding of accents is even more difficult, since the second dimension introduced by accents can be handled in different ways.

Since the Greek characters contained in standard TeX are intended for, and used in math mode, it is possible to introduce abbreviations in the following way:

```
\mathcode'a=\alpha
```

and then typeset Greek as math. But interword spacing is ignored, and so this would not be a particularly good way to solve the problem.

A new font may also be defined using an existing one. The following code first gives a new name to an existing math italic font, then repeats the `\fontdimen1..7` parameters for that fontname.

```
\font\grft=ammi10             \fontdimen1\grft=0.25pt
\fontdimen2\grft=3.58pt       \fontdimen3\grft=1.67pt
\fontdimen4\grft=1.11pt       \fontdimen5\grft=4.31pt
\fontdimen6\grft=10.0pt       \fontdimen7\grft=1.11pt
```

Since this method inherits some of the problems of math mode, and also would require different definitions for different font sizes, it was not pursued any further.

Our approach is to typset each character as a piece of math on its own. Though this method may increase the overhead costs, it is most flexible regarding all other

---

16 See Leclercq A. A.: A Note on the Transliteration of New Testament Greek. New Testament Studies 19 (1972/73) 187-90. Transliteration for several languges is discussed in J. Longton: Codage des écritures non-latines. Paper read at the conference "Informatique et Bible", Louvain La-Neuve, Août 1985, see also note 42. For Hebrew see note 19.

aspects. For the time being, we can only use those Greek letters that are available as math characters in TEX and also as math mode control sequences provided by PLAIN.[17]

In the math character set, the normal forms $\epsilon\theta\rho\phi$ are replaced by the variant forms $\varepsilon\vartheta\varrho\varphi$, whereas π is preferred to its variant form ϖ. In the case of *sigma*, ς should be considered as an additional letter, since it is used instead of σ at the end of a word. *Iota subscriptum* is nothing but a smaller ι. From a typesetting point of view, it behaves like an accent, but from a semantic point of view, it is a letter, and it becomes a normal *iota* called *iota adscriptum*, if its vowel is capitalized.

Although lowercase Greek letters in italics might be combined with uppercase straight letters, we preferred italics. They are taken from the `mit` font. A switch to *italic* is done to affect those characters that are not defined separately, like *omikron* and the uppercase letters *ABEZHIKMNOPTX* shared with Latin.

While accents are prefixes in TEX, they are suffixes in our scheme in order to be compatible with our existing texts, which are based on the concept of *zero-width-*characters. 'Zero width' means that these characters are simply overlaid over the previous character without any adjustment (rf. note 8 and note 10). For Hebrew, this requires that letters are shaped in such a way that punctuation will remain visible.

To implement accents coming after their letter, one might take advantage of the fact that accents can only occur in connection with vowels. So vowels might be made active to let them inspect what follows. An example of this technique is the activation of `\prime` in PLAIN ('The TEXbook', p. 357). Unfortunately this would mean to look ahead in vain in the more frequent cases of unaccented vowels and also would involve complicated tests inside the macros. So we decided to accentuate characters *afterwards*. In principle, the TEX philosophy to precede a character with its accent seems to be superior, because an accent might change the width of the accented character. Thus, for Greek words starting with a single uppercase vowel, the accents have to be placed *in front of the letter*, i.e. to its left side.

The TEX method of accenting, using an `\accent` primitive as a prefix to the letter to be accented, would only work with the existing accent characters and therefore not cover all possibilities. So we had no choice but to simulate accenting by explicit graphic movements. From a graphic point of view, this task is made difficult in two respects: first, vowels differ in width, second, the bending of italic letters would require some trigonometric calculations, a problem we solved by ignoring it. To obtain at least some symmetry, however, we made the vowels pass their width to an accent macro that might follow.

Accents like *acutus* or *gravis* are already provided by TEX. The *spiritūs* are, in some common fonts, represented as right and left quotes (' ') for *lenis* and *asper*,

---

[17] Rf. note 11 p.154f, p.434. A *digamma*, which might be useful for the purposes of etymology, and a *varkappa* are contained in the MSYx fonts published by *Barbara Beeton* in TUGboat 6 (1985/3) 124-128.

in some others as semi-circles, the latter of which we preferred. To achieve this shape, we used the \rhook and \lhook (ˀ ˁ) normally used only in compound math symbols. Smaller *spiritūs* are needed to place a *circumflexus* above them.[18]

In general, the accents are produced from normal math or math italic characters, which are taken from a smaller fontsize and which are raised or lowered according to need. They are overlaid on the preceding character by means of the \llap macro. The corresponding macro takes into account the width passed to it by the preceding vowel.

Most Greek characters are related to their Latin counterparts in an obvious way. The remaining codes were chosen also for reasons of compatibilty with our earlier texts. Since *sigma finalis* was coded as the '¢' (cent) character from the EBCDIC character set before, it had to be changed to some ASCII character, 'v' in this case.

a	b	g	d	e	z	h	q	i	j	k	l	m	n	c	o	p	r	s	v	t	y	f	x	u	w
α	β	γ	δ	ε	ζ	η	ϑ	ι	ͺ	κ	λ	μ	ν	ξ	ο	π	ϱ	σ	ς	τ	υ	φ	χ	ψ	ω
A	B	G	D	E	Z	H	Q	I		K	L	M	N	C	O	P	R	S		T	Y	F	X	U	W
A	*B*	*Γ*	*Δ*	*E*	*Z*	*H*	*Θ*	*I*		*K*	*Λ*	*M*	*N*	*Ξ*	*O*	*Π*	*P*	*Σ*		*T*	*Υ*	*Φ*	*X*	*Ψ*	*Ω*

Table 1: Codes for Greek Characters.

Keyboard characters now represent the Greek alphabet as shown in Tbl. 1. It turns out that the whole Latin alphabet and figures are used up, with the exception of 'V' and 'J', since *sigma finalis* and *iota subscriptum* do not exist in uppercase. This fact can be used to build macro names which are to be used inside Greek text.

```
\let\VVVVVVVVV=\underline       % underlining
```

This example was used to underline certain keywords in Greek quotations, since emphasis cannot be achieved by switching from Greek italic to Greek roman, because the latter is not yet available.

A slightly different problem is posed by the coding of accents. In the program mentioned in note 6, I tried to minimize the keystrokes for accents. Every word is prefixed there with a figure that indicates its accent class according to Greek grammar. The correspondence is shown in Tbl. 2. A zero for unaccented words is required to make sure that no word has slipped classification. The program will than analyse the words into syllables and determine which combination of accents and *spiritūs* is to be used and where it is to be placed.

Though this method is rather elegant, it requires knowledge of grammar and increases the overhead costs, because accenting has to be computed over and over again. So both in SCRIPT and TeX, we coded accents as figures as shown in Tbl. 3

[18] These combinations will be higher than normal letters, but will not cause problems in normal text. To avoid problems as in Tbl. 3, a \strut could be used, cf. also Barbara N. Beeton: How to build a \strut. TUGboat 4 (1983/1) 35-36.

Syllable	Class	Code	Greek
-1 & 1	0 atonon	0ge	γε
-1	1 oxytonon	1de ...	δὲ
-2	2 paroxytonon	2eiper	εἴπερ
-3	3 proparoxytonon	3anqrwpov	ἄνθρωπος
-1	4 perispomenon	4brontaj	βροντᾷ
-2	5 properispomenon	5bhma	βῆμα
-3, -1	6 proparoxytonon	6anqrwp'ov 0tiv	ἄνθρωπός τις
-2	7 properispomenon	7bhma 0ti	βῆμά τι
-1	8 oxytonon	8tiv	τίς
1	9 aspiration	9wv	ὥς

Table 2: Codes for Accent Classes.

and placed them where they belong. A slight disadvantage is the interruption of the typing flow.

spiritus	atonon	acutus	circumflexus	gravis
none	α	1 ά	2 ᾶ	3 ὰ
lenis	> ἀ	4 ἄ	5 ἆ	6 ἂ
asper	< ἁ	7 ἅ	8 ἇ	9 ἃ

Table 3: Codes for Greek Accents.

Mapping Latin keys to Greek characters is normally done by a construction of the form:

```
{\catcode`x=13 \gdefx{$\alpha$}}
```

Character 'x' is made active (catcode=13) and then defined to a new meaning. This definition must be global to transcend the group it is contained in. This group will reset automatically the activation of 'x' when left. It should also be noted that this construction can be used only on input level, because characters once read cannot change their category code any more. There is, however, a way to circumvent this problem if certain restrictions are met, as we shall see in connection with the index problem. To use the character with its new meaning, it is sufficient to make it active again.

Unfortunately our construction would not work for 'a' instead of 'x', because this letter also occurs in the definition and will be active at the time it is read. To solve this problem, we use intermediate names for our Greek characters. A safe building convention for these names is to use the active character in folded and doubled form. So *alpha* will become `AA`.

We have also to consider the similar problem that characters contained in the names `\catcode` or `\gdef` will also have to be made active. For them we may use different names that definitely will not contain active characters. With these two modifications, our construction will look like this:

```
\let\@@=\catcode
\let\@@@=\gdef
{\@@`a=13 \@@@a{\@AA}}
{\@@`b=13 \@@@b{\@BB}}
...
{\@@`A=13 \@@@A{\@aa}}
```

Our next step is to define these intermediate names for every Greek character in the well known way:

```
...          \def
\@BB{$\beta$}\def
...
```

The funny line breaking helps to avoid unwanted blanks. Lower case vowels are put into a box, the width of which is kept for later use by possible following accents, and then they are unboxed again:

```
\def\deftgreek{\def\vdef##1##2{\def##1{\setbox
\@tempboxg=\hbox{##2}\@tempdimg=\wd\@tempboxg
\unhbox\@tempboxg}}\vdef
   \@AA{$\alpha$}\def
   ...
```

To do this, a `\vdef` (define vowel) macro is defined, and this definition and its repeated execution are combined in a `\deftgreek` (define text Greek) macro together with definitions for the conconants and the accents. As the meaning of active characters will be different for other languages like Hebrew that might be used in the same text, we have to confine this meaning to the scope of the groups containing Greek text. So this macro will allow Greek to start anew every time it is needed.

Greek text will look like normal fontswitching. A left brace is followed by the `\greek` macro, which does the switching, then by the text itself, followed by a right brace. A previous loading of the corresponding macros is required. To give an example, the Greek text *VII: 2.Ko 9,5*

NTG *ἀναγκαῖον οὖν ἡγησάμην παρακαλέσαι τοὺς ἀδελφούς, ἵνα προέλθωσιν εἰς ὑμᾶς καὶ προκαταρτίσωσιν τὴν προεπηγγελμένην εὐλογίαν ὑμῶν ταύτην, ἑτοίμην εἶναι οὕτως ὡς εὐλογίαν καὶ μὴ ὡς πλεονεξίαν.*

from our book (note 1, p. 162) will be produced by the following input:

```
\begin{description}
\item[{NTG}] {\greek
a>nagkai2on oy5n h<ghsalmhn parakale1sai toy3v a>delfoy1v,
i7na proe1lqwsin ei>v y<ma2v kai3 prokatarti1swsin th3n
```

```
\VVVVVVVVVV{%
pro\-ep\-hg\-gel\-me1-}
\VVVVVVVVVV{%
nhn}
ey>logi1an y<mw2n tay1thn,
e<toi1mhn ei5nai oy7twv w>v ey>logi1an
kai3 mh3 w<v pleoneci1an.}
\end{description}
```

Explicit hyphenation will work, but not in connection with underlining, where we had to do hyphenation explicitely.

Like this, Greek will be rather similar to normal font-switching, and the text will not be read as a parameter, so that there are no restrictions of length. It should be remembered, that normal macros can only be used inside Greek text after their names have been redefined, as was explained earlier.

3. Reverted Hebrew

Typesetting Hebrew, like Greek, also needs a mapping of characters.[19] Accentuation, however, is much more complicated, since vowels are handled as a sort of accent called *punctuation*, and, in addition to them, there is another layer of accents in their proper sense called *cantilation*, which give a sort of segmentation and hints for singing the text aloud.

First, there was the question of Hebrew characters. Only a few of them are available because they are used for mathematical purposes.[20] An example letter using a complete font as far as consonants are concerned was published by *Lynne A. Price* in TUGboat 2 (1981/1) 122-123.[21] By chance we had available a similar Hebrew font, but only in two sizes.[22]

The real problem with Hebrew is its different running direction, from right to left, shared with other semitic scripts.[23] When Hebrew is to be mixed with some language using the Latin alphabet, this problem is further complicated, since opposite running directions have to be combined dynamically into lines.

The printer's rules for typesetting mixed texts are quite simple to state, if we distinguish between the *forward* direction of a text, being its running direction in

---

19 See Wolfgang Richter: Transliteration und Transkription. Objekt- und metasprachliche Metazeichensysteme zur Wiedergabe hebräischer Texte. ATSAT 19. München 1983; rf. also note 16.

20 While *aleph* (ℵ) is standard, *bet*, *gimel*, and *dalet*, are contained in the MSYx fonts published by *Barbara Beeton* in TUGboat 6 (1985/3) 124-128.

21 Since no automatic reversion was done, the input had to be entered in reverse order depending on how much would fit on the output line. There was also no explanation of the fact that the baseline of the Hebrew font was different from the normal baseline.

22 It might be interesting to compare the size of these fonts, which also depends on the output device, with a standard: in BHS, Hebrew in the main text has a height of 3 mm, and in the apparatus 2 mm.

23 See Pierre A. MacKay: Typesetting Problem Scripts. Computer typesetting provides a solution for Arabic and other scripts. Byte 11 (1986/2) 201-218. Cf. also his earlier project description in TUGboat 4 (1981/2) p. 76.

time, on the one hand, and its graphic representation, being *ltr* (left to right) or *rtl* (right to left), on the other hand:

> Take as much Hebrew text in forward direction as will fit on the line and revert it relative to this line.

If this is done on the computer, it requires the Hebrew text to be coded forward in the normal *ltr* direction of the environment and reverted later on in the program. Here we have to cope with a design problem of text processing systems, because normally you cannot change output lines *after* they have been broken by the processing system. For SCRIPT, we were lucky enough to have a plot-driver written by *P. K. Schilling* in PL/1 (see note 10) that could be modified rather easily. Though the algorithm is quite simple in principle, one has to find a way to mark the Hebrew parts uniquely and to deal with such cases that start in one line and end in another. Another problem is posed by delimiting blanks.

Since the problem of reversion was mentioned both in 'The TEXbook' and in an early 'Dreamboat' article (TUGboat 2,2 p. 58.), one may safely assume that there is no obvious solution in TEX.[24] Though this is a good approach in practice, it is inappropriate in principle because reversion should already be present in the `dvi` file. It also requires rewriting the output driver for the `dvi`-File, which was impossible in our case as we had no access to the source code. So we had to look for a solution that could use the normal instruments of TEX, without either modifying TEX or the output driver.

The list macros given in Appendix D of 'The TEXbook' provide a guide for writing the actual reversion macros. Unlike Greek, the text to be reverted will be read in as a parameter and scanned by these macros character by character. Input characters, however, cannot remain what they are. They should print as Hebrew letters, some of which might be associated with different positions in the font table. The problem now is to get hold of these characters. This problem is due to the fact that the inspection macros use `\futurelet`, a macro built on the `\let` philosophy, which allows us to make comparisons, but no redefining or the like.

To bypass this problem, we used a trick which might be rated "very dirty": the `\meaning \next` control sequence will produce "`the letter a`", if `\next` was `\let` to "a". So we can construct a macro `\strip` inspired by a similar one from 'The TEXbook' (p. 382), that will just strip off the describing words "`the letter`".

```
\def \strip #1 #2 {} % remove text 'the letter'.
```

The first parameter will swallow the word '`the`' and the second parameter the word '`letter`'. The character we want is then left over, and we can use the following code to make it the definition of `\thischar`:

---

[24] *Pierre MacKay* at first studied the possibilies of changing TEX itself, but now prefers a solution similar to our CALLIGRA approach, i.e. doing reversion in the output driver (rf. note 23).

```
\edef \thischar {\expandafter \strip \meaning \next}.
```

With macros like this, I prefer to 'believe' in them than to try and explain them.[25]

t y r q ? 4 P p (s N n M m l K k j v x z w h d g b)
אבגדהוזחטיכךלמםנןסעפףצץקרשת

Table 4: Arbitrary codes for Hebrew Characters.

However this technique requires that we are sure to have only such material in our revert-parameter, which will produce just the type of two-word descriptions that our strip macro can handle. For example, this would not be the case for macros. Much could be gained therefore if someone could write a more sophisticated `\strip` macro that could handle different types of input.

To produce Tbl. 4, we used a `\revert{...}` macro acting like a `\hebrew{...}` macro, but leaving input characters untouched. Character mapping is *ad hoc* and should be replaced as soon as a convincing standard is available.In our Hebrew texts we actually used '%' instead of '4' and '$' instead of 'y', but this will only work if the `\hebrew{...}` macro does not become part of a parameter of another macro.

To produce the Hebrew part of the text *I: Nu 30,7* in our book (note 1, p. 150):

BHS ואם־היו תהיה לאיש ונדריה עליהאו מבטא טפתיה

אשר אסרה על־נפשה׃

V Si maritum habuerit et voverit aliquid et semel de ore eius verbum egrediens animam eius *obligaverit* iuramento.

1545 Hat sie aber einen Man, vnd hat ein gelůbd auff jr, oder entferet jr aus jren lippen ein *verbůndnis* v̊ber jre Seele ....

the following input was used:

```
\item[{BHS}] \hebrew
{w')iM-h+jwo tih'j'h l')ij$
w!n'd+r'jh+ (+l'j|h)wo mib'v+) v'p!+t'jh+}
\par\noindent\hebrew
{)H$'r )+s'r+h (al-nap'$+Sh!E}
```

There is no problem with reversion as long as line breaking is explicitly controlled. It will be interesting to learn from the wizards whether some sort of semi-automatic linebreaking might be implemented that allows reversion to be confined to one line at a time.

[25] Unfortunately there is no WEB-like system for the production of TeX macros.

4. Gothic and Fraktur

Before we finish our discussion of different scripts, we should mention in passing our applications for *Gothic* and *Fraktur*.

In general, the *Gothic* script corresponds to Gothic architecture:[26]

> Die Buchstaben der Gotik sind höher als breit. Sie lassen sich in ein hohes schmales Rechteck einordnen und stehen eng beeinander. Alle Buchstaben stehen mit wenigen Ausnahmen auf der Grundlinie. Die Ober- und Unterlängen erscheinen verkürzt. Das untere Ende des Schaftes ist angebrochen und durch kurze Verbindungsstriche an den nächsten Buchstaben herangezogen.

One of its highlights is reached in the 42-line Bible of Johannes Gutenberg (1397-1468). It should be noted in passing that the outstanding quality of his work is also due to the letter variants with different widths, a technique that, in connection with TEX, is considered for Arabic (rf. note 23 p. 217).

In our book, Gothic is used to quote from medieval authors like *Martin Luther*, and we already saw an example from his translation of 1545 above. Typesetting of Gothic will help a lot when German and Latin are mixed in a text. From a typesetting point of view, some peculiarities are involved, e.g. a long and a short form of the letter 's', ligatures like 'tz', or the umlaut 'e' written as a small letter in the position of an accent. Since we had no Gothic font available, I tried to simulate some of these effects with the `\sf` font.[27]

Fraktur (literally: 'broken script') is a collective term for forms of script in the Gothic tradition, coming from the end of the Gothic period, from the Renaissance, Baroque, classicism and Biedermeier. In developing a rich choice of forms, it corresponds particularly to the architecture of Baroque (rf. note 26 p. 144-147).

Fraktur capitals are often used in textual criticism to denote some of the main sources, for example in "Biblia Hebraica Stuttgartensia" (rf. note 7).

5. Indexing

While reading a book only gives 'sequential access', an index will give 'direct access' to its contents. One of the main purposes of indexes is therefore to help with *not* reading a book.[28] While everbody can work with an index, it is by no means trivial to give a general definition of what an index is like. Neither TEX

---

[26] See also the examples in Sepp Jakob / (P.) Donatus M. Leicher: Schrift + Symbol in Stein, Holz und Metall. München: Callwey 1977. p. 134-143, the quotation is on p. 134. Interesting aspects of typography may be gained from this book, since it presents scripts from a mason's point of view.

[27] It is standard in LATEX, but is not simply a different style, but a completly different script, which also is available in 'slanted' and 'bold' and should not be mixed with *computer modern* fonts for æsthetic reasons. We used slanted sans-serif for the motto texts and straight sans-serif for their authors (cf. also the mottos of 'The TEXbook'). Both for æsthetic and handling considerations, it would seem more appropriate to have a concept that allows to switch between several base scripts, giving the full range of script styles for each of them.

[28] Cf. also G. Knorz / G. Putze: Textverarbeitung zur Vorbereitung und Durchführung einer automatischen Indexierung. Peter R. Wossidlo (ed.): Textverarbeitung und Informatik. Fachtagung der Gesellschaft für Informatik 1980. Informatik Fachberichte 30. Berlin: Springer 1980. P. 139-163

nor LaTeX provide automatic indexing, but allow collection of index material in a file.[29] It is then up to the user to write his own sorting program or to use one from others.[30]

To produce an index as in the 'Leitfaden' (note 7) requires a lot of programming effort. So it seemed wise to rely on what had already been developed. Index handling in SCRIPT was also required since the automatic search of items for the bibliography is based on output coming from the author part of the index.[31] Normally the index has to be run with two purposes, one to give the requests for the bibliography, and the other to produce TeX input for typesetting the index.

The `\index` macro that I wrote will produce input for SCRIPT. In the following code

```
\ix z [Jes 65,17 A-C]{Jes 65,17}
```

the first parameter `z` denotes a biblical quotation. The text in brackets is an optional parameter according to LaTeX conventions; it is used to specify an alternative form of the index term that is to be used in the text, but is also typeset in the predefined style for index terms. If empty, the parameter in curly brackets will appear only in the index.

If our example is the first index entry, it will cause a comment card containing 'come-from' information to be written to the file `\jobname.idx`.[32] Then it will produce the index entry in SCRIPT format:

```
.* index entries for TEXOL of August 20, 1985 at 1156
:s p='1'.zA Jes 65,17
```

The '`:s`' is my GML-tag for indexing, '`p='1'`' is a keyword parameter giving the location, here page 1, '`z`' denotes biblical quotations as before. The '`A`' means to regard all the rest of the line as index entry, whereas in my SCRIPT texts normally the number of words for this entry is given.

Although this approach gives acceptable results and might be further improved, it seems important to look for a more algorithmic description of the problem that may lead to solutions which will conform to the high standards of problem description reached in TeX itself. The following considerations are only a first step to pin down some of our experience with indexing. Let us start with a few informal definitions.

---

29 Rf. 'The TeXbook', p.423-425; cf. also the index macros of *Max Díaz'* Fácil TeX (TUGboat 2 (1981/2) A-28.

30 Terry Winograd / Bill Paxton: An Indexing Facility for TeX. TUGboat 1 (1980/1) A 1-12. Sorting is done here with INTERLISP programs. According to the index in TUGboat 4 (1983/2) p.79-80, no other sorting programs have been published.

31 Though collect volumes, which get a separate entry, are not necessarily in the index, they are also found in the first pass, because they contain information on the parts of them contained elsewhere in the bibliography, and will search the list of requests coming from the index for a match.

32 This concept is part of ***manuscript support***, a topic we shall come back to further on.

1. A Main Index, or 'Register' is a set of indexes representing different *sets of index terms* or different *principles of order.*
2. An Index is an *ordered* list of main index entries.
3. A main index entry is a *hierarchy* of one index entry and its subentries.
4. An index entry consists of one index term and an *aggregated* list of index *addresses.*
5. An index address can be a *logical* or *physical* location or a *reference.*

An index term will belong to a certain class, e.g. 'biblical reference' or 'cited author', or 'subject'. Every class will be associated with a certain principle of order. Biblical references have to be ordered according to their canonical sequence, while subjects are ordered according to the alphabet. Different classes with the same ordering may as well appear in one index as in different ones. Individual index terms can also be classified according to different degrees of importance or different kinds of use, and associated with different typesetting styles, as in 'The TEXbook'. So it can be desirable to know whether a biblical text was just mentioned or was commented upon. In some cases it may be necessary to ignore certain elements in the sorting process; so control sequences should be sorted according to their names and not be collected under '\' (backslash). A reference can be exclusive, saying 'see ...', or additional, saying 'see also ...'.

A physical location is normally a page number. It can also be a file name. A logical location may be the number of a heading or a figure or the like.[33] A reference will refer the reader to a different index term. In the index of the *Leitfaden*, we also used footnote numbers to give a more precise access to the information.[34]

Producing an index will involve the following steps: 1. index term mark-up; 2. collection of index term and index address pairs; 3. sorting index terms; 4. aggregating index terms and index addresses; 5. typesetting. Aggregation of index addresses will normally be done according to their natural (collecting) sequence. In SCRIPT, the '`order`' parameter of the '`.pi`' control word will place the address in front of the others, and the '`start`' and '`end`' parameters will form an address range. Sorting can be influenced by explicit sorting keys, and we used them heavily. In order to achieve the canonical sequence of Biblical books, our index macro has to prefix every single quotation term with its sequence number. To improve efficiency, one should be able to influence sorting *after* aggregation.

Typesetting the index can also be rather complicated.[35] We wrote macros that would cause SCRIPT to produce TEX input instead of printing the index. These

---

33 Some historical and theoretical aspects of the logical and physical arrangement of texts are discussed in my paper: Normaltext und Normalsynopse. Zeitschrift für Sprachwissenschaft 3 (1984) 201-233.

34 The failure to use also §-numbers as announced on p.117 was detected too late to be corrected.

35 See the example of *Mathematical Reviews*, which is described in 'The TEXbook' in the appendix "Dirty Tricks" p. 392-394.

macros are fairly general. So they will put a symbol between an index entry term and its address list. In TEX, this symbol can be used to produce blank space, a colon, of even leaders. We chose the latter to separate page numbers very clearly from the chapter and verse numbers of biblical quotations, and also to improve the formal quality of the index.

It should be noted that an index, at least with larger manuscripts, will help a lot during the development phase. In this case it is desirable to use as addresses the names of the files in which the source text is kept. One also should like to see which terms have been chosen for indexing. This can be done with different fonts or with `\marginpar` (rf. note 11 p. 423).

Normally an index term will be the same as a piece of text, so that it will be convenient to produce both text and index entry by one macro, as it is done in the format used to produce 'The TEXbook'. For German and other inflecting languages, there will often be a slight morphological difference between the two forms. The expression 'im Alten Testament' should be indexed as 'Altes Testament' or even as 'Testament, Altes'.

6. On Symbols

An additional problem is posed by non-standard characters contained in index terms. If an index term contains symbols, they should not be expanded on the `.idx`-file, since the task of sorting expressions like '`z{\accent nn e}ro`' will not be considered a favourite occupation by programmers. Avoiding expansion is not trivial, as symbols occur at random inside the terms. What efforts are necessary to avoid expansion can be learned from the LATEX `\index` macro. Basically, the escape character is to be recatcoded from 0 to 12 (other), *before* the term is read from the file. Therefore such macros must not be inside the arguments of other macros. Since the LATEX `\footnote` macro reads the footnote text as a parameter, `\index` macros do not work correctly inside footnotes. Even worse is a `\verb` macro inside a footnote. This restriction is not imposed by the `\footnote` macros from 'The TEXbook', App. B, and so we re-introduced the PLAIN footnote philosophy into LATEX.

The problem is due to the fact that characters once read in from the input file can no longer change their category code. It might be worth discussion if such a restriction is acceptable. In SCRIPT, three different methods to translate characters are provided by the '`.ti`' (translate input), '`.ts`' (translate string) and '`.tr`' (translate output) control words.

Our problem can, at least, be partially solved, provided we use delimited symbols only. TEX allows symbols, or `\cs-names`, to be either delimited by their context or to be declared with explicit delimiters. The period used in SCRIPT as a delimiter seems to be a good choice, as it does not disturb the appearance of the source text too much. So we shall say e.g. `\def\TeX.{...}`, or `\def\o.{...}` for the German Umlaut. Afterwards we have to use only the delimited form. As such delimiters can also be used to delimit parameters of macros, we can use a little trick to solve our problem: 1. the *escape character* of TEX, normally *backslash*, is set active and mapped to a macro `\backsl` in the following way `{\catcode'\|=0 \catcode'\\=13 |gdef\{|backsl}}`; 2. *backslash* is activated while the argument of the index macro is read; 3. the argument is stored in a token register, which is done in unexpanded form; 4. while the token register is used to write the index file, the `\backsl` macro is defined to the desired character, e.g. to `\escapechar`; 5. while the token register is used to make text, the `\backsl` macro is defined in the following way: `\def\backsl#1.{\csname#1\endcsname.}`; the name is scanned up to the delimiter and then used as a control sequence; so the initial symbol is re-established.

Though such manipulations are possible with this specific type of control sequence, which we call 'symbol' for convenience, they seem to be hardly acceptable in view of the general importance of symbols for almost all languages besides English and Latin.[36] To overcome shortcomings of TEX concerning the use of several languages,[37] it seems necessary to further investigate the complex nature of symbols, both in practice and on a theoretical level, as will become clear from the following remarks on their rôle in hyphenation,[38] and sorting.

Unfortunately the hyphenation algorithm cannot handle accentuation reasonably. Accents in a word will not only inhibit hyphenation, but also make it impossible to add such words to the hyphenation dictionnary. A ligature approach on the other hand would require a new hyphenation dictionnary. Assuming that accented words normally will hyphenate like their unaccented counterparts, one should like to have a hyphenation algorithm that can simply *ignore* accents. The few errors that might be caused by this approach could then be corrected by explicit hyphenation.

As we learned from the index problem, it will often be better to handle special and accented characters as symbols. In TEX, accented characters are produced dynamically by overlaying normal characters with accents. There are two ways to accomplish that: 1) using special control sequences like in PLAIN or some other macro package; 2) defining active characters. 3) using ligatures. In case (1), these macros will precede the accented character and are somewhat clumsy to type. In case (2), easy typing is paid for by restrictions in the variety of accents that can be handled this way. There is also a static way to produce accented characters, which is based on the concept of ligatures. In this case, special fonts are needed, and ligature analysis will increase overhead costs (rf. note 23 p.214).

---

36 The very simplicity of English seems to have a spoiling influence, cf. Pierre MacKay (rf. note 23 p.201): *The complications of typesetting non-Latin scripts offer a challenge to the typesetter who has been spoiled by the English language.*

37 Michael J. Ferguson: A Multilingual TêX. TUGboat 6 (1985/2) 57-58.

38 Bernd Schulze: German hyphenation and Umlauts in TEX. TUGboat 5 (1984) 103-104; Jacques Désarménien: How to run TeX in a French environment. Hyphenation, fonts, typography. TUGboat 5 (1984) 91-102; G. Canzii / F. Genolini / D. Lucarella: Hyphenation of Italian words. TUGboat 5 (1984/1) 14-15.

To keep source texts independent of such technical problems, special characters should be coded as macros following these specifications: a. *unique:* all characters should be possible at the same time; b. *semantic:* the meaning and not the face is to be coded, e.g. Umlaut vs. diaeresis, or right quote vs. apostrophy; c. *context free:* looking for these characters in the source should give a unique result.

While much has been done to make programs perfect in typesetting, these programs do not normally properly reflect other properties of symbols. Even plain characters are complex symbols that have a printing quality, but also have other qualities more difficult to describe. One of them is their sorting quality. The collating sequence of the Latin alphabet is traditional, while the sequence of the special characters is somewhat arbitrary and needs additional conventions.

As we have already seen, the distinction between upper and lower case is essential for making indexes. In English keyword indexes, both should be considered the same, but a distinction should be made in an index of special terms.[39]

The distinction between upper and lower case is also necessary sometimes in German. So the verb *versprechen* (to promise) will become a homograph to the noun *Versprechen* (the promise) when occuring at the head of the sentence. To cover this problem, a third case should be introduced, which might be called *raised.* A lower case letter will have the type *raised,* if it is to print as uppercase for reasons of context (e.g. at the head of a sentence) or style (e.g. in running headings). This problem also occurs when main words are capitalized in English book titles.

7. Operating

To make operating TEX and its dialects safe and easy in an MVS environment, a lot of support is needed. While becoming acquainted with TEX and LATEX, I gradually developed a public command list to provide this support.[40] This command list will combine members of partitioned datasets into sequential files acceptable for TEX, run TEX and the corresponding output drivers in foreground or submit batch jobs, and assist with the production of style files and the handling of `\includeonly` in LATEX. Though these functions depend on the local environment, some specific connections between TEX and NEWLIB (note 40) might be of a more general interest.

One of these connections helps to recall datasets that have been migrated by the storage managing system. Recall at run time will cause long delays for the user, because files are recalled one after the other when they are used for the first time. So it is desirable to recall them in bulk in advance and use the waiting time for some editing. To recall datasets based on the TEX `\jobname` is rather

---

[39] The index of the 'Leitfaden' (note 7) can be recommended as a test case to anyone trying to write index programs, though this index by no means contains all the possibilities to be dealt with in that area of research.

[40] It is based on the DESY general editing system NEWLIB, developed by *Harald Butenschön*, and the FSP fullscreen panel device, developed by *Dietrich Mönkemeyer*.

trivial,[41] but to do the same for datasets based on `\includeonly` names is not. Our solution makes NEWLIB read the central `.aux` file and change it so that it can be executed as a command list that will recall all datasets mentioned in it.

Though LaTeX gives the possibility of running each part of a book on its own, it does not allow the production of the whole book in independent pieces, because only Cross Reference and Table of Contents information is written on a file `\partname.aux`, i.e. a file associated with the specific part; all other information, including Index information, is written on the files `\jobname.dvi`, `-.log`, `-.idx`. This means that finally the manuscript has to be processed in one piece in spite of the parts. To circumvent this problem, we developed a replacement procedure, which will rename `\jobname` files to `\partname` files after one part has been run. Unfortunately, this will only work in foreground for reasons of dynamic file allocation. In SCRIPT, we wrote macros that allow the running of a whole book in parts also with a job-net, which can save a lot of stupid terminal work. Judging from this experience, we should prefer a filename solution that would generally allow a manuscript to be processed in parts.

8. Manuscript Support

There is also the field of *manuscript support*, which so far has not had the attention it deserves. This term refers to all facilities which help to change and develop a manuscript, to keep track of different versions or to link paper output to its electronic sources. A first step already implemented in LaTeX is a switch for whether overful lines should be marked or not. The next step might be to produce 'come-from' information when generating a file, as we do when writing an index file (see example above). But it seems worthwile to go a little further in this field. During manuscript development, one should like also to know the file, date and time of a source text. Instead of giving this information manually, we rely upon the automatic services of NEWLIB. If a language like PL/1 or TeX is specified, NEWLIB will prefix a member with a so-called *zero-card*. Though this record becomes part of the data in the file, it will be updated automatically, and it will be invisible to the program because it comes as a comment card, like in the following examples:

```
%  11/04/86 604141427  MEMBER NAME  PVO     (LVT)      M  TEX
 (* 14/04/86           MEMBER NAME  PVO     (LVT)      M  PASCAL   *)
\QQ 14/04/86           MEMBER NAME  PVO     (LVT)      M  LATEX
```

This feature is extended for TeX in the following way: if a `language` different from, but containing the string '`TEX`' is specified, the comment delimiter will be replaced by the control sequence `\QQ`. So date of creation, date and time of update (if applicable), member name, datset name (in part), an '`M`' to indicate an upper and lower case character set, and the TeX dialect can be read by an appropriate

41 In LaTeX, it will be wise to name the style file for the specific project `\jobname.sty` to support automatic recall.

macro. The information can then be used in the text. A straightforward way would be to use `\marginpar`, but in some cases, printing has to be postponed, e.g. if a heading that follows the source information causes a page break. Printing such information should not disturb line and page breaking either, so that it can safely be left out in the final output. Thus, more convincing solutions still wait to be found.

9. Conclusions

The problems we encountered during the production of 'Verheißung und Versprechen' seem to be typical of this area of typesetting, and they contain some interesting aspects of using and adapting TEX. The solutions discussed here are only a first try, developed under the pressure of time and without previous experience with TEX. To judge from several communications during the last months, there is a growing demand for non-mathematical applications of TEX, and although our solutions are not perfect, they may give a start to people with similar problems.

But for me, there is more to TEX than just solving problems of typesetting. In a paper presented at a meeting on "The Bible and Computers",[42] I suggested that Biblical computer projects could improve a lot if they adopted the principles guiding TEX (as explained in note 13), above all the algorithmic approach and the publishing of fully documented source code, and that TEX might even be used as a common output standard for the different projects, provided the problems described here could be solved. Thus, the preceding lines intend to encourage philologists and to challenge the wizards to join their gifts in further development in this field.

[42] Überlegungen zu einer maschinenlesbaren Ausgabe der Biblia Hebraica. Actes du Colloque "Informatique et Bible", Louvain La-Neuve, Août 1985, in press.

PARTICIPANTS

J. ANDRÉ	*IRISA, Campus de Beaulieu,* F-35042 Rennes Cedex
W. APPELT	*Gesellschaft für Mathematik und Datenverarbeitung mbH, Schloß Birlinghoven, Postfach 1240,* D-5205 Sankt Augustin 1
G.-D. BARG	*Fern Universität, Rechenzentrum, Feithstr. 140,* D-5800 Hagen
K. BAZARGAN	*Optics section, Blackett Laboratory, Imperial College,* GB-London SW7 2BZ
B. BEETON	*American Math. Society, PO Box 6248,* USA-Providence, RI 02940
J.-Y. BIDAN	*EDF, 1, av. du Général-de-Gaulle,* F-92141 Clamart Cedex
A. BINDING	*Kaiserstr. 61,* D-6900 Heidelberg
C. BOOTH	*University of Exeter Computer Unit, Math and Geology Building, North Park Road,* GB-Exeter EX4 4QE
P. BRIANÇON	*EDF, 1, av. du Général-de-Gaulle,* F-92141 Clamart Cedex
N. BROUARD	*INED, 27, rue du Commandeur,* F-75675 Paris Cedex 14
A. BRÜGGEMANN-KLEIN	*Institut für Andgewandte Informatik, und Formale Beschreibungsverfahren, Universität Karlsruhe (TH), Postfach 6380,* D-7500 Karlsruhe 1
J. BRÜNING	*Universität Konstanz, Rechenzentrum, Universitätstr., Postfach 5560,* D-7750 Konstanz
G. CANZII	*Te.Co.Graf. snc, via Pacini 11,* I-20131 Milano
L. CARNES	*Personal TEX, Inc., 20, Sunnyside Ave., Suite H,* USA-Mill Valley, CA 94941

D. CARTON — *EDF, 1, av. du Général-de-Gaulle,*
F-92141 Clamart Cedex

F. CHAHUNEAU — *INRA, Laboratoire de Biométrie, CRJJ,*
F-78350 Jouy-en-Josas

K. CHEMLA — *3, square Bolivar,*
F-75019 Paris

P. CHEN — *Computer Science Division, 517 Evans Hall, Univ. of California, Berkeley,*
USA-Berkeley, CA 94720

K. CHRISTIANSEN — *Computer Science Dept., Univ. Aarhus, Ny Munkegade,*
DK-8000 Aarhus

D. CLAR — *Service informatique, Supélec, Plateau du Moulon,*
F-91190 Gif-sur-Yvette

M. CLARK — *Imperial College Computer Centre, Exhibition Road,*
GB-London SW7 2BX

J. COKER — *Computer Science Division, 517 Evans Hall, Univ. of California, Berkeley,*
USA-Berkeley, CA 94720

E. CRISANTI — *Te.Co.Graf. snc, via Pacini 11,*
I-20131 Milano

S.G.H. DANIELS — *Open University, Walton Hall,*
GB-Milton Keynes MK7 6AA

M. DEBAR — *Faculté N.-D. de la Paix, Rue Grandgagnage 21,*
B-5000 Namur

F. DÉSARMÉNIEN — *PROBE, 26, av. des Frères-Lumière, BP 90,*
F-78194 Trappes Cedex

J. DÉSARMÉNIEN — *Labo. typographie informatique, Université Louis-Pasteur, 7, rue René-Descartes,*
F-67084 Strasbourg Cedex

P. DOLLAND — *Institut für Andgewandte Informatik, und Formale Beschreibungsverfahren, Universität Karlsruhe (TH), Postfach 6380,*
D-7500 Karlsruhe 1

T. EHRHARD — *École Polytechnique, Centre de mathématiques, 10, route de Saclay,*
F-91128 Palaiseau Cedex

S. FARAUT — *11, rue Schweighaeuser,*
F-67000 Strasbourg

M. FERGUSON — *INRS-Télécommunications, 3, Place du Commerce, Île des Sœurs,*
CDN-Verdun, PQ H3E 1H6

D. Foata	*Labo. typographie informatique, Université Louis-Pasteur, 7, rue René-Descartes,* F-67084 Strasbourg Cedex
G. Friesland-Köpke	*FB Informatik, Universität Hamburg, Schlüterstr. 70,* D-2000 Hamburg 13
W. Gander	*Neu-Technikum,* CH-9470 Buchs
J. G. Garbeson	*CIBA-GEIGY AG, R-1032.5.84, Postfach,* CH-4002 Basel
J. Glöckner	*In der Hessel 23,* D-6908 Wiesloch
K. Guntermann	*Technische Hochschule Darmstadt, Institut für Theoretische Informatik, Fachbereich Informatik, Alexanderstr. 24,* D-6100 Darmstadt
R. Hainebach	*Terhorst 19,* NL-6262 NA Banholt
A. Heinz	*Institut für Andgewandte Informatik, und Formale Beschreibungsverfahren, Universität Karlsruhe (TH), Postfach 6380,* D-7500 Karlsruhe 1
E. Hentschel	*Fäutlingsgasse 2,* D-3400 Göttingen
P. Jacobsen	*EDP-Consultant, University of Oslo, USE, PO Box 1059, Blindern,* N-0316 Oslo 3
K. Kautz	*Technische Universität Berlin, Institut für Angewandte Informatik, Franklinstr. 28/29,* D-1000 Berlin 10
M. Kettler	*EDY Consulting, Postfach 1345,* D-8172 Lenggries
G.-H. Knauf	*RRZN/Universität Hannover, Schlosswenderstr. 5,* D-3000 Hannover 1
H. Kröger	*Zentralblatt für Mathematik, Hardenbergstr. 29c,* D-1000 Berlin 12
P. La Bruna	*Te.Co.Graf. snc, via Pacini 11,* I-20131 Milano
A. Lampen	*Technische Universität Berlin, Institut für Angewandte Informatik, Franklinstr. 28/29,* D-1000 Berlin 10

M. Lannes	*CNRS, Laboratoire d'optique électronique, 29, rue Jeanne-Marvig,* F-31055 Toulouse Cedex
S. Larsen	*UNI-C, Ny Munkegade, Bldg. 540,* DK-8000 Aarhus
Y. Legrandgérard	*LITP, UER Math., Univ. Paris 7, 2, place Jussieu,* F-75005 Paris
D. Lucarella	*Dip. di Scienze dell'Informazione, Univ. Milano, Via Moretto da Brescia 9,* I-20133 Milano
M. Manili	*Istituto Enciclopedia Italiana, Piazza Paganica 4,* I-00186 Roma
K. Mattes	*Springer-Verlag, Tiergartenstr. 17,* D-6900 Heidelberg
D. Maurer	*Informatik II, Universität des Saarlandes,* D-6600 Saarbrücken
J. McCarrell	*Computer Science Division, 517 Evans Hall, Univ. of California, Berkeley,* USA-Berkeley, CA 94720
M. Morris	*Addison-Wesley, De Lairessestraat 90,* NL-1071 PJ Amsterdam
J. Navia Rosenmann	*CISI Télématique, CEN BP 24,* F-91190 Gif-sur-Yvette
F. Paracchini	*Dip. Scienze dell'Informazione, Univ. Milano, Via Moretto da Brescia 9,* I-20133 Milano
P. Penny	*CNET, 38–40, rue du Général-Leclerc,* F-92131 Issy-les-Moulineaux
H. Petersen	*RWTH, Rechenzentrum, Seffenter Weg 23,* D-5100 Aachen
J. Picart	*INRA, Laboratoire de Biométrie, CRJJ,* F-78350 Jouy en Josas
W. Pieper	*Union Internationale des Télécommunications, Place des Nations,* CH-1211 Genève 20
S. Procter	*Computer Science Division, 517 Evans Hall, Univ. of California, Berkeley,* USA-Berkeley, CA 94720
V. Quint	*Laboratoire de génie informatique, IMAG, BP 68,* F-38402 St-Martin-d'Hères Cedex

R. RABENSEIFNER — *Rechenzentrum Universität Stuttgart, Allmandring 30,* D-7000 Stuttgart

H. ROHNERT — *FB 10, Universität Saarbrücken,* D-6600 Saarbrücken

J. RÖHRICH — *Universität Karlsruhe, Institut für Informatik II,* D-75 Karlsruhe I

Y. ROY — *Labo. typographie informatique, Université Louis-Pasteur, 7, rue René-Descartes,* F-67084 Strasbourg Cedex

P. SCHERBER — *Gesellschaft für wissenschaftliche, Datenverarbeitung, Am Faßberg,* D-3400 Göttingen

P.-K. SCHILLING — *DESY-R02, Notkestr. 85,* D-2000 Hamburg 52

F. SCHOEN — *CNR-IAMI, via Cicognara 7,* I-20129 Milano

R. SEROUL — *Labo. typographie informatique, Université Louis-Pasteur, 7, rue René-Descartes,* F-67084 Strasbourg Cedex

R. SOUTHALL — *Labo. typographie informatique, Université Louis-Pasteur, 7, rue René-Descartes,* F-67084 Strasbourg Cedex

K. THULL — *Inst. für Mathematik III der FU, Arnimallee 2–6,* D-1 Berlin 33

T. TSCHEKE — *Universitätsdruckerei H. Stürtz AG, TUG-Mitglied, Beethovenstr. 5,* D-8700 Würzburg

I. VATTON — *Laboratoire de génie informatique, IMAG, BP 68,* F-38402 St-Martin-d'Hères Cedex

D. VIGNAUD — *84, av. Secrétan,* F-75019 Paris

G. WEIL — *Centre de calcul de Cronenbourg, 23,rue du Lœss,* F-67200 Strasbourg

H. WENDT — *Springer-Verlag, Tiergartenstr. 17,* D-6900 Heidelberg

M. WERSHOFEN — *Gesellschaft für Mathematik, und Datenverarbeitung, Postfach 1240, Schloß Birlinghoven,* D-5205 St Augustin 1

R. Wonneberger — *Drachenstieg 5,* D-2000 Hamburg 63

M. Zocchi — *Te.Co.Graf. snc, Via Pacini 11,* I-20131 Milano